CASEBOOK SERIES

PUBLISHED

Jane Austen: *Emma* DAVID LODGE
Jane Austen: *'Northanger Abbey'* and *'Persuasion'* B.C. SOUTHAM
Jane Austen: *'Sense and Sensibility'*, *'Pride and Prejudice'* and *'Mansfield Park'* B.C.
  SOUTHAM
William Blake: *Songs of Innocence and Experience* MARGARET BOTTRALL
Charlotte Brontë: *'Jane Eyre'* and *'Villette'* MIRIAM ALLOTT
Emily Brontë: *Wuthering Heights* MIRIAM ALLOTT
Browning: *'Men and Women'* and *Other Poems* J.R. WATSON
Bunyan: *The Pilgrim's Progress* ROGER SHARROCK
Byron: *'Childe Harold's Pilgrimage'* and *'Don Juan'* JOHN JUMP
Chaucer: *Canterbury Tales* J.J. ANDERSON
Coleridge: *'The Ancient Mariner'* and *Other Poems* ALUN R. JONES AND WILLIAM TYDEMAN
Congreve: *'Love for Love'* and *'The Way of the World'* PATRICK LYONS
Conrad: *'Heart of Darkness'*, *'Nostromo'* and *'Under Western Eyes'* C.B. COX
Conrad: *The Secret Agent* IAN WATT
Dickens: *Bleak House* A.E. DYSON.
Dickens: *'Hard Times'*, *'Great Expectations'* and *'Our Mutual Friend'* NORMAN PAGE
Donne: *Songs and Sonets* JULIAN LOVELOCK
George Eliot: *Middlemarch* PATRICK SWINDEN
George Eliot: *'The Mill on the Floss'* and *'Silas Marner'* R.P. DRAPER
T.S. Eliot: *Four Quartets* BERNARD BERGONZI
T.S. Eliot: *'Prufrock'*, *'Gerontion'*, *'Ash Wednesday'* and *Other Shorter Poems* B.C. SOUTHAM
T.S. Eliot: *The Waste Land* C.B. COX AND ARNOLD P. HINCHLIFFE
Farquhar: *'The Recruiting Officer'* and *'The Beaux' Stratagem'* RAYMOND A. ANSELMENT
Henry Fielding: *Tom Jones* NEIL COMPTON
E.M. Forster: *A Passage to India* MALCOLM BRADBURY
Hardy: *The Tragic Novels* R.P. DRAPER
Hardy: *Poems* JAMES GIBSON AND TREVOR JOHNSON
Gerard Manley Hopkins: *Poems* MARGARET BOTTRALL
Jonson: *Volpone* JONAS A. BARISH
Jonson: *'Every Man in His Humour'* and *'The Alchemist'* R.V. HOLDSWORTH
James Joyce: *'Dubliners'* and *'A Portrait of the Artist as a Young Man'* MORRIS BEJA.
John Keats: *Odes* G.S. FRASER
D.H. Lawrence: *Sons and Lovers* GAMINI SALGADO
D.H. Lawrence: *'The Rainbow'* and *'Women in Love'* COLIN CLARKE
Marlowe: *Doctor Faustus* JOHN JUMP
Marlowe: *'Tamburlaine the Great'*, *'Edward the Second'* and *'The Jew of Malta'* JOHN
  RUSSELL BROWN
Marvell: *Poems* ARTHUR POLLARD
The Metaphysical Poets GERALD HAMMOND
Milton: *Comus'* and *'Samson Agonistes'* JULIAN LOVELOCK
Milton: *Paradise Lost* A.E. DYSON AND JULIAN LOVELOCK
John Osborne: *Look Back in Anger* JOHN RUSSELL TAYLOR
Peacock: *The Satirical Novels* LORNA SAGE
Pope: *The Rape of the Lock* JOHN DIXON HUNT
Shakespeare: *Antony and Cleopatra* JOHN RUSSELL BROWN
Shakespeare: *Coriolanus* B.A. BROCKMAN
Shakespeare: *Hamlet* JOHN JUMP

Tragedy
Developments in Criticism

A CASEBOOK

EDITED BY

R. P. DRAPER

First edition 1980
Reprinted 1983

Published by
THE MACMILLAN PRESS LTD
London and Basingstoke
Associated companies in Delhi Dublin
Hong Kong Johannesburg Lagos Melbourne
New York Singapore and Tokyo

Printed in Hong Kong

British Library Cataloguing in Publication Data

Tragedy, developments in criticism. – (Casebook series).
  1. Tragedy – History and criticism – Addresses,
essays, lectures
I. Draper, Ronald Philip
II. Series
809'.91'6   PN1892

ISBN 0–333–25822–3
ISBN 0–333–25823–1 Pbk

CONTENTS

ACKNOWLEDGEMENTS

The editor is grateful to Professor Charles Chadwick for help with the translations from Racine and A. W. von Schlegel.

The editor and publishers wish to thank the following, who have kindly given permission for the use of copyright material: Northrop Frye, extracts from 'Historical Criticism: Theory of Modes' from *The Anatomy of Criticism: Four Essays*, Copyright © 1957 by Princeton University Press (Princeton Paperback, 1971), reprinted by permission of the publishers; G. W. F. Hegel, extracts from *Aesthetics: Lectures on Fine Arts*, translated by T. M. Knox, by permission of Oxford University Press, © OUP 1975; Humphry House, extracts from *Aristotle's Poetics* by permission of Hart-Davis MacGibbon Granada Publishing Ltd; Aldous Huxley, essay 'Tragedy and the Whole Truth' from *Music at Night* by permission of Mrs Laura Huxley and Chatto and Windus Ltd; John Jones, extracts from *On Aristotle and Greek Tragedy* by permission of the author and Chatto and Windus Ltd; James Joyce, an extract from *A Portrait of the Artist as a Young Man* (1960) by permission of the Executors of the James Joyce Estate and Jonathan Cape Ltd; Jeannette King, extracts from *Tragedy in the Victorian Novel* (1978) by permission of the author and Cambridge University Press; Dorothea Krook, extract from *Elements of Tragedy* (1969) by permission of Yale University Press; Arthur Miller, extract from the Introduction to *Collected Plays*, copyright © 1958 by Arthur Miller, published by Secker and Warburg Ltd, reproduced by permission of Elaine Greene Ltd; Friedrich Wilhelm Nietzsche, extracts from *The Birth of Tragedy* translated by William Kaufman, in *Basic Writings of Nietzsche* (1968) by permission of Alfred A. Knopf Inc.; I. A. Richards, extract from *Principles of Literary Criticism* (1924) by permission of Routledge & Kegan Paul Ltd; George Steiner, extracts from *The Death of Tragedy* (1961) by permission of Faber and Faber Ltd; August Strindberg, extract from Preface to *Miss Julie* from Collected Volume *Miss Julie, The Father and The Ghost* (1976) translated by Michael Meyer, published by Eyre Methuen and reproduced by permission of David Higham Associates Ltd; J. L. Styan, extract from *The Dark Comedy* (1968) by permission of the author and Cambridge University Press; Raymond Williams, extracts from *Modern Tragedy* (1966), by permission of the author and Chatto and Windus Ltd; Virginia Woolf, extract from 'On Not Knowing Greek' from *The Common Reader*, vol. 1. (1925), by permission of The Hogarth Press Ltd and the Literary Estate of Virginia Woolf; W. B. Yeats, extract from 'The Tragic Theatre' in *Essays and Introductions* (1961), by permission of A. P. Watt Ltd, on behalf of Michael B. Yeats and Miss Anne Yeats.

GENERAL EDITOR'S PREFACE

The Casebook series, launched in 1968, has become a well-regarded library of critical studies. The central concern of the series remains the 'single-author' volume, but suggestions from the academic community have led to an extension of the original plan, to include occasional volumes on such general themes as literary 'schools' and genres.

Each volume in the central category deals either with one well-known and influential work by an individual author, or with closely related works by one writer. The main section consists of critical readings, mostly modern, collected from books and journals. A selection of reviews and comments by the author's contemporaries is also included, and sometimes comment from the author himself. The Editor's Introduction charts the reputation of the work or works from the first appearance to the present time.

Volumes in the 'general theme' category are variable in structure but follow the basic purpose of the series in presenting an integrated selection of readings, with an Introduction which explores the theme and discusses the literary and critical issues involved.

A single volume can represent no more than a small selection of critical opinions. Some critics are excluded for reasons of space, and it is hoped that readers will pursue the suggestions for further reading in the Select Bibliography. Other contributions are severed from their original context, to which many readers will wish to turn. Indeed, if they take a hint from the critics represented here, they certainly will.

A. E. DYSON

INTRODUCTION

'Tragedy', almost as much as the more broadly inclusive word 'poetry', is impossible to define satisfactorily. All of us in the end have to rely on our intuition of its meaning – though I would hasten to add that there is an immense difference between the educated and uneducated intuition of this meaning. As a literary-critical term it is complicated by the fact that it is also in common use to describe an incident or experience which arouses feelings of shock, horror, distress and sympathy. The 'educated' response is very often to dismiss this use of the word as a journalistic de-basement. This is what Stephen Dedalus does in his homily on tragedy in Joyce's *A Portrait of the Artist as a Young Man.* [*] The death of the girl in the hansom cab was called 'tragic' by a newspaper reporter, but, says Stephen, in his arrogant way, 'It is not. It is remote from terror and pity according to the terms of my definitions.' Stephen, however, is not Joyce. There are many indications in his *Portrait of the Artist as a Young Man* and *Ulysses*, not least among them the attitude which in the latter he adopts to the 'tragedy' of his own mother's death, that Stephen is becoming walled up in his own hyper-aesthetic self-consciousness, and that as an artist he is in danger of losing contact with the common experience which is necessary to nurture his art. To that extent his is a 'pseudo-educated' rather than 'educated' response. It has some of the elements necessary to the distinction between the educated and the uneducated: for example, a capacity for making careful intellectual discriminations and relating them to an overall philosophical concept, and, by implication, a breadth of reading, which enables him to understand the features which make tragedy an aesthetic experience, i.e. something derived from the contemplation of a work of art, as distinct from an experience in real life. But the degree of emphasis placed on that distinction is in danger of eliminating the spontaneous emotional reaction which is common to both the educated and uneducated response. If a universally satisfactory definition of tragedy were possible (and I repeat that this seems not to be so), it would certainly have to include this instinctive upsurge of feeling which links the artistic to the non-artistic experiences of 'tragedy' and forms a continuity between the educated and uneducated intuitions of its meaning.

[*] Here and elsewhere in the Introduction an asterisk within square brackets indicates reference to material included in the relevant Part of this Casebook.

Raymond Williams [*] argues that the separation of tragedy from common experience is an illusion. For him the very theory which would maintain this separation – claiming that so-called 'tragic' happenings only become tragedy proper 'through shaped response' and 'that significant response depends on the capacity to connect the event with some more general body of facts' – is itself the product of an ideology which seeks to universalise itself through some such 'general body of facts'. What is claimed as a permanent order of things, to which, if it is to become 'tragedy', the particular instance of suffering must be related via the work of art, is in reality a temporary expression of the socially determined culture of the day. Thus tragedy is 'not a single and permanent kind of fact, but a series of experiences and conventions and institutions'; and, in particular, 'the ordinary academic tradition of tragedy is in fact an ideology'.

There is much force in this argument. When one takes a view of the whole tragic tradition from Aristotle to the present day, it becomes quite apparent that tragedy does alter its shape and meaning from one century to another with chameleon variability, reinforcing the sense that a single, unchanging definition of tragedy is unattainable. But it does not account for the equally strong sense of an underlying unity beneath diversity, of a continuity which makes the word 'tradition' applicable, and which makes many (though certainly not all) of the insights of earlier critics and commentators relevant not only to the tragic literature of their own times, but also to that of other times, including our own.

At the heart of this continuity is the preoccupation with suffering, the experience from which tragedy springs and to which it seeks to give a meaningful context. My original version of that last clause was 'and which it seeks to explain'. Some tragedies do precisely this, but not by any means all. The effect of a tragedy may well be to underline the inexplicability of suffering, to ask the question to which no answer is expected:

> Why should a dog, a horse, a rat have life,
> And thou no breath at all?

The context, however, is still a meaningful one, even though the meaning, as in *Waiting for Godot*, may be one of apparent meaninglessness. No tragedy is simply a cry of pain. It is an apprehension of pain in relation to a sense – perhaps bleak, perhaps consolatory – of what it is to be human and therefore to belong to a species which must not only endure suffering, but also give voice to its awareness of suffering as its destiny. Theories of tragedy likewise centre (though they may also move to many seemingly remote points on the circumference) on this dual core of suffering and its meaning. For the critic, however, the duality may be reduced to two kinds of basic question: 'By what means is suffering presented so that it most deeply engages audience or reader?' and 'What are the values which emerge from the context provided for suffering by the tragic work of art?' In practice, individual critics tend to focus their attention on one or other of these basic questions: that is, they become commentators on either tragic form or tragic vision, and as such many of them may seem to give an unduly one-sided account of tragedy. The ideal critic would place an equal emphasis on both form and vision; and, as Raymond Williams implies, he would also be aware of the dependence of the work of art on the period to which it belongs, and of the influence which his own time exerts on the judgements he himself makes. Such perfection, however, is as elusive as the complete definition of tragedy. With most critics the insights which they achieve are only made possible by an energy and concern which is unbalanced. Their eagerness to answer one of the basic questions usually leads to neglect, or comparative neglect, of the other, and in the process they make assumptions which to later generations may seem unwarrantable, but which for them are necessary platforms from which to launch themselves towards discovery. What they reveal therefore is not Tragedy, but facets of tragedy; and we can admit this relativity without necessarily concluding that all is relative.

☆

Aristotle stands at the head of those who focus on tragic form. What he has to say about tragedy is part, though a very considerable part, of a larger treatment of poetry which has, according to Humphry House, a more practical bent than most of his earlier work.[1] The *Poetics* [*] is concerned with how the ends appropriate to the different kinds of poetry (epic, tragedy, comedy, etc.) are best achieved, the end of tragedy being to present an action which will arouse the emotions of pity and fear and in so doing accomplish 'the proper purgation (*catharsis*) of these emotions'. Unfortunately very little is said within the *Poetics* to explain the meaning of *catharsis*. As House shows [*], it is necessary to refer to other works by Aristotle if one is to understand the fuller implications of the word. Either because the *Poetics* is an incomplete text – perhaps a series of lecture notes which would have been expanded in actual delivery – or because Aristotle assumed that his terms of reference would be understood by students who had already been schooled in other aspects of his philosophy, he passes over the subject of *catharsis*, important as it is, and concentrates on the main business of the *Poetics*, i.e. the study of the means by which tragedies can be so constructed as to maximise the cathartic effect which is their end. Here he is emphatic that it is *muthos*, or 'plot' (in modern critical parlance 'structure' might be the better term), rather than character or stylistic embellishment, which contributes most to the achievement of this purpose:

> But most important of all is the structure of the incidents. For Tragedy is an imitation, not of men, but of an action and of life, and life consists in action, and its end is a mode of action, not a quality. Now character determines men's qualities, but it is by their actions that they are happy or the reverse. Dramatic action, therefore, is not with a view to the representation of character: character comes in as subsidiary to the actions. Hence the incidents and the plot are the end of a tragedy; and the end is the chief thing of all. Again, without action there cannot be a tragedy; there may be without character. . . . Again, if you string together a set of speeches expressive of character, and well finished in point of diction and thought, you will not produce the essential tragic effect nearly so well as with a play which, however deficient in these respects, yet has a plot and artistically constructed incidents.

Elsewhere Aristotle says that fear and pity may also be aroused by spectacle, but less effectively than by structure. If the latter is properly designed it will achieve at least some of its purpose independently of actual dramatic performance: 'For the plot ought to be so constructed that, even without the aid of the eye, he who hears the tale told will thrill with horror and melt to pity at what takes place.' In this ideal structure – of which the best example, cited by Aristotle himself, is *Oedipus Rex* – the most strongly recommended constituents are *anagnorisis* ('recognition') and *peripeteia* ('reversal'): those contrivances of plot which lead to the climactic moment when Oedipus realises that despite all his attempts to evade the predictions of the oracle he has indeed killed his father and married his mother, and as a consequence of which the action of the play goes into reverse. Oedipus's heroic determination to solve the mystery surrounding the disappearance of Laius turns into the intolerable knowledge which makes him pluck out his own eyes. Such a combination of recognition and reversal is to be preferred because it gives the greatest possible heightening to the emotions of pity and horror; the instrument is by this means screwed to the highest pitch, and the notes which it then emits have the utmost tragic vibration.

Tragic vibration, that is, for the Greeks. For in this respect there seems to be a difference between ancient and modern conceptions of the tragic experience. Plot may be all-important for the Greeks, but modern man (more especially nineteenth- and twentieth-century man, whose responses are profoundedly influenced by the dominance of the novel as a literary form) vibrates more intensely than Aristotle seems to think possible to a tragic movement which is hidden in the depths of the soul rather than embodied in structure and action. Shakespeare points the way when he makes Hamlet exclaim:

> But I have that within which passeth show;
> These but the trappings and the suits of woe.[2] (i ii 85–6)

But it is in the novel that the tragic experience is most interiorised, as may be seen in Henry James's *The Portrait of a Lady*. Here the tragedy is entirely a matter of psychological mutation. With some adjustment the Aristotelian terms may still be applied: for example, a powerful variation of recognition and reversal is involved when Isabel Archer at last realises that she has been deceived and exploited by her husband and Madame Merle (though James chooses to present this to the reader through Isabel's retrospective understanding rather than direct action, a procedure which puts it more firmly 'within').[3] But 'the house of darkness' which she now knows herself to have entered, symbolised by the forbidding villa which Osmond inhabits, is a gloomy, inward-looking house of the mind; and the ultimate decision she makes, to return to Italy and fulfil her obligations as the wife of Osmond, is the expression of an essentially tragic acceptance that, although her attempt to 'affront her destiny' has been defeated, she will abide by the melancholy wisdom that her disillusionment has brought her. Outwardly there is no great difference, but inwardly the change is profound. The reader feels that the meaning of the novel resides less in what is done than in the change which suffering has wrought in the mental world of Isabel; it is this which constitutes the tragic 'portrait'.

Greek tragedy, however, as seen through the *Poetics*, has its meaning realised in the action. As John Jones [*] observes: 'To our sense of characteristic conduct' (and Isabel's return to Osmond is a perfect example of such 'characteristic conduct'), 'Aristotle opposes that of characterful action: the essence of conduct being that it is mine or yours; of action, that it is out there – an object for men to contemplate.' To some extent, of course, this is a difference between the novel and the drama in general. In a staged play thought and feeling necessarily become exteriorised in a way that is by no means inevitable in the novel. But there is also a difference between play and play. Without going to the extreme of an over-psychologised, Coleridgean *Hamlet* (Shakespeare's play is one of vigorous action as well as brooding melancholy), the character of Hamlet belongs to a mental world which has a reality at least as substantial as that of the plotted action. To quote Jones again: 'Aristotelian man cannot make a portentous gesture of "I have that within which passes show" because he is significantly himself only in what he says and does.' The gulf between this and the drama of Chekhov or Beckett is greater still. Here the mental world fills the stage, and action reaches a condition of frustrated stasis. Man is only significantly himself in what he says; what he does is nugatory or irrelevant. In this sense, although there is a common ground of human suffering arousing pity and terror, it is a long way over from modern to Greek tragedy.

There is also a marked difference in the theatrical environment of modern and ancient Greek plays. The open-air amphitheatre of the Greeks and the indoor proscenium arch of the moderns are both physically and symbolically contexts conditioning the tragic experiences which they surround.[4] This, as Jones reminds us, is brought home vividly by the use of the mask. For the Greek, 'mask and face were at one in their sufficiency; unlike the modern face and modern mask, they did not owe their interest to the further realities lying behind them, because they declared the whole man. They stated; they did not hint or hide.' The consequence is a bold, explicit tragedy, generic and representative rather than private and idiosyncratic: a tragedy, of larger-than-life, idealised types, and their actions, as Hegel perceived, not the expression of personality, but the embodiment of values and forces which have a universal significance.[5]

☆

If the bent of Aristotle in the *Poetics* was practical, it was not prescriptive. He merely drew inferences from what he observed to be the custom of the Greek theatre. It was later commentators who erected these into 'rules' and, especially in the Renaissance period, gave them a codified formalisation which isolated them from the conditions to which they were appropriate.[6] Hence the supposed 'unities', of time, place and action, only the last of which (and the most sensible since it presupposes an organic connectedness between the parts of a play) is given serious emphasis by Aristotle.[7] These rules are important because of the influence which they exerted on major writers of tragedy in the seventeenth and eighteenth centuries, producing a formal exactitude which was self-consciously learned, aristocratic and opposed to popular tradition. Sir Philip Sidney's contempt, in his *Apologie for Poetrie* (1580–81), for Elizabethan violations of time and place is in this respect prophetic [*]; and the scholary Milton, nearly a hundred years later, is both deliberately correct in his composition of *Samson Agonistes* and makes a virtue of it in his Preface [*]: 'The circumscription of time wherein the whole Drama begins and ends, is according to antient rule, and best example, within the space of 24 hours.'

But the 'rules' are not of great critical importance in themselves. In their more naïve form, which supposed the total inability of an audience to transcend the actualities of time and place in the theatre where they saw the drama being performed, they were effectively demolished by Samuel Johnson in his *Preface to Shakespeare* (1765). 'It is false', he said, 'that any representation is mistaken for reality.' Any play requires an

act of imagination by its audience, and if it can imagine itself
transported from London to the Alexandria of the Ptolemies, it can
imagine further changes of scene and of time. As he acutely perceived,
'The delight of tragedy proceeds from our consciousness of fiction . . . .'[8] The kind of realism that led to the 'rules' is a misplaced
realism.

It is true, however, that there are more sophisticated arguments for
the unities, based on concentration and economy of effect. These are
more genuinely Aristotelian since they relate to the basic question of
structure and the intensification of pity and fear. The unities practised
in this spirit produce a drama that is genuinely classical in that it is
single-minded and restrained, focused upon its end, and pruned of all
that is irrelevant.[9] As Dryden puts it [*], 'there must be a point of sight
in which all the lines terminate'. To further this, the Aristotelian
emphasis on unity of action often became, in the hands of neo-classicists,
a rigid insistence on the single theme and the single line of plot. Dryden,
echoing received opinion, makes this his first 'ground of criticism in
tragedy,' and as a consequence of it he must formally condemn not only
Shakespeare's histories, but 'all double action of plays' (including,
presumably, the Gloucester second-plot in *King Lear*). Being very much
a man of the theatre, however, he is conscious that double plots are the
custom of the English stage, and he seems caught a little uneasily
between Greek purity and 'the pleasure of variety'. Similarly,
Aristotle's preoccupation with the appropriate end of tragedy, and his
concern that it should be differentiated from comedy (in II 4 of the
Poetics, for example, he speaks of Comedy's aim being to represent 'men
as worse, Tragedy as better than in actual life'), gives rise among later
Aristotelians to the doctrine of the rigid separation of the genres. The
mixing of comedy with tragedy was despised as impure. Thus, in
Sidney's view the idealised dignity of tragedy should not be con-
taminated by 'mingling Kings and Clownes'; and the sardonic neo-
classicist, Thomas Rymer, author of *A Short View of Tragedy* (1692),
mocked at Shakespeare as an inveterate mixer who could not see the
folly of his lack of decorum: 'But to him a Tragedy in *Burlesk*, a merry
Tragedy was no Monster, no absurdity, nor at all preposterous: all
colours are the same to a Blind man.'[10]

Decorum – i.e. appropriateness and consistency, and, where tragedy
is concerned, a suitable elevation in both language and character –
becomes the hallmark of neo-classical criticism. With the narrowing
and refining of the audience for which the dramatist writes (a tendency
which sets in strongly in seventeenth-century France, and influences,
but very imperfectly, the revived English theatre after the Restoration)
comes an insistence, not only, as in Aristotle, on the dignity and high
position of the tragic protagonist, but on a mannerliness and delicacy

which borders on the finicky. Thus, Racine, in his Preface to *Andromaque* [*] has to call Aristotle in aid against detractors who find his characterisation of Pyrrhus falling beneath the standards set by current refinement; and he shows a degree of hypersensitivity himself when he declares, in the Preface to *Phèdre* [*], that he gave the words accusing Hippolyte of immorality to Phèdre's nurse rather than Phèdre herself since it seemed to him 'that calumny was something too wicked and degrading to be put in the mouth of a princess whose feelings are otherwise so pure and noble'.

The assumption that the tragic protagonist must be a person of exalted rank goes unquestioned in classical, Elizabethan and neo-classical tragedy alike – though neo-classical critics felt that the Elizabethans, not excluding Shakespeare, often failed to maintain an appropriate dignity in both the manners and diction of their heroes. It is not until the nineteenth and twentieth centuries (if one discounts occasional exceptions such as *Arden of Feversham*) that a bourgeois or working-class figure is felt to be worthy enough for the role of tragic protagonist. Lessing [*] points the way forward with his quotation from Jean-François Marmontel (1723–99) to the effect that 'We wrong the human heart, we misread nature, if we believe that it requires titles to rouse and touch us'; and Wordsworth's practice in such poems as 'Michael' and 'The Thorn', reinforced by his Preface to the second edition of *Lyrical Ballads*,[11] contributes to the Romantic reassessment of what is meant by the dignity of man. But it is the nineteenth-century novelists, especially George Eliot, Hardy and James in England, Flaubert and Zola in France, and Turgenev and Tolstoy in Russia, who firmly establish the tragedy of the common man (or, remembering the sex of the greatest of these figures – Maggie Tulliver, Dorothea, Tess, Isabel, Emma Bovary, Anna Karenina – one perhaps ought to say 'woman'). None the less, as Jeannette King has shown [*], critical resistance to this change was strong, particularly where novelists sought to transcend the class barriers. With regard to lower-class characters it was felt that: 'Their social position deprives their fall of any wider significance, and therefore of any element of real catastrophe. And their limited mental range deprives their suffering of any greatness.'[12] There is an element of snobbishness in this which it is easy enough for the egalitarian twentieth century to dismiss without further thought, but behind the snobbishness are more serious issues which touch the fundamentals of tragedy.

Some of these are encountered when one reads Arthur Miller's defence of *Death of a Salesman* [*] against the charge that Willy Loman (the very name is a symbolic gesture of defiance) lacks 'the "stature" for the tragic hero.' Miller first of all denies that 'rank' has the same significance today as it had in earlier centuries. What matters, he says, is whether the hero has the capacity to choose, and whether his choice is between alternatives of sufficient seriousness: 'So long as the hero may be said to have had alternatives of a magnitude to have materially changed the course of his life, it seems to me that in this respect at least, he cannot be debarred from the heroic role.' Secondly, there is 'the question of intensity'. For Miller this seems to mean the extremism of the protagonist, 'the fanatic insistence upon his self-conceived role' – a concept profoundly relevant to Antigone, or Othello when wound up to belief in his overriding 'cause', but less obviously embodied in Willy Loman. Thirdly, there is 'the so-called tragic victory'; and this, as Miller goes on to insist, is 'a question closely related to the consciousness of the hero'. As far as *Death of a Salesman* is concerned there is a difficulty here, of which Miller seems aware, but which he is unable to face completely. Death throws human values into relief. This is obviously true in 'a society of faith', but less obviously so, in a 'secular society', for the 'tragic victory', if there is to be one, must come out of the essential humanity of the character, not out of the transcendent values which 'faith' presupposes. One important implication of this is that the tragedy of 'a secular society' must be exceptionally effective in creating and articulating a sense of self-generated values. But, as Miller disarmingly says, *Death of a Salesman* is a play in which nobody 'stops to make a speech objectively stating the great issues', and the hero lacks 'the intellectual fluency to verbalise his situation'. While, as Miller also claims, this does not mean that Willy necessarily lacks awareness, it does make adequate communication of that awareness to the audience virtually impossible. The further claim, that 'Complete consciousness is possible only in a play about forces, like *Prometheus*, but not in a play about people', contains a basic truth, but uses it misleadingly to suggest that *Death of a Salesman* only falls short of completeness in the way that all plays about people do. This argument overlooks the mythic potency usually possessed by the traditionally exalted hero and the enrichment of meaning which traditional tragedy derives from this. The dignity of such a protagonist and the focus which he provides for significant issues enables the play in which he appears to approximate far more closely to the 'play about forces' than the modern tragedy of the humble, inarticulate hero. Complete consciousness may still not be achieved, but the difference in the degree of consciousness is much greater than Miller seems willing to allow.

For Dorothea Krook [*] the stature of the protagonist is certainly important. In her discussion of the qualifications of the ideal tragic hero – i.e. the kind of hero necessary to enable the work in which he appears (play or novel) to achieve the maximum tragic effect – she places first a modified form of the traditional requirement of high rank. Actual social status may not be important, but representativeness is.

However, what the tragic hero represents is not commonplace humanity, but 'some fundamental, persistent aspect of man's nature'. He
must therefore be not ordinary, but extraordinary; and among the
extraordinary qualities he must possess are those of charisma, courage
(the moral being more important than the physical variety), nobility of
spirit, and the capacity to learn through suffering and thereby achieve
self-knowledge.

Such a frankly Platonic approach to tragedy, though it serves
splendidly to illuminate *Hamlet* or the trio of rich and intricate works
which are the culmination of Henry James's career as a novelist,[13] is too
selective to be entirely satisfactory. It leaves little room for plays like
Medea or *Macbeth*; and even a work such as James's *The Turn of the
Screw* does not quite fit: it has nobility and suffering, but the outcome is a
very curious knowledge. In effect, it is a particular kind of tragedy that
Dorothea Krook is advocating, which might be called 'heroic tragedy'.
Criticism which centres on this kind of tragedy (a further example is
Yeats's 'The Tragic Theatre' [*] with its preference for 'the moment of
exaltation' as against the more realistic 'daily mood') tends to look for
triumph in defeat, a tragedy that reassures rather than depresses. The
tragedy which comes from distortion and perversion of the vital forces
sustaining humanity,[14] or the tragedy of bleakness deriving from a
Schopenhauerian sense of the delusiveness of life itself [15] – these are not
catered for, or they are demoted to the level of non-tragedy.[16]

This discussion of 'heroic tragedy' finds its origin in the distinction
between 'high mimetic' and 'low mimetic' modes made by one of the
most influential of modern critics, Northrop Frye. Frye himself,
however, is less committed than Dorothea Krook to the hero of the high
mimetic mode, even though he states that this is the kind of hero to be
found in most epic and tragedy, and 'primarily the kind of hero that
Aristotle had in mind'. In his *Anatomy of Criticism* [*] Frye attempts
what may be described as a neo-Aristotelian categorising of literature
into genres, but one that takes into account the far more complex
variations which the vast extension of post-Aristotelian literature has
introduced to the field. In his 'First Essay', devoted to the 'Theory of
Modes', Frye begins with an attempt at classifying fictions into five
different 'modes' according to the hero's power of action compared with
other men and their environment: if this is superior in *kind*, the result is
(1) a myth about a god; if in *degree* only, (2) a romance. Superiority in
degree, but not in environment, produces the heroic figure already
mentioned in (3) the high mimetic mode; similarity in both respects the
hero of (4) the low mimetic mode; and inferiority (5) the ironic mode.
Each of these modes has its appropriate genre – the high mimetic, for
example, has tragedy, and the low mimetic, comedy (and realistic
fiction); but within the genres the five modes again appear, complicat-

ing and sometimes confusing the seemingly simple pattern of order.

It is because it recognises this complexity, however, that Frye's scheme is able to cope with the rich profusion of actual literary works. This is an important modification of genre criticism. The bane of such criticism in the past, and especially as it operated in the neo-classical period of the seventeenth and eighteenth centuries, was that it tended to rigidify into 'kinds' which were considered to have their appropriate 'decorum', and any lapse from decorum was correspondingly regarded as a failure to realise the proper potentiality of the genre. We have already seen examples of this in the scorn of Sidney and Rymer for mixed tragedies. Frye's genres are more flexibly adaptable. Tragedy, for example, is not seen as exclusively 'high mimetic'. In the case of a novel such as *Tess of the D'Urbervilles* it may be 'low mimetic', and, because of the element of the '*pharmakos* or scapegoat' in the way Tess is presented, it may also participate in the 'ironic'. There is thus not one uniform category of tragedy, but a variety of modes of tragedy, and, furthermore, variable modality within each particular mode.

Some readers may feel that the logical outcome of this recognition of variety is to throw away classification altogether and simply deal with individual works on their own merits. The fundamental critical argument which this raises is considered by Frye in his 'Polemical Introduction'; all that can be said here is that it concerns the very nature of criticism as an ordered body of knowledge and not just a series of disparate individual experiences. The value of Frye's, tentatively advanced, scheme to the student of tragedy is that it develops formal criticism to the point where it can both recognise tragedy as a genre with characteristic features, and avoid the pitfall of seeking to make these into defining features. The family resemblance is preserved without the tyranny of the family. And this is not merely an academic exercise, for, to refer again to the example of *Tess of the D'Urbervilles*, it is part of the complex response which one has to that novel that it seems both a departure from traditional tragedy of the heroic sort, involving both affirmation of the common humanity of its central figure and embittered assertion of her role as victim of society and of fate, and at the same time to be claiming kinship for Tess with the dignified Aristotelian protagonist and demanding an equal status for her. A system such as Frye suggests constitutes a formal acknowledgment of the complex relationship which this novel has with other tragic fictions, which sustain it, and which by being a vigorous latter-day example of the kind, *Tess of the D'Urbervilles* in its turn also helps to sustain.

☆

Answers to the question, 'What are the values which emerge from tragedy?' are already implicit in some of the comments on the means by which suffering is presented. Racine's belief that to accuse Hippolyte would have been unworthy of Phèdre, because her 'feelings are otherwise so fine and noble', suggests not only decorum, but a moral position as well. And this is equally true of his remark in the Preface to *Bérénice* [*] that 'Bloodshed and death are not absolutely indispensable to a tragedy. It is enough if the action is impressive, if the characters are heroic, if the passions are aroused, and if everything is charged with that feeling of majestic sadness which constitutes the true pleasure of tragedy.' In both these instances the implication is that tragedy is an ennobling experience belonging to a region of the mind freed from the contamination of the commonplace. The values are those of Milton: 'Tragedy, as it was antiently compos'd, hath been ever held the gravest, moralest, and most profitable of all other Poems'; and of Addison [*]: 'Diversions of this kind wear out of our Thoughts every thing that is mean and little.' Arthur Miller, on the other hand, reveals a democratic radicalism quite at odds with this sense of the loftiness of tragedy when he claims that it is possible, if the right issues are engaged, for 'the corner grocer' to outdistance the President of the United States as a tragic figure.

Aristotle again points the way (though, as already indicated, he does little to clarify his exact meaning) when he speaks of *catharsis* as the end of tragedy. This is an effect upon the audience – and, as Milton suggests, can be extended to the reader; but, of course, no attempt is made to investigate what actually happens to audience or reader. Research of that kind is unknown to the classical mind; it is purely a twentieth-century phenomenon, and even now usually the business of sociologists and psychologists rather than literary critics. *Catharsis* must be regarded as a tentative conception of the ideal effect of tragedy on an ideal audience. This is how it is interpreted by Humphry House in the study mentioned earlier. Tragedy, he suggests, exercises the emotions and 'controls them by directing them to the right objects in the right way'; and 'When they subside to potentiality again after the play is over, it is a more "trained" potentiality than before. . . . Our responses are brought nearer to those of the good and wise man.' Tragedy might well have no such effect on most members of most audiences, but, even if this could be proved by statistical evidence, that would not, by itself, invalidate the idea of *catharsis*. What House's interpretation of Aristotle outlines is a response to tragedy which can serve as both a controlling purpose for the writer and a criterion of judgement for the critic. It has implications – such as the need to arouse deep feeling about painful human experiences, without recourse to sensationalism; and the need to modulate these feelings towards a normative conclusion – which are moral as well as methodological. Thus, House refers to 'Artistotle's educative and "curative" theory'. Such a phrase may well go beyond what can be indisputably established from Aristotle's text, but it is in keeping with Aristotle's evaluative attitude. And if House is importing values of his own, he is in good and extensive company, for the emotional theory of *catharsis* has, at least since the Renaissance rediscovery of Aristotle, been an emotive subject round which a wealth of literary ideology has accumulated.

Samuel Johnson, as reported by Boswell [*], gives *catharsis* a distinctively moral twist, as his example of the man motivated by ambition makes clear: 'but by seeing upon the stage, that a man who is so excessively ambitious as to raise himself by injustice, is punished, we are terrified at the fatal consequences of such a passion'. However, for Addison (whom we have already cited) pity and fear create an almost smug *catharsis*. Borrowing his interpretation from Dacier's commentary on the *Poetics*,[17] Addison suggests that we take delight in the artistic representation of suffering 'from the secret Comparison which we make between ourselves and the Person who suffers'; and the effect is to 'make us prize our good Fortune which exempts us from the like Calamities'.

Burke [*] examines the issue more deeply. For him, 'the influence of reason in producing our passions is nothing near so extensive as it is commonly believed'. He denies that the distinction is between real and imagined misfortunes, for he insists that we take as much pleasure in historical as fictitious examples. Immunity may be a condition, but it is not the cause. Furthermore, he argues, we might not choose to be the agents of certain kinds of destruction and suffering (his example is London destroyed by fire or earthquake), but we would be irresistibly drawn to the spectacle of their consequences. The cause must therefore be sought in the nature of the human mind, which is so constructed that it sympathises with (i.e. experiences an instinctive outflow of pleasurable emotion towards) even that of which it may consciously disapprove.

The danger with thinking of this kind, however fascinating it may be, is that it tends away from the work of art and towards the psychology of the spectator. As Geoffrey Brereton reminds us, the study of *catharsis*, with its direction of attention to the effect which tragedy produces on an audience, 'must eventually lead to the conclusion that the significance of a work of art is dependent on the emotions which it generates'.[18] This can only be so if the emotions have a relevant and proportionable relationship to the properly interpreted stimulants within the text, or text-in-performance, which arouse them. Both the fascination and the dangers of such an approach are illustrated by I. A. Richards's observations on tragedy in *Principles of Literary Criticism*. [*] The ideal tragic effect is postulated as a balance of responses: 'Pity, the impulse to approach, and Terror, the impulse to retreat, are brought in Tragedy to a reconciliation which they find nowhere else.' Richards, therefore, like

Lessing [*], insists on the equal importance of both pity and terror: 'It is the relation between the two sets of impulses, Pity and Terror, which gives its specific character to Tragedy, and from that relation the peculiar poise of the Tragic experience springs.' The curious thing, however, about this theory is that it seems to combine an intensely elevated view of tragedy ('Tragedy' – in, that is, such rare examples as 'Shakespeare's six masterpieces' – 'is perhaps the most general, all-accepting, all-ordering experience known') with a quite disconcerting effect of bathos ('The joy which is so strangely the heart of the experience . . . is an indication that all is right here and now in the nervous system'). This is a fault inherent, perhaps, in psychological explanations of literary experience. They deflect attention from the work of art itself and risk seeming to reduce it to an instrument of mental health. It may be that the medical interests of Aristotle himself are ultimately to blame for this; *catharsis* being, of course, originally a medical term. (But see House, pp. 52–6 below.)

☆

David Hume [*], like Addison and Burke, also finds in tragedy the paradox of pleasing pain; but for him the explanation of the paradox is to be found in the aesthetic transformation which is brought about when suffering is eloquently expressed. The subject-matter may be ugly and repulsive, but the beauty generated by art takes over the ugly substance of what is being represented and converts it to its own nature. Needless to say, there are limitations to this process, as Hume properly recognises. For example, the loss of a favourite child cannot be mitigated, but only intensified, by dwelling upon it with elocution; and passive suffering beautifully rendered amounts to pathos rather than tragedy. The attraction of this theory is that it offers an interesting account of the positive force of the emotion aroused by tragedy. Violence and suffering when fused with the more purely aesthetic pleasures associated with a work of art ('the force of imagination, the energy of expression, the power of numbers, the charms of imitation', all of which are 'naturally of themselves, delightful to the mind') do, indeed, become something different from violence and suffering in the real world, and more capable of stimulating a pleasurable response. But the weakness of the theory, or at least in Hume's expression of it, is that the resultant of this fusion is characterised too sentimentally: the passion, says Hume, is 'so smoothed, and softened, and mollified . . . that it affords the highest entertainment'. 'Smoothed, and softened, and mollified' unfortunately suggests an effect of emasculation rather than heightening.

An instance that might well be used to illustrate Hume's theory is Lear's apostrophe of the storm in Act III, scene ii ('Blow, winds, and crack your cheeks . . .'). Here violence becomes superbly stimulating imaginative vision. But it is not 'smoothed, and softened, and mollified'. An apostrophe such as 'And thou, all-shaking thunder / Strike flat the thick rotundity o' th' world' is eloquent (one feels that sheer destruction has been made to sing out with a Beethovian music) and yet with an eloquence that sharpens, rather than softens, the cutting edge of the storm. If 'rotundity' is full and rounded and, in its academic overtones, a learned and self-consciously civilised word, its qualification by the blunt, vulgar 'thick' – echoing the monosyllabic curtness of 'strike' and 'flat' – shows that these more effete qualities are suggested only in order to be debased (giving 'rotundity' now the character of grossness and obesity) and crushed down in a spirit of vindictive and malicious levelling. Art thus enhances the nihilistic energy of 'all-shaking thunder', and transforms it, by hyperbolic magnification, into a mythic being (the vocative 'thou' contributing a personifying effect). All this is indeed 'delightful to the mind', but alien to the 'man-of-feeling' terms in which Hume expresses himself. Keats is nearer the mark, when, in his sonnet 'On Sitting Down to Read King Lear Once Again' (1818), he speaks of leaving 'golden tongued Romance' behind and willingly involving himself in 'the fierce dispute / Betwixt damnation and impassion'd clay'. This is something which must be 'burnt through'; it is still a kind of pleasing pain, but one which is best summed up in the line, 'The bitter-sweet of this Shakespearian fruit'.

Hume, the philosopher of the Enlightenment, also serves as an introduction to those Romantic writers for whom the conviction that suffering witnesses to human dignity becomes an article of faith. Thus, Schlegel [*], taking up again the question of the pleasure–pain paradox of tragedy, offers a rather different resolution of it from Hume. In his opinion, 'what makes us feel . . . a kind of fundamental satisfaction arising from our sympathy with the violent situations and afflictions represented on stage is either the sense of the dignity of human nature aroused in us by great examples of humanity, or the intimation of an order of things which is supernatural . . .'. Through suffering the man of noble soul, precisely because he is forced back on his own resources, discovers 'that store of unconquerable resolution which the heavens seem to have put there for such occasions as these', and his soul comes to know its affinity with the infinite. Shelley [*], too, passes from the agony and degradation of tragic man to his transformation through suffering. Drama 'of the highest order', he says, in a typically complex and idealised image from a passage in his *Defence of Poetry* dealing with Greek tragedy, 'teaches . . . self-knowledge and self-respect'; it becomes 'a prismatic and many-sided mirror, which collects the brightest rays of human nature, and divides and reproduces them from the simplicity of their elementary forms, and touches them with majesty and beauty . . .'. This fundamentally optimistic view also informs Shelley's own dramatic writing. His characteristic tragedy is the triumphant *Prometheus Unbound* rather than *The Cenci*. Prometheus is heroic in his apparent defeat and sustained by the conviction of ultimate victory. Shelley's vision is fixed on a point beyond suffering, as in the trajectory of Demogorgon's final stanza, which follows a path through misery and injustice, but is always aiming towards the final 'Victory':

> To suffer woes which Hope thinks infinite;
> To forgive wrongs darker than death or night;
> To defy Power, which seems omnipotent;
> To love, and bear; to hope till Hope creates
> From its own wreck the thing it contemplates;
> Neither to change, nor falter, nor repent;
> This, like thy glory, Titan, is to be
> Good, great and joyous, beautiful and free;
> This is alone Life, Joy, Empire, and Victory.

This optimistic belief in the dawning of light, no matter how black the present darkness may be, as George Steiner argues in *The Death of Tragedy* [*], is basically anti-tragic. Despite the continuing esteem accorded to tragedy by the Romantics, and the efforts which many of them made to contribute to the genre, their 'Rousseauist belief in the perfectibility of man' undermined the very foundations on which tragedy is built. In Steiner's words:

The romantic vision of life is non-tragic. In authentic tragedy, the gates of hell stand open and damnation is real. The tragic personage cannot evade responsibility. . . . Where a tragic conception of life is in force, moreover, there can be no recourse to secular or material remedies. . . . In tragedy, the twist of the net which brings down the hero may be an accident or hazard of circumstance, but the mesh is woven into the heart of life.

The position here taken up is something like that of the Christian who believes in original sin (for whom 'damnation is real') in opposition to the secular-minded agnostic, or the liberal Christian who accepts a heaven, but not a hell. But, in Steiner's view, Christianity, too, is 'an anti-tragic vision of the world'.[19] The promise of redemption undercuts the finality of tragedy: that 'Never, never, never, never, never' which makes the death of Cordelia, not a gateway to eternity, but an enormous prospect of waste. Her death and that of Milton's Samson are poles apart. Manoa may overstate the mood when he says of Samson's emergence from defeat and humiliation to victorious self-destruction,

> Nothing is here for tears, nothing to wail
> Or knock the breast,

for that sense of humiliation sticks in the reader's mind as an expression of the bewildered Job-like suffering which is a real and lasting part of the human condition; nevertheless, the final Chorus places the immediate here-and-now of evil in a sublime perspective which substitutes divine benevolence for tragic loss:

> All is best, though we oft doubt,
> What th' unsearchable dispose
> Of highest wisdom brings about,
> And ever best found in the close.

And this undoubtedly is the view that Milton himself endorses for his reader.

Christian tragedy in the Middle Ages tended towards a simpler concept than this. The formulation of which the extract from Chaucer's *Monk's Tale* is representative [*] belongs to the *de casibus virorum illustrium* tradition ('concerning the falls of famous men'). It emphasises that nothing sublunar (beneath the sphere of the changing moon) is stable; all is subject to Fortune, who will turn her wheel and bring those who now enjoy prestige and prosperity tumbling down to wretchedness and misery. In itself this is a secular idea; its Christian dimension consists in the accompanying advice to fix the heart on everlasting things, which are not subject to this process of mutability: to wean attention from the inherently unstable conditions of earthly life and focus, instead, on the eternal world, of which death is the gateway:

> O yonge, fresshe folkes, he or she,
> In which that love up groweth with youre age,
> Repeyreth hom fro worldly vanyte,
> And of youre herte up casteth the visage
> To thilke God that after his ymage
> Yow made, and thynketh al nys but a faire
> This world, that passeth soone as floures faire.
>
> (Chaucer, *Troilus and Criseyde*, v 1835–41)

In *Paradise Lost*, which, though cast in epic form, Milton originally intended to write as a tragedy, the fall from bliss to misery is also the major theme. At the beginning of Book iv Satan, taking his first prospect of Eden, remembers his own fall from Heaven, and speaks with the accents of a tragic protagonist:

> to thee I call,
> But with no friendly voice, and add thy name
> O Sun, to tell thee how I hate thy beams

That bring to my remembrance from what state
I fell, how glorious once above thy Spheare.

And at the beginning of Book IX, when the action is about to shift to the
fall of man from Paradise, Milton comments, 'I now must change /
Those Notes to Tragic'. Each of these falls is related to offences
committed by the respective protagonists; mutability, therefore, gives
way to culpability. But there is even greater change, since, in man's case
at least, the fall is not final. He is redeemed by Christ; indeed, the
Incarnation would not have occurred without the Fall, and this is so
great a blessing that Adam, when the future is unfolded to him by
Michael, hesitates between feeling guilt and remorse for the evil which
will follow his sin and rejoicing at the greater good that will ultimately
spring from it:

                                    full of doubt I stand,
Whether I should repent me now of sin
By mee done and occasiond, or rejoyce
Much more, that much more good thereof shall spring,
To God more glory, more good will to Men
From God, and over wrauth grace shall abound.[20] (XII 473-8)

The message is fundamentally the same as that of *Samson Agonistes*. Both
works see beyond tragedy, which belongs to the temporal perspective,
and, by placing it in the perspective of eternity, convert it into divine
comedy.

    The material on which the religious mind dwells is thus productive of
tragedy, but the interpretation which Christianity places upon it draws
the tragic sting. This paradox is discussed by Laurence Michel in an
interesting essay on 'The Possibility of a Christian Tragedy'. The
religious sense as such is not incompatible, he says, with tragedy, but the
specifically Christian sense is:

For the religious person, the problem of evil, which is the root of tragedy,
becomes the conviction of sin; the tension, the qualm, the psychomachia, the
agon-izing, all result from 'the dream of innocence confronted by the fact of
guilt'. Thus tragedy can get a start in a religious vision of human life, and of the
cosmos, which is 'Jewish' or Manichean. But Christians believe in the efficacy of
the Incarnation and the Resurrection and the Redemption: that the hegemony
of the devil was destroyed once and for all. The Gordian tragic knot has been
cut. Sin remains, although the devastating effect of Original Sin has been
removed, and each man must work out his salvation with diligence, if not in fear
and trembling; but his life is no longer in the proper sense a predicament or a
dilemma.[21]

The problems raised by this comment are perhaps more complex than at first appears. 'Christian' is itself too widely embracing for the assertion that Christianity is incompatible with tragedy to stand unqualified. Less optimistic forms of Christianity, such as Calvinism or Jansenism, or the Kierkegaardian 'fear and trembling',[22] to which Michel alludes in the above quotation, induce an awareness of possible exclusion from grace which in the guilty consciousness of certain protagonists may work to intensify a tragic sense of damnation.[22] Thus, if Marlowe's *Dr Faustus* is a 'Christian tragedy' it is of this kind; and Racine's *Phèdre*, despite its classical setting, reflects the dark side of a 'Christian' sense of sin which has taken on the aspect of irremediability. Hogg's *Confessions of a Justified Sinner*, on the other hand, is sardonic tragical satire on a Calvinistic over-confidence of election: a 'redemption' that becomes tragic because it damns. Christianity of this kind belongs to that wider category of religious consciousness which, far from undermining tragedy, in fact, becomes essential to it. (The possibility of Christian tragedy of this kind is also entertained by Schlegel, despite his generally Romantic view.) 'Religious' in this sense involves a commitment of the entire being, a wholeheartedness and singlemindedness the lack of which, in the view of J. L. Styan [*], makes the twentieth century unsuited to tragedy 'in the full sense of the word':

Our present-day mongrel conventions . . . do not encourage the exclusive consistency of purpose we ask of tragedy. Twentieth-century currents of contradictory thought and the mood of audiences do not permit it; the laws of tragedy belong to a world which is religious in its affirmation of human greatness.

☆

We therefore reach the seemingly paradoxical conclusion that Christianity is anti-tragic, but that tragedy belongs to a world which is religiously committed. One mode of resolving this paradox is to say that it is the incomplete quality of the religious commitment which makes for tragedy. This does not mean, of course, that tragedy is only possible in a bigoted age. It is to the protagonist that the incompleteness belongs, but the 'religious' consciousness of the author or audience must be such that the protagonist's incompleteness does not present itself as mere folly or pitiable ignorance. The protagonist is justified, and only incomplete by some further, overarching standard. Basically, this is the Hegelian view of tragedy – ultimately as optimistic as the supposedly anti-tragic Christian view, but lacking the Christian emphasis on revealed religion and personal salvation.

Hegel [*] exalts this distinction between the overarching standard and the incompleteness of the protagonist to the level of the governing principle of tragedy. He posits, on the one hand, a universal order, blameless, neutral and passive, in which all is ideally justified and harmonised; and, on the other, particular ethical powers which are partial expressions of the universal order, and which become embodied in active, self-confident individuals who assert their incomplete ethical truths with unrelenting energy and conviction. It is out of the conflict of such individuals with each other that tragedy – and more especially Greek tragedy, which Hegel tends to regard as a purer and weightier form of tragedy than the modern – comes into being. Or, as Clark Butter puts it, in his exposition of Hegel's conception of tragedy:

Tragic conflict arises out of the circumstance that an individual identifies with a finite, limited end with such single-minded passion that other, related ends are blindly ignored and stomped under foot. In the language of Hegelian dialectics, we should say that the tragic hero *abstracts* and absolutises some limited end essentially related (*internally related*) to *other* ends which he thereby *negates*, calling forth his own *self-negation* through those other excluded ends.[23]

The favourite example, both for Hegel and his followers, is the conflict in Sophocles's *Antigone* between Antigone herself, determined to honour her dead brother with burial, and Creon, equally determined to disallow her. (See the extracts from Hegel's *Aesthetics* and from George Eliot included in the present selection.) According to this interpretation (though in the judgement of C. M. Bowra it contradicts Sophocles's text[24]), both are right and both are wrong. In opposing each other, though they are incapable of recognising it, they are opposing an ethical principle which has a valid claim upon them, and therefore inevitable destruction follows, as much from within as from without. In Hegel's own words: 'So there is immanent in both Antigone and Creon something that in their own way they attack, so that they are gripped and shattered by something intrinsic to their own actual being.'[25]

   This sense that one party to a conflict is opposed by another who is 'ethically justified' is essential in Hegel's view to the full effect of tragedy. Without it tragedy is merely subjective, as in modern (i.e. post-classical) examples such as *Hamlet*. Comparing the Greek treatment of Orestes's situation (a son duty-bound to avenge the murder of his father by his mother) with that of Hamlet (a son bound to avenge the murder of his father by his uncle), Hegel argues that 'whereas in the Greek poets the King's death does have an ethical justification, in Shakespeare it is simply and solely an atrocious crime'. Since there is nothing for Hamlet to respect in Claudius, he is not in the tragic situation which yields the greatest intensity: i.e. when the portagonist, pursuing 'an ethically justified revenge', is compelled thereby to violate some other ethically justified position. It is different with Orestes. His dilemma is that he must, at the instigation of Apollo, avenge the murder of his father Agamemnon, but by so doing he will spill the blood of his own mother, Clytemnestra, and therefore outrage the Furies. Because there is no equivalent dilemma for Hamlet, his conflict becomes mainly a matter of personality. As Hegel puts it,

His noble soul is not made for this kind of energetic activity; and, full of disgust with the world and life, what with decision, proof, arrangements for carrying out his resolve, and being bandied from pillar to post, he eventually perishes owing to his own hesitation and a complication of external circumstances.

Leaving aside the arguments which can be advanced against this particular view of *Hamlet*, one can see that a tragedy of this subjective nature, though it may be very moving, lacks the weightiness which belongs to the tragedy of equally valid claims; and, what is especially significant for Hegel, it lacks a catastrophe which satisfies the audience as inevitable and ultimately just. 'In Greek tragedy', he says, 'it is eternal justice which, as the absolute power of fate, saves and maintains the harmony of the substance of the ethical order against the particular powers which were becoming independent and therefore colliding, and because of the inner rationality of its sway we are satisfied when we see individuals coming to ruin.' The incomplete protagonists are thus resolved back by their deaths into the complete ethical substance from which they divided themselves, and though the feeling of suffering and agony is still acute in the minds of the audience, there is also a countervailing, and ultimately over-riding, sense that it is fundamentally just that they should die.

George Eliot probably intended such an ending for *The Mill on the Floss*. Maggie, justified according to her lights, and her brother, Tom, equally justified according to his, have come into tragic opposition in the latter part of the novel, but their perishing together in the flood transcends this opposition, giving the final catastrophe of the novel a sense of division overcome: 'In their death they were not divided.' Unfortunately the intended effect is marred by a certain sentimentality which creeps into the closing pages, and a feeling that other, more serious, issues have been evaded.

One of the difficulties in the way of writing Hegelian tragedy is that it can seem to offer too easy a consolation for the suffering which has been depicted; and as a means of interpreting earlier tragedy, even the Greek, on which Hegel so much depends for his evidence, it is likewise open to the objection that it blunts powerfully presented individual suffering in the interest of a remote and abstract sense of final justice. It does not, of course, reduce tragedy to the banal level of so-called 'poetic justice', which demands an appropriate distribution of rewards and punishments to the good and the wicked characters respectively,[26] but it can lead to a slightly spurious sense that 'all's for the best in the best of all possible worlds' which undermines, if not defeats, the sense in all great tragedy that human suffering is immitigable. In the words which express the growing sense of suffering that led Keats to recast his epic of Hyperion in a form nearer to that of 'high tragedy',

> None can usurp this height . . .
> But those to whom the miseries of the world
> Are misery, and will not let them rest.[27]

For Hegel there is a formal correspondence to the contrast between individual ethical positions and the overarching ethical substance in the contrast, as it is found in Greek tragedy, between protagonists and Chorus. However, the Chorus, he says, 'is not at all a moralist', and the extent to which it can be regarded as enacting the role of the 'ethical substance' is strictly limited. This has to be so, because, as Hegel would recognise, the Chorus hardly ever transcends the protagonists in its foresight and wisdom and capacity to view the events of the tragedy *sub specie aeternitatis*. Nevertheless, Hegel does regard the Chorus as 'the actual substance of moral life and action of the heroes themselves', and, he says, 'in contrast to these individuals it is the people as the fruitful soil out of which they grow (just as flowers and towering trees do from their own native soil) and by the existent character of which they are conditioned'. As the protagonists separate off from the Chorus, they are thrown into relief against its background, in a contrast which is at least dramatically parallel to the separation of their incomplete moral values from the ethical substance; and just as the ethical substance persists beyond the destruction which the clash of incomplete values brings about, so the Chorus outlives the deaths of the protagonists, remaining, after the fall of the 'flowers and towering trees', as 'the fruitful soil' which represents the unbroken continuity of life.

☆

Precise examination of the function of the Chorus from play to play would probably reveal a more variable role than this, but the fundamental idea of the protagonist as an individual detaching himself in his more intense consciousness and commitment from the surrounding mass of the Chorus is valid for many Greek tragedies and also for various works which are influenced by them, such as *Samson Agonistes*, *Murder in the Cathedral* and Hardy's tragic novels.[28] It is, however, completely at variance with another major, and possibly even more influential, theory concerning the Chorus – that which Nietzsche expresses in his disconcertingly original *The Birth of Tragedy*. [*]

Nietzsche's Chorus has nothing to do with the moral life; it is non-moral, or better still, pre-moral. Moreover, it is conceived by Nietzsche, not in contrastive relationship to the protagonist, but as that from which tragedy itself derives. In other words, he is concerned with origin rather than form – though, one must hasten to add, not with origin examined in a disciplined, scholarly fashion. Nietzsche makes a bold intuitive leap, to claim that this originating principle was a chorus of satyrs, followers of Dionysus, expressing through their dithyrambic utterances an immediate, irrational sensation of the surging chaos of existence: something which undercuts the whole edifice of reason and order which man in his sophistication has built up for himself. Consequently, it gives a sense both of annihilation and vitality, of destruction and release, comparable to that which Wagner claims for music:

> ... the satyr, the fictitious natural being, bears the same relation to the man of culture that Dionysian music bears to civilisation. Concerning the latter, Richard Wagner says that it is nullified by music just as lamplight is nullified by the light of day. Similarly, I believe, the Greek man of culture felt himself nullified in the presence of the satyric chorus ....

To counter this anarchic Dionysian principle the man of culture has recourse to the antithetical Apollonian* principle – named from Apollo, the god of the sun and of poetry – which by articulating it and re-creating it into the dream-world of art makes it bearable for man. It is at this point that tragedy is born, delicately poised between the irrational and rational, the Dionysian and Apollonian, worlds. While it sustains this balance tragedy, as J. P. Stern explains, has 'a vital function: to protect men from a full knowledge of the life-destroying doom that surrounds them, and at the same time to refresh their zest for life from tragedy's own dark Stygian sources'.[29] The balance is precarious, however, and in Nietzsche's view is already disturbed in the work of Euripides, which succumbs to 'an altogether newborn demon, called *Socrates*'. '*Aesthetic Socratism*', he protests, holds that 'To be beautiful everything must be intelligible', and, as a result of the determined application of this principle, tragedy, with Euripides, dies through 'audacious reasonableness'.

The full title of Nietzsche's book is *The Birth of Tragedy from the Spirit of Music*, and its inspiration, as hinted by the quotation from Wagner

---

* The form 'Apollinian' is employed in the excerpts from Nietzsche, in Part Two of this selection, but I use here the form more frequent among English-speaking writers—Ed.

above, is Wagnerian opera. Nietzsche has comparatively little to say about particular works of literature – though there is, for example, an interesting comment on the way Dionysian man resembles Hamlet. But his sense of the underlying, disturbing force of tragedy is strong, and it is this which he calls music. In particular, the Wagnerian effect of a continuous flow of orchestral and choral music from which the individual singers' voices emerge, and into which they seem to die again, is the best analogy for his Dionysian/Apollonian conception of tragedy. It is, however, only analogy. As Stern shows, Nietzsche's thinking is indirect, metaphorical thinking which eschews dogmatic absoluteness.[30] If the world is to be explained, it is only as some kind of vast artistic construction, an opera or a symphony, which does not have meaning, but which nevertheless meaningfully relates sounds and rhythms to each other. And the work of art being Apollonian, dedicated to making the Dionysian destructive vitality bearable, its composition is a fusion of beauty and ugliness, a 'musical dissonance':

In this sense, it is precisely the tragic myth that has to convince us that even the ugly and disharmonic are part of an artistic game that the will in the eternal amplitude of its pleasure plays with itself. But this primordial phenomenon of Dionysian art is difficult to grasp, and there is only one direct way to make it intelligible and grasp it immediately: through the wonderful significance of *musical dissonance*.

☆

Cloudy and generalised though this may be (one is dealing, as stated at the beginning of this Introduction, with a subject that does not lend itself to clear and simple definitions), it nevertheless expresses an important insight into the nature of tragedy. Tragedy does not yield moral lessons. Where they are offered, as in the closing lines of *Dr Faustus*, they are apt to seem superficially inadequate, and even, in the deepest sense, irrelevant, to the experience which the tragedy has caused the audience (whether spectator or reader) to live through. It articulates, with subtlety and power, the disturbing resonances of suffering and injustice, and often does so in a way that modulates initial protest into final acceptance, but it stops at the point where philosophy might want to begin. For philosophy could only falsify the experiential effect of tragedy. If there is a sense in which tragedy 'explains' suffering, that explanation is essentially non-discursive. The terrible and beautiful are emotionally co-ordinated in the cathartic effect of tragedy, as in Nietzsche's 'wonderful significance of *musical dissonance*', and the result is an intuition of the meaning of suffering on a level which is, however, inaccessible to reason as such. The work of art experienced *as* a work of art is the explanation; any other is at best an attempt to create the conditions in which that artistic explanation may work more effectively on the imagination of the audience or reader. When the tragic curve has been completed, then, in Hamlet's words, 'the rest is silence'.

That curve is most often completed within the confines of a play or a novel, for it usually needs the space for development and interaction of opposed characters afforded by more extended literary forms. (Though excessive length – and this is perhaps true of Hardy's *The Dynasts* – may dissipate the effect.) But certain poems and lyrics manage to achieve moving expression of the tragic experience within a much smaller compass. The essay with which this Casebook concludes [*] is an attempt to explore the possibilities of such 'lyric tragedy'. It is a tentative, and perhaps over-compressed, essay and has room for analysis of a few examples only; a proper consideration of the subject would require a book of its own. But I hope that enough is done to serve as a useful complement to the rest of the extracts, which are, inevitably, devoted exclusively to drama and the novel; and to underline the point already made, that the 'explanation' of tragic experience is inherent in the distinctively literary quality of the means by which it is expressed. The meaning of suffering is only understood when the reader is made to 'see it feelingly'; and though that phrase belongs to a play, it aptly describes the response evoked by such poems as Keats's Odes, Hopkins's 'terrible sonnets' and Philip Larkin's 'The Building'.

The essay on 'Lyric Tragedy', in common with the extracts which precede it, examines only a corner of the huge area covered by tragedy. None of the separate items in this Casebook can claim to be a comprehensive treatment of tragedy. In each one individually tragedy is refracted and incomplete. But collectively they may help to compensate for their separate deficiencies, and it is with this hope that they are here gathered together and offered to the reader. Ranging from Aristotle to the present day, they necessarily reflect very diverse attitudes and are conditioned by the prevailing tastes and assumptions of the different periods from which they come; but they also represent a remarkable co-operative effort of criticism which has built up across the centuries a fascinating body of thought about the nature and meaning of tragedy. A great deal has been modified, but little actually superseded. The result is, I believe, a highly diverse, and sometimes contradictory, but still living tradition.

NOTES

1. According to House, both the *Rhetoric* and the *Poetics* belong to the third stage of Aristotle's career (post–335 BC, after his return to Athens). They come at the end of the Lyceum course, assuming considerable previous theoretical

training, and 'They are the kind of works suitable for men about to go into public life; partly theoretical, partly practical': *Aristotle's Poetics* (London, 1956), p. 36.

2. Cf. the extract from John Jones in Part One, below.

3. Henry James, *The Portrait of a Lady*, ch. 42.

4. Cf. the extract from Virginia Woolf in Part Three, below.

5. See the extract from Hegel in Part Two, below, and the remarks on the Hegelian concept of tragedy in this Introduction below.

6. For an account of the Renaissance interpretation, and distortion, of Aristotle, see Bernard Weinberg, 'From Aristotle to Pseudo-Aristotle', *Comparative Literature*, v (Spring 1953), 97–104; reprinted in Elder Olson (ed.), *Aristotle's 'Poetics' and English Literature* (Chicago, 1965), pp. 192–200.

7. The so-called 'unity of time' derives from Aristotle's comment that 'Tragedy endeavours, as far as possible, to confine itself to a single revolution of the sun, or but slightly to exceed this limit' (*Poetics*, v 4: Butcher's trans., p. 23) – a practice which probably derives from the continuous presence of the Greek Chorus in the orchestra. The 'unity of action', however, is given lengthy treatment in VII, VIII and IX. (See the extracts from the *Poetics*, headed 'Plot and Unity of Action', in Part One, below.)

8. See Walter Raleigh (ed.), *Johnson on Shakespeare* (Oxford, 1908; reprint of 1946), pp. 25–8.

9. Cf. the title of Odette de Mourgues's book on Racine: *Racine, or The Triumph of Relevance* (Cambridge, 1967) and her statements: 'Everything in his tragedies is directed towards one single aim: to bring the tragic emotion to the highest degree of intensity. . . . In fact the most striking aspect of Racine's art . . . might be described as the triumph of relevance.' (pp. 6–7).

10. Curt A. Zimansky (ed.), *The Critical Works of Thomas Rymer* (New Haven, Conn., 1956), p. 170.

11. Thomas Hutchinson (ed.), *The Poetical Works of Wordsworth*, revised by Ernest de Selincourt (Oxford, 1904; rev. edn 1942). The most relevant passage is that which begins (p. 935): 'The principal object, then, proposed in these Poems was to choose incidents and situations from common life, and to relate or describe them, throughout, as far as was possible in a selection of language really used by men. . . . Humble and rustic life was generally chosen, because, in that condition, the essential passions of the heart find a better soil in which they can attain their maturity, are less under restraint, and speak a plainer and more emphatic language . . . .'

12. Jeannette King, *Tragedy in the Victorian Novel* (Cambridge, 1978), pp. 7–8.

13. The three novels are: *The Wings of the Dove* (1902), *The Ambassadors* (1903) and *The Golden Bowl* (1904).

14. The ambiguous position which Dorothea Krook gives to *Hedda Gabler* illustrates the weakness of her Platonic approach to what is one of the most powerful tragic experiences of the modern theatre.

15. For an interesting discussion of examples of Schopenhauerian tragedy, see David Lenson, 'The Other Tragedy': ch. 7 of his *Achilles' Choice* (Princeton, N.J. 1975), pp. 137–58.

16. The shift from the use of 'tragedy' as a term merely denoting genre to one implying favourable literary-cum-moral status is traced by Clayton Loelb in

' "Tragedy" as an Evaluative Term', *Comparative Literary Studies*, XI, 1 (March 1974), 69–84. As far as Dorothea Krook is concerned, it would perhaps be fairer to say that she differentiates between higher and lower forms of tragedy rather than that she reserves the term exclusively for her Platonic kind of tragedy.

17. According to Dacier, tragedy 'disposes the most miserable, to think themselves happy, when they compare their own Misfortunes, with those, which Tragedy has represented to them': quoted by Donald F. Bond in his edition of *The Spectator* (Oxford, 1965), p. 568.

18. Geoffrey Brereton, *Principles of Tragedy* (Coral Gables, Florida, 1968), p. 31. The whole of Brereton's discussion of *catharsis*, including some speculation on the psychology of the audience (which, however, is not allowed to get out of hand) is an interesting contribution to the subject: see pp. 28–34.

19. George Steiner, *The Death of Tragedy* (London, 1961), p. 331; this passage is not in the excerpt included in Part Three, below.

20. Although I have been concerned to stress the difference between Milton's version of Christian tragedy and that of the Middle Ages, I ought in fairness to point out that this *felix culpa* theme was itself a commonplace in the Middle Ages – witness the lyric, 'Adam lay ibowndyn': see T. Silverstein (ed.), *Medieval English Lyrics* (London, 1971), p. 100. It is, however, the building of this into a structure which 'justifies' the Fall, retaining its tragic meaning, but also transcending it, which distinguishes the Miltonic version.

21. Laurence Michel, article in *Thought* (Autumn 1956), 428. Another view of Christian tragedy, that it is the 'tragedy of possibility' as opposed to the Greek 'tragedy of necessity', is to be found in W. H. Auden's 'The Christian Tragic Hero', *New York Times Book Review* (16 Dec. 1945); reprinted in Robert W. Corrigan (ed.), *Tragedy: Vision and Form* (San Francisco, 1965), pp. 143–7. This, however, fails to engage with the *felix culpa* theme which essentially undercuts the tragic finality of loss.

22. See Kierkegaard, *Fear and Trembling*, trans. Robert Payne (Oxford, 1939); also 'The Ancient Tragical Motif as Reflected in the Modern' in *Either/Or: A Fragment of Life*, reprinted in Corrigan (ed.), op. cit., pp. 451–70. For Kierkegaard the typically religious tragic figure is Abraham caught between the ethical command not to murder his son Isaac and God's command to sacrifice him. His tragic hero is above all a guilt-ridden figure.

23. Clark Butter, *G. W. F. Hegel* (Boston, 1977), p. 111.

24. See C. M. Bowra, *Sophoclean Tragedy* (Oxford, 1944).

25. The translator is T. M. Knox, who makes the following gloss: 'His [Hegel's] point is that the *Antigone* is the finest portrayal of what he regards as the greatest tragic conflict . · . . one where both parties are under the necessity of trangressing; they are divided against themselves; neither of them can obey *both* the valid *laws* to which they are subject': *Aesthetics* (Oxford, 1975), vol. 2, p. 1218.

26. See Addison's refutation of this morally naïve view of tragedy in the extract from *Spectator*, No. 40 (16 April 1711), reproduced in Part Two, below.

27. *The Fall of Hyperion: A Dream*, lines 147–9. This poem was an attempt by Keats, at the end of 1819, to reconstruct the earlier, more Miltonic *Hyperion*. The words are attributed to Moneta, goddess of Memory, and it is in connection with her that the phrase 'high tragedy' is later used:

So at the view of sad Moneta's brow
I ach'd to see what things the hollow brain
Behind entomb'd: what high tragedy
In the dark secret chambers of her skull
Was acting . . .   (275–9)

28. Groups of minor rustic figures such as those who gather round the bonfire
in *The Return of the Native*, or comment on the major characters from the safety of
their inn seats in *Far From the Madding Crowd* or *The Mayor of Casterbridge*, form a
nineteenth-century Dorset equivalent, *mutatis mutandis*, of the Greek chorus;
and like the Chorus they also participate in the action.

29. J. P. Stern, *Nietzsche* (London, 1978), p. 45; ch. 3 gives an excellent
account of *The Birth of Tragedy*, to which I am much indebted.

30. Ibid., ch. 7, 'Aesthetic Re-interpretation'.

PART ONE

The *Poetics* of Aristotle

Aristotle   Extracts from the 'Poetics'
(c. 335–22 BC)

The Definition of Tragedy

Tragedy, then, is an imitation of an action that is serious, complete, and of a certain magnitude; in language embellished with each kind of artistic ornament, the several kinds being found in separate parts of the play; in the form of action, not of narrative; through pity and fear effecting the proper purgation of these emotions. By 'language embellished',I mean language into which rhythm, 'harmony', and song enter. By 'the several kinds in separate parts', I mean, that some parts are rendered through the medium of verse alone, others again with the aid of song. . . . (VI 2–3)*

The Constituents of Tragedy

Again, Tragedy is the imitation of an action; and an action implies personal agents, who necessarily possess certain distinctive qualities both of character and thought; for it is by these that we qualify actions themselves, and these – thought and character – are the two natural causes from which actions spring, and on actions again all success or failure depends. Hence, the Plot is the imitation of the action: for by Plot I here mean the arrangement of the incidents. By Character I mean that in virtue of which we ascribe certain qualities to the agents. Thought is required wherever a statement is proved, or, it may be, a general truth enunciated. Every Tragedy, therefore, must have six parts, which parts determine its quality: namely, Plot, Character, Diction, Thought, Spectacle, Song. Two of the parts constitute the medium of imitation, one the manner, and three the objects of imitation. And these complete the list. These elements have been employed, we may say, by the poets to a man; in fact, every play

---

* The references at the conclusion of each extract relate to the section and subsection numbering in the translation, which is cognate with the ordering of the Greek text. The captions for the extracts are supplied for this Casebook and do not figure in the original (Ed.).

contains Spectacular elements as well as Character, Plot, Diction, Song, and Thought.

But most important of all is the structure of the incidents. For Tragedy is an imitation, not of men, but of an action and of life, and life consists in action, and its end is a mode of action, not a quality. Now character determines men's qualities, but it is by their actions that they are happy or the reverse. Dramatic action, therefore, is not with a view to the representation of character: character comes in as subsidiary to the actions. Hence the incidents and the plot are the end of a tragedy; and the end is the chief thing of all. Again, without action there cannot be a tragedy; there may be without character. The tragedies of most of our modern poets fail in the rendering of character; and of poets in general this is often true. It is the same in painting; and here lies the difference between Zeuxis and Polygnotus. Polygnotus delineates character well: the style of Zeuxis is devoid of ethical quality. Again, if you string together a set of speeches expressive of character, and well finished in point of diction and thought, you will not produce the essential tragic effect nearly so well as with a play which, however deficient in these respects, yet has a plot and artistically constructed incidents. Besides which, the most powerful elements of emotional interest in Tragedy – Peripeteia or Reversal of the Situation, and Recognition scenes – are parts of the plot. A further proof is, that novices in the art attain to finish of diction and precision of portraiture before they can construct the plot. It is the same with almost all the early poets.

The Plot, then, is the first principle, and, as it were, the soul of a tragedy: Character holds the second place. A similar fact is seen in painting. The most beautiful colours, laid on confusedly, will not give as much pleasure as the chalk outline of a portrait. Thus Tragedy is the imitation of an action, and of the agents mainly with a view to the action.

Third in order is Thought – that is, the faculty of saying what is possible and pertinent in given circumstances. In the case of oratory, this is the function of the political art and of the art of rhetoric: and so indeed the older poets make their characters speak the language of civic life; the poets of our time, the language of the rhetoricians. Character is that which reveals moral purpose, showing what kind of things a man chooses or avoids. Speeches, therefore, which do not make this manifest, or in which the speaker does not choose or avoid anything whatever, are not expressive of character. Thought, on the other hand, is found where something is proved to be or not to be, or a general maxim is enunciated.

Fourth among the elements enumerated comes Diction; by which I mean, as has been already said, the expression of the meaning in words;

and its essence is the same both in verse and prose.

Of the remaining elements Song holds the chief place among the embellishments.

The Spectacle has, indeed, an emotional attraction of its own, but, of all the parts, it is the least artistic, and connected least with the art of poetry. For the power of Tragedy, we may be sure, is felt even apart from representation and actors. Besides, the production of spectacular effects depends more on the art of the stage machinist than on that of the poet. (VI 5–19)

Plot and Unity of Action

These principles being established, let us now discuss the proper structure of the Plot, since this is the first and most important thing in Tragedy.

Now, according to our definition, Tragedy is an imitation of an action that is complete, and whole, and of a certain magnitude; for there may be a whole that is wanting in magnitude. A whole is that which has a beginning, a middle, and an end. A beginning is that which does not itself follow anything by causal necessity, but after which something naturally is or comes to be. An end, on the contrary, is that which itself naturally follows some other thing, either by necessity, or as a rule, but has nothing following it. A middle is that which follows something as some other thing follows it. A well constructed plot, therefore, must neither begin nor end at haphazard, but conform to these principles.

Again, a beautiful object, whether it be a living organism or any whole composed of parts, must not only have an orderly arrangement of parts, but must also be of a certain magnitude; for beauty depends on magnitude and order. Hence a very small animal organism cannot be beautiful; for the view of it is confused, the object being seen in an almost imperceptible moment of time. Nor, again, can one of vast size be beautiful; for as the eye cannot take it all in at once, the unity and sense of the whole is lost for the spectator; as for instance if there were one a thousand miles long. As, therefore, in the case of animate bodies and organisms a certain magnitude is necessary, and a magnitude which may be easily embraced in one view; so in the plot, a certain length is necessary, and a length which can be easily embraced by the memory. The limit of length in relation to dramatic competition and sensuous presentment, is no part of artistic theory. For had it been the rule for a hundred tragedies to compete together, the performance would have been regulated by the water-clock – as indeed we are told was formerly done. But the limit as fixed by the nature of the drama itself is this: the greater the length, the more beautiful will the piece be by reason of its size, provided that the whole be perspicuous. And to define the matter roughly, we may say that the proper magnitude is comprised within such limits, that the sequence of events, according to the law of probability or necessity, will admit of a change from bad fortune to good, or from good fortune to bad.

Unity of plot does not, as some persons think, consist in the unity of the hero. For infinitely various are the incidents in one man's life which cannot be reduced to unity; and so, too, there are many actions of one man out of which we cannot make one action. Hence the error, as it appears, of all poets who have composed a Heracleid, a Theseid, or other poems of the kind. They imagine that as Heracles was one man, the story of Heracles must also be a unity. But Homer, as in all else he is of surpassing merit, here too – whether from art or natural genius – seems to have happily discerned the truth. In composing the Odyssey he did not include all the adventures of Odysseus – such as his wound on Parnassus, or his feigned madness at the mustering of the host – incidents between which there was no necessary or probable connexion: but he made the Odyssey, and likewise the Iliad, to centre round an action that in our sense of the word is one. As therefore, in the other imitative arts, the imitation is one when the object imitated is one, so the plot, being an imitation of an action, must imitate one action and that a whole, the structural union of the parts being such that, if any one of them is displaced or removed, the whole will be disjointed and disturbed. For a thing whose presence or absence makes no visible difference, is not an organic part of the whole. . . . (VII 1–7; VIII 1–4)

Recognition and Reversal

But again, Tragedy is an imitation not only of a complete action, but of events inspiring fear or pity. Such an effect is best produced when the events come on us by surprise; and the effect is heightened when, at the same time, they follow as cause and effect. The tragic wonder will then be greater than if they happened of themselves or by accident; for even coincidences are most striking when they have an air of design. We may instance the statue of Mitys at Argos, which fell upon his murderer while he was a spectator at a festival, and killed him. Such events seem not to be due to mere chance. Plots, therefore, constructed on these principles are necessarily the best.

Plots are either Simple or Complex, for the actions in real life, of which the plots are an imitation, obviously show a similar distinction. An action which is one and continuous in the sense above defined, I call

Simple, when the change of fortune takes place without Reversal of the Situation and without Recognition.

A Complex action is one in which the change is accompanied by such Reversal, or by Recognition, or by both. These last should arise from the internal structure of the plot, so that what follows should be the necessary or probable result of the preceding action. It makes all the difference whether any given event is a case of *propter hoc* or *post hoc*.

Reversal of the Situation is a change by which the action veers round to its opposite, subject always to our rule of probability or necessity. Thus in the Oedipus, the messenger comes to cheer Oedipus and free him from his alarms about his mother, but by revealing who he is, he produces the opposite effect. Again in the Lynceus, Lynceus is being led away to his death, and Danaus goes with him, meaning to slay him; but the outcome of the preceding incidents is that Danaus is killed and Lynceus saved.

Recognition, as the name indicates, is a change from ignorance to knowledge, producing love or hate between the persons destined by the poet for good or bad fortune. The best form of recognition is coincident with a Reversal of the Situation, as in the Oedipus. There are indeed other forms. Even inanimate things of the most trivial kind may in a sense be objects of recognition. Again, we may recognise or discover whether a person has done a thing or not. But the recognition which is most intimately connected with the plot and action is, as we have said, the recognition of persons. This recognition, combined with Reversal, will produce either pity or fear; and actions producing these effects are those which, by our definition, Tragedy represents. Moreover, it is upon such situations that the issues of good or bad fortune will depend. Recognition, then, being between persons, it may happen that one person only is recognised by the other – when the latter is already known – or it may be necessary that the recognition should be on both sides. Thus Iphigenia is revealed to Orestes by the sending of the letter; but another act of recognition is required to make Orestes known to Iphigenia. . . . (IX 11–12; X 1–3; XI 1–5)

The Nature of the Tragic Hero

A perfect tragedy should, as we have seen, be arranged not on the simple but on the complex plan. It should, moreover, imitate actions which excite pity and fear, this being the distinctive mark of tragic imitation. It follows plainly, in the first place, that the change of fortune presented must not be the spectacle of a virtuous man brought from prosperity to adversity: for this moves neither pity nor fear; it merely shocks us. Nor, again, that of a bad man passing from adversity to prosperity: for nothing can be more alien to the spirit of Tragedy; it possesses no single tragic quality; it neither satisfies the moral sense nor calls forth pity or fear. Nor, again, should the downfall of the utter villain be exhibited. A plot of this kind would, doubtless, satisfy the moral sense, but it would inspire neither pity nor fear; for pity is aroused by unmerited misfortune, fear by the misfortune of a man like ourselves. Such an event, therefore, will be neither pitiful nor terrible. There remains, then, the character between these two extremes – that of a man who is not eminently good and just, yet whose misfortune is brought about not by vice or depravity, but by some error or frailty. He must be one who is highly renowned and prosperous – a personage like Oedipus, Thyestes, or other illustrious men of such families.

A well constructed plot should, therefore, be single in its issue, rather than double as some maintain. The change of fortune should be not from bad to good, but, reversely, from good to bad. It should come about as the result not of vice, but of some great error or frailty, in a character either such as we have described, or better rather than worse. The practice of the stage bears out our view. At first the poets recounted any legend that came in their way. Now, the best tragedies are founded on the story of a few houses – on the fortunes of Alcmaeon, Oedipus, Orestes, Meleager, Thyestes, Telephus, and those others who have done or suffered something terrible. A tragedy, then, to be perfect according to the rules of art should be of this construction. Hence they are in error who censure Euripides just because he follows this principle in his plays, many of which end unhappily. It is, as we have said, the right ending. The best proof is that on the stage and in dramatic competition, such plays, if well worked out, are the most tragic in effect; and Euripides, faulty though he may be in the general management of his subject, yet is felt to be the most tragic of the poets. . . . (XIII 2–6)

Spectacle and the Deed of Horror

Fear and pity may be aroused by spectacular means; but they may also result from the inner structure of the piece, which is the better way, and indicates a superior poet. For the plot ought to be so constructed that, even without the aid of the eye, he who hears the tale told will thrill with horror and melt to pity at what takes place. This is the impression we should receive from hearing the story of the Oedipus. But to produce this effect by the mere spectacle is a less artistic method, and dependent on extraneous aids. Those who employ spectacular means to create a sense not of the terrible but only of the monstrous, are strangers to the purpose of Tragedy; for we must not demand of Tragedy any and every kind of pleasure, but only that which is proper to it. And since the pleasure which the poet should afford is that which comes from pity and fear through imitation, it is evident that this quality must be impressed upon the incidents.

Let us then determine what are the circumstances which strike us as terrible or pitiful.

Actions capable of this effect must happen between persons who are either friends or enemies or indifferent to one another. If an enemy kills an enemy, there is nothing to excite pity either in the act or the intention – except so far as the suffering in itself is pitiful. So again with indifferent persons. But when the tragic incident occurs between those who are near or dear to one another – if, for example, a brother kills, or intends to kill, a brother, a son his father, a mother her son, a son his mother, or any other deed of the kind is done – these are the situations to be looked for by the poet. He may not indeed destroy the framework of the received legends – the fact, for instance, that Clytemnestra was slain by Orestes and Eriphyle by Alcmaeon – but he ought to show invention of his own, and skilfully handle the traditional material. Let us explain more clearly what is meant by skilful handling.

The action may be done consciously and with knowledge of the persons, in the manner of the older poets. It is thus too that Euripides makes Medea slay her children. Or, again, the deed of horror may be done, but done in ignorance, and the tie of kinship or friendship be discovered afterwards. The Oedipus of Sophocles is an example. Here, indeed, the incident is outside the drama proper; but cases occur where it falls within the action of the play: one may cite the Alcmaeon of Astydamas, or Telegonus in the Wounded Odysseus. Again, there is a third case: to be about to act with knowledge of the persons and then not to act. The fourth case is when some one is about to do an irreparable deed through ignorance, and makes the discovery before it is done. These are the only possible ways. For the deed must either be done or not done – and that wittingly or unwittingly. But of all these ways, to be about to act knowing the persons, and then not to act, is the worst. It is shocking without being tragic, for no disaster follows. It is, therefore, never, or very rarely, found in poetry. One instance, however, is in the Antigone, where Haemon threatens to kill Creon. The next and better way is that the deed should be perpetrated. Still better, that it should be perpetrated in ignorance, and the discovery made afterwards. There is then nothing to shock us, while the discovery produces a startling effect. The last case is the best, as when in the Cresphontes Merope is about to slay her son, but, recognising who he is, spares his life. So in the Iphigenia, the sister recognises the brother just in time. Again in the Helle, the son recognises the mother when on the point of giving her up. This, then, is why a few families only, as has been already observed, furnish the subjects of tragedy. It was not art, but happy chance, that led the poets in search of subjects to impress the tragic quality upon their plots. They are compelled, therefore, to have recourse to those houses whose history contains moving incidents like these. . . . (xiv 1–9)

Characterisation

In respect of Character there are four things to be aimed at. First, and most important, it must be good. Now any speech or action that manifests moral purpose of any kind will be expressive of character: the character will be good if the purpose is good. This rule is relative to each class. Even a woman may be good, and also a slave; though the woman may be said to be an inferior being, and the slave quite worthless. The second thing to aim at is propriety. There is a type of manly valour; but valour in a woman, or unscrupulous cleverness, is inappropriate. Thirdly, character must be true to life: for this is a distinct thing from goodness and propriety, as here described. The fourth point is consistency: for though the subject of the imitation, who suggested the type, be inconsistent, still he must be consistently inconsistent. As an example of motiveless degradation of character, we have Menelaus in the Orestes: of character indecorous and inappropriate, the lament of Odysseus in the Scylla, and the speech of Melanippe: of inconsistency, the Iphigenia at Aulis – for Iphigenia the suppliant in no way resembles her later self.

As in the structure of the plot, so too in the portraiture of character, the poet should always aim either at the necessary or the probable. Thus a person of a given character should speak or act in a given way, by the rule either of necessity or of probability; just as this event should follow that by necessary or probable sequence. It is therefore evident that the unravelling of the plot, no less than the complication, must arise out of the plot itself, it must not be brought about by the *Deus ex Machina* – as in the Medea, or in the Return of the Greeks in the Iliad. The *Deus ex Machina* should be employed only for events external to the drama – for antecedent or subsequent events, which lie beyond the range of human knowledge, and which require to be reported or foretold; for to the gods we ascribe the power of seeing all things. Within the action there must be nothing irrational. If the irrational cannot be excluded, it should be outside the scope of the tragedy. Such is the irrational element in the Oedipus of Sophocles.

Again, since Tragedy is an imitation of persons who are above the common level, the example of good portrait-painters should be followed. They, while reproducing the distinctive form of the original, make a likeness which is true to life and yet more beautiful. So too the poet, in representing men who are irascible or indolent, or have other defects of character, should preserve the type and yet ennoble it. In this way Achilles is portrayed by Agathon and Homer. . . . (xv 1–8)

Kinds of Recognition

What Recognition is has been already explained. We will now enumerate its kinds.

First, the least artistic form, which, from poverty of wit, is most commonly employed – recognition by signs. Of these some are congenital – such as 'the spear which the earth-born race bear on their bodies', or the stars introduced by Carcinus in his Thyestes. Others are acquired after birth; and of these some are bodily marks, as scars; some external tokens, as necklaces, or the little ark in the Tyro by which the discovery is effected. Even these admit of more or less skilful treatment. Thus in the recognition of Odysseus by his scar, the discovery is made in one way by the nurse, in another by the swineherds. The use of tokens for the express purpose of proof – and, indeed, any formal proof with or without tokens – is a less artistic mode of recognition. A better kind is that which comes about by a turn of incident, as in the Bath Scene in the Odyssey.

Next come the recognitions invented at will by the poet, and on that account wanting in art. For example, Orestes in the Iphigenia reveals the fact that he is Orestes. She, indeed, makes herself known by the letter; but he, by speaking himself, and saying what the poet, not what the plot requires. This, therefore, is nearly allied to the fault above mentioned: for Orestes might as well have brought tokens with him. Another similar instance is the 'voice of the shuttle' in the Tereus of Sophocles.

The third kind depends on memory when the sight of some object awakens a feeling: as in the Cyprians of Dicaeogenes, where the hero breaks into tears on seeing the picture; or again in the 'Lay of Alcinous', where Odysseus, hearing the minstrel play the lyre, recalls the past and weeps; and hence the recognition.

The fourth kind is by process of reasoning. Thus in the Choëphori: 'Some one resembling me has come: no one resembles me but Orestes: therefore Orestes has come'. . . . Again, there is a composite kind of recognition involving false inference on the part of one of the characters, as in the Odysseus Disguised as a Messenger. A said that no one else was able to bend the bow; hence B (the disguised Odysseus) imagined that A would recognise the bow which, in fact, he had not seen; and to bring about a recognition by this means – the expectation that A would recognise the bow – is false inference.

But, of all recognitions, the best is that which arises from the incidents themselves, where the startling discovery is made by natural means. Such is that in the Oedipus of Sophocles, and in the Iphigenia; for it was natural that Iphigenia should wish to despatch a letter. These recognitions alone dispense with the artificial aid of tokens or amulets. Next come the recognitions by process of reasonings. . . . (xvi 1–6, 7–8)

SOURCE: extracts from *The Poetics of Aristotle*, translated by S. H. Butcher (London, 1895), pp. 23, 25–35, 39–43, 45–7, 49–53, 53–7, 57–9, 61.

Humphry House   Catharsis and the Emotions (1956)

Pity and Fear

These two emotions are described by Aristotle as peculiarly and specially the tragic emotions and he nearly always uses them in conjunction with each other, as a pair. (This conjunction of the two is probably traditional and is found in Gorgias, *Helenae Encomium*, 8.)

The main passage in which he writes about the nature of these emotions in the *Poetics* is in ch. XIII, where he says: 'pity is occasioned by undeserved misfortune, and fear by that of one like ourselves' (i.e., by the misfortune of one like ourselves).

This very short treatment of these emotions can be expanded and explained by what Aristotle says in Book II of the *Rhetoric*. There, in ch. 5, fear is defined as 'a kind of pain or disturbance due to a mental picture of some destructive or painful evil in the future'. (W. Rhys Roberts's translation.) And he adds that this impending evil must be near at hand, not distant. A little later in the same chapter he says further that 'speaking generally, anything causes us to feel fear that when it happens to or threatens others causes us to feel pity'.

This pity and fear are very closely linked; and this becomes still clearer from the definition of pity in *Rhetoric*, II, 8, as

a sort of pain at an evident evil of a destructive or painful kind in the case of somebody who does not deserve it, the evil being one which we might expect to happen to ourselves or to some of our friends, and this at a time when it is said to be near at hand.

And this again is related to fear a little further on, where he says that pity turns into fear when the object is so nearly related to us that the suffering seems to be our own, and we pity others in circumstances in which we should fear for ourselves.

Thus in Aristotle's treatment pity is not an altruistic and disinterested emotion. There can be no pity, in his view, where there is not also fear. Both pity and fear are derived from the self-regarding instinct, and pity springs from the feeling that a similar suffering might happen to ourselves. And this has its obvious bearing on the third requirement for Character in Tragedy in ch. xv of the *Poetics* – that it should be 'like'. This is the basis of the very possibility of sympathy: of the 'feeling with' somebody else. When the good prosper we rejoice with them. When the good suffer or expect to suffer, we share their pains and fears; and that is pity.

If we do not have a tendency to fear for ourselves we cannot share the fear of others. Rash and presumptuous people therefore tend to be incapable of pity. And at the other extreme, if we ourselves are already in terrible suffering and have nothing worse to suffer or fear, we also for this reason tend to be incapable of pity, because we are absorbed in our own fear and cannot share any more with others.

Ideally, according to justice, the two scales of goodness and badness and of pleasure and pain should be in harmony, so that the good have pleasure and the bad pain. Tragedy illustrates a dislocation of this harmony; for it is of the essence of the situation which calls forth pity, that the misfortune and suffering are undeserved. Tragic pity is felt only for the good; it is therefore not a patronising or sentimental feeling by which we look down on the sufferer: we continue to look up at him. Aristotle's pity and fear are sympathy for the good part of mankind in the bad part of their experiences: this ($\phi\iota\lambda\alpha\nu\theta\rho\omega\pi\iota\alpha$) is the emotional side of justice.

You will thus see that no theory of catharsis makes sense which speaks of purging away a 'painful element' in pity and fear. Aristotle does not say that pity and fear have a 'painful element'; he says of both of them in the definitions in the *Rhetoric* that they *are* species of 'pain' or 'disturbance'; therefore to get rid of the 'pain' would be to get rid of the emotion altogether. That would throw over the whole of Aristotle's ethical theory; there are things which the good and wise man *ought* to fear. To deprive him of any part of his emotional equipment would be to make him a useless ethical cipher without even the potentiality of goodness.

Still less is it possible to accept a theory of catharsis which says that by Tragedy pity and fear are to be purged of their 'self-regarding' element; as if catharsis were some kind of process by which pity and fear were converted from being self-regarding emotions into being altruistic emotions. That would, on Aristotle's theory, sweep away the very possibility of having any sympathy at all. For pity is based on a fear which is, though not for ourselves, yet *as if* for ourselves.

The tragic character (personage in the play) has to be far enough removed from ourselves to allow for the possibility of pity; but near enough to ourselves to allow for the possibility of fear.

Neither the personage in the play nor the spectator should be too far removed from a supposed emotional 'norm'; otherwise there is no common emotional ground, and the interaction of feeling (which is sympathy) becomes impossible. . . .

Catharsis

In this technical sense Aristotle uses the word κάθαρσις only once in the whole of the *Poetics* as we have it; that is, in the formal definition of Tragedy in ch. VI: Bywater translates: 'with incidents arousing pity and fear, wherewith to accomplish its catharsis of such emotions.' It is certainly best to keep the word 'catharsis' as a technical term, simply transliterating it from Greek into English, as Bywater has done: any attempt to translate it by one single English word prejudices the whole interpretation.

But I must in this passage warn . . . against Bywater's extraordinary predilection for the word 'incidents'; there is no equivalent of this in the Greek, and the use of the word again here has the unfortunate effect of making the matter seem 'incidental', almost unimportant. Bywater himself translates much better in ch. XIII, where he writes of 'actions arousing pity and fear'.

In fact the Greek word κάθαρσις does occur once more in the text of the *Poetics*, though not in this technical, special sense of Aristotle's. In ch. XVII, in the summary of the plot of Euripides's *Iphigenia in Tauris*, it is the word used for the 'purifying' of Orestes. This is one of the word's frequent normal meanings in Greek; it means ceremonial purification from a religious impurity.

There has been great controversy whether the term in this context of ch. VI is to be treated as a 'metaphor' from religion *or* from medicine. It is extremely useful to keep these two other contexts of the term in mind, because they are convenient points of reference for the understanding of it, and one cannot go far in reading discussions of catharsis without finding this distinction between medicine and religion offered as a dilemma, as if it required the choice of one *or* other of the two alternatives.

The theory that Aristotle's use of the term was a metaphor from medicine was cogently revived in modern criticism by Weil in 1847 and by Bernays in 1857. Both the most influential English interpreters of the *Poetics* in modern times – Butcher and Bywater – have accepted this view in one of its several forms; but it is not in itself modern; it was known to the Italian Renaissance critics, and Milton showed in his Preface to *Samson Agonistes* that he was familiar with it, although he did not by any means accept it as a wholly adequate explanation of Aristotle's meaning. In simpler and more popular works than Butcher's or Bywater's editions, there occur phrases that imply a tacit acceptance of the medical origin of the term almost always in one sense, without any hint that the question is open to debate: thus, when Hamilton Fyfe uses phrases like 'as strong a purge' 'a powerful aperient' and 'a good clearance', he is uncritically perpetuating one form of the medical associations of the term. Mr F. L. Lucas, in his *Tragedy*, asserts (p. 24) dogmatically and emphatically that catharsis, as Aristotle uses it, 'is a definitely medical metaphor – a metaphor of an aperient', and he expresses his distaste for the theory which this involves, in the summary and too memorable epigram: 'the theatre is not a hospital' (p. 29).

These widely current forms of the medical interpretation of 'catharsis' are based on the mistaken notion that the only medical uses of the word are equivalent to the English word 'purging' in the sense of evacuating something undesirable by the use of an aperient. I have already asked (and I hope answered) this question. What is it that can be evacuated? It cannot be the emotions of pity and fear themselves, because it is good that people should have them; it cannot be a 'morbid element' in them because nothing is said about their having a morbid element.

But the word is used in a medical sense not only of a quantitative evacuation of this kind; it is also used of a qualitative change in the body, in the restoration of the proper equilibrium (e.g., between heat and cold) in the body; and a state of health depends on the maintenance of this proper equilibrium. In the *Problems*, a work of Aristotle's school rather than of Aristotle himself, but not much later than Aristotle and reasonably good evidence of his teaching, we find (Problem xxx) this question of the heat and cold in the 'black bile' of the body expressly linked with the emotions. And coldness in the black bile is said to be the physical accompaniment of the emotions of 'despair and fear'. This state is corrected by the restoration of the equilibrium, the balance, the mean of temperature. And this is a medical form of catharsis.[1]

The most difficult passage in which Aristotle mentions catharsis is in the *Politics*, viii, 7. He is there discussing music, and says that one of the functions of music is to effect a 'catharsis'; and he says: 'we use this term without explanation for the present; when we come to speak of poetry, we shall give a clearer account of it.' The trouble is that, when he *does* come to speak of poetry, he does not make this promise good. We are thus forced, paradoxically, to try to use the passage in the *Politics*, which Aristotle himself admitted to be inadequate, as a means of interpreting the even more inadequate passage in the *Poetics*.

The *Politics* passage is the one which gives the strongest justification to the view that the catharsis is a 'relief to overcharged feeling':

We accept the classification of melodies given by some philosophers into melodies of character, melodies of action, and orgiastic melodies. They say further that each of these has a scale which naturally corresponds to it. We say, however, that music is to be studied for the sake of many benefits and not of one only. It is to be studied with a view to education, with a view to catharsis – we use this term without explanation for the present; when we come to speak of poetry, we shall give a clearer account of it – and thirdly with a view to the right use of leisure and for relaxation and rest after exertion. It is clear, then, that we must use all the scales, but not all in the same way. For educational purposes we must use those that best express character, but we may use melodies of action and enthusiastic melodies for concerts where other people perform. For every feeling that affects some souls violently affects all souls more or less; the difference is only one of degree. Take pity and fear, for example, or again enthusiasm. Some people are liable to become possessed by the latter emotion, but we see that, when they have made use of the melodies which fill the soul with orgiastic feeling, they are brought back by these sacred melodies to a normal condition as if they had been medically treated and undergone a catharsis. Those who are subject to the emotions of pity and fear and the feelings generally will necessarily be affected in the same way; and so will other men in exact proportion to their susceptibility to such emotions. All experience a certain catharsis and pleasant relief. In the same manner cathartic melodies give innocent joy to men.

(J. Burnet's translation, pp. 124–6, with 'catharsis' and 'cathartic' substituted for 'purge', 'purgation' and 'purgative'.)

Though Aristotle does there say that such feelings as pity and fear, 'or again enthusiasm', exist very strongly in some souls, and have more or less influence over all, it is particularly the 'enthusiasm' or 'religious frenzy' that he gives his attention to, and to its cure by music (of which he has little to say in the *Poetics*).

Religiously excited persons are liable to fall into a frenzy. This 'enthusiasm' is not to be dealt with by suppression, which merely makes it stronger; nor by letting it have uncontrolled sway, where it becomes disordered and wild. But it is to undergo a catharsis by means of religious ritual and music. And the 'soul' of a person so affected is thus to be brought back to a balanced state.

As he describes it, this is a sort of homeopathic treatment; as Butcher says: 'it consisted in applying movement to cure movement, in soothing the internal trouble of the mind by a wild and restless music'.

Aristotle then says that 'those who are influenced by pity and fear have a like experience . . . they all undergo a catharsis of some kind and a lightening, with pleasure'.

The point is that he says the experience is of the same kind and they have *some kind* of catharsis, τινὰ κάθαρσιν: he does not say they are always formally identical. The instance of the religious enthusiasm is *one* example of a group of experiences of much wider range.

To ask if 'catharsis' is a *metaphor from* medicine or religion is to put the question in the wrong form. For it is not *a metaphor derived from* either. The point is that illustrations of the same general principle are found in relation to physical states in medicine, to some emotional states in religion and to some emotional states in poetry. In Tragedy in particular to the emotional states of pity and fear.

In English we may also use the word 'healthy' about moral and emotional states and in a sense it can be thought of as a metaphor from medicine. But that does not exclude the general principle of 'well-being' which can be physical, moral, mental, emotional and so on. This broader principle, to which the medical, the religious and the poetic catharsis has to be referred, is to be looked for in the wider context of Aristotle's thought as a whole, and the guide to it is the principle of 'the Mean', 'the intermediate'.

I shall approach this from the ethical side, because it is that which concerns the *Poetics* most. We go back . . . to the opening books of the *Nicomachean Ethics*; and what follows is a summary of Aristotle's doctrine there:

Virtue of character is about pleasures and pains; pleasures and pains are the results of successful or thwarted activities, and activities are movements towards a *desired* end. Hence nothing is more important in the education of character than training to rejoice and feel pain rightly, at the right things and times, and to the right extent. It is not right to be afraid of nothing or to be angry at nothing: there are things the wise man should fear and be angry at.

The passage which expresses Aristotle's general conception most clearly is in *Nicomachean Ethics*, II, vi (Ross's translation):

If it is thus, then, that every art does its work well – by looking to the intermediate and judging its works by this standard (so that we often say of good works of art that it is not possible either to take away or to add anything, implying that excess and defect destroy the goodness of works of art, while the mean preserves it; and good artists, as we say, look to this in their work), and if, further, virtue is more exact and better than any art, as nature also is, then virtue must have the quality of aiming at the intermediate. I mean moral virtue; for it is this that is concerned with passions and actions, and in these there is excess, defect and the intermediate. For instance, both *fear* and confidence and appetite and anger and *pity* and in general pleasure and pain may be felt both too much and too little, and in both cases not well; but to feel them at the right times, with reference to the right objects, towards the right people, with the right motive, and in the right way, is what is both intermediate and best, and this is characteristic of virtue.

The Aristotelian idea of the 'mean' is derived ultimately from the Pythagoreans, who discovered that the musical scale is based on simple mathematical proportions; and the idea of right proportion is not, in the musical scale, merely a matter of quantity. It is a quantitative method of expressing a qualitative difference between one note and another.

So too in ethics the idea of 'the mean', 'harmony', 'balance', is not purely quantitative; it is rather a theory of the relation between quantity and quality. Virtue and goodness are themselves not measurable; but they lie in a balance of things that are, if not measurable by an exact scale, yet amenable to quantitative statements: it makes sense to say a man is more or less pleased, more or less angry, more or less fearful. The goodness does not lie alone in the adjustment of quantities of pleasure, anger or fear, but in the balance and rightness resulting from such adjustments.

A tragedy rouses the emotions from potentiality to activity by worthy and adequate stimuli; it controls them by directing them to the right objects in the right way; and exercises them, within the limits of the play, as the emotions of the good man would be exercised. When they subside to potentiality again after the play is over, it is a more 'trained' potentiality than before. This is what Aristotle calls κάθαρσις. Our responses are brought nearer to those of the good and wise man. And this is the view which Milton puts forward in his Preface to *Samson Agonistes* [see Part Two, below–Ed.]; for though he translates the cathartic process by the verb 'purge' he explains his translation thus:

that is, to temper and reduce them to just measure with a kind of delight, stirr'd up by reading or seeing those passions well imitated.

Milton's phrase 'just measure' is the 'mean', the standard of the good and wise man, of which I have been speaking. The result of the catharsis is an emotional balance and equilibrium; and it may well be called a state of emotional health. . . .

SOURCE: extracts from *Aristotle's Poetics* (London, 1956), pp. 100–3, 104–10.

NOTE

1. See especially D. S. Margoliouth, *The Poetics of Aristotle* (1911), pp. 57ff.

John Jones   'Character and Action' (1962)

Aristotle warns us in his own way that the tragic action advanced in the *Poetics* is not abstract and bloodless. Tragedy, he says, is an imitation 'of action and life', and this coupling is supported by the analogue of the soul and by the reiterated metaphor of the living creature. Action, the soul-like form, is more than a principle of perfect intelligibility. But still it is a form, and if somebody had asked him what is action the form *of*, Aristotle would surely have reckoned the question fair. I believe he would have answered that the *praxis* contemplated by the tragedian is the form of an event in life, sometimes close in time and known immediately, but usually received from an historical or mythological source: history and myth are never distinguished in the *Poetics*, there is no problem of relative authenticity.[1] Thus tragic action presents the translucent and vital quiddity of a life-event; it makes sense of experience. Aristotle's treatise begins and ends, as any sane aesthetic might, with art confronting life in an effort of interpretation.

And yet he says that Tragedy is not an imitation of human beings. By this he cannot mean that Tragedy lacks what we loosely call human interest; somehow the imitation of action and life must carry human interest without being an imitation of human beings. An abrupt and ugly passage explains, lecture-note fashion, how this is so:

> Tragedy is an imitation not of human beings but of action and life, of happiness and misery. Happiness and misery are realised in action; the goal of life is an action, not a quality. Men owe their qualities to their characters, but it is in their actions that they are happy or the reverse. And so the stage-figures do not act in order to represent their characters; they include their characters for the sake of their actions.[2] [VI]*

Human interest enters the *Poetics* at this point, and the difference between its legitimate and illegitimate treatment in Tragedy is foreshadowed by 'they include their characters for the sake of their

---

* The roman numerals within square brackets relate to the main sections in Butcher's translation, excerpted as the first item in Part One. They are inserted for the convenience of the reader. Jones's citations here from Aristotle appear to be his own translation, following (as he indicates in a note) 'the second edition of Rostagni's text' (Ed.).

actions'. Here Aristotle switches from the action of the play to the actors in the play so that he can present us with the histrionic correlate of the dramaturgy that conceives and articulates an action rich in human interest, but does not imitate human beings. Actor and dramatist both include character for the sake of action, each in his separate sphere; and, shifting back again to the dramatist's standpoint, Aristotle likens his case to that of the painter:

The analogy of painting is very close: if someone were to cover his canvas with the most beautiful colours laid on at random, he would please us less than if he drew a monochrome sketch on a white ground. [vi]

Among the major issues raised by Aristotle's comparison, the most important is the service which one element in the artistic process renders to another, and through which its very existence is justified. Having said that character is included for the sake of action, and next that 'a tragedy is impossible without an action, but there may be one without characters', Aristotle now introduces a 'very close' analogy in which the full literal application of these assertions is unavoidable, thus making it as hard as possible for us to play them down in relation to Tragedy. As the monochrome sketch is to bare tragic action, colour is to character.[3] The painter who strives after a likeness of his subject can rest assured, however thin and poor the result, that he is working within the bounds of his art: not so the painter of a medley of beautiful colours, for no Greek could have denied (since all the painting he knew and dreamed of was representational) that the end-product is at best an agreeable chaos, not a work of art at all.

Similarly with the tragedian; and Aristotle's analogy bears mainly upon the function of character: he wants to make the proposition that character serves action seem no less assured than is (for a Greek) the proposition that the only legitimate use of colour in painting is to support the finished likeness. He is saying that character is included for the sake of the action; he is not saying, or he is saying only incidentally, that character is less important than action. This crucial inflexion of argument has not been acknowledged, either in close professional analysis, where stress falls on the 'subordinate significance'[4] of character and on the 'superiority of activities over states',[5] or in the general and popular expositions with their antithetical talk of Plot and Character, those capital-letter fixtures of commentary. It needs to be said that the plot-character dichotomy is radically false to Aristotle's understanding of Tragedy, that character, like colour, must be denied even the most primitive autonomy.

The task of a tragic plot (*muthos*) is, we recall, to render an ideal action in terms of stage-event; and it may succeed in this without having recourse to character. But the clear implication is that a tragedy is the richer for containing character, just as an executed likeness is the richer for being coloured. Not only is the analogy of colour and character firmly invoked; it is also less forced, more happy and natural, than is at once obvious to ourselves; for Aristotelian character (*ēthos*) is almost precisely ethical colouring. Its discriminations are exclusively moral, and it is applied two-dimensionally to the surface of the realised action.

Aristotle duly confines *ēthos* when he declares: 'Character in a tragedy is that which reveals a moral choice.'[6] All familiar thought of the characters of friends or the characters in books must be set aside, since *ēthos* is without the ambition of inclusiveness (character in its various modern contexts casts a net around personality), and it yields nothing to naturalistic expectation. We even find *ēthos* working against a general naturalistic tendency when Aristotle remarks that 'the tragedies of most of our modern writers are characterless', whereas 'nearly all the early men' had greater success with character than with action. The fuller psychology and relative closeness to nature of the post-Euripidean drama – the drama called modern in the *Poetics* – could and did go with extreme ethical poverty. Nor did the brilliant verisimilitude of Zeuxis's painting (the story survives from antiquity that he painted some grapes so like the life that the birds flew down and pecked at the paint) save his work from being, as Aristotle tells us, 'empty of character'.[7]

Again it is true that *ēthos*, this narrow moral spectrum, has an outwardness of application which brings it unexpectedly close to colour. When Aristotle defines *ēthos* as 'that which reveals a moral choice' the modern reader anticipates an exposure of consciousness; instinctively he stresses *reveals*, because he has inherited – from Socratic-Platonic, Euripidean, Jewish, Roman, Christian, humanist and Romantic sources – an image of the human self and its working which he accepts for a universal *donnée* of life, and never questions. If he were to question it, he would observe that Aristotle has already issued a very emphatic warning against the mentality that unthinkingly stresses *reveals*. He would recall that the eye of Tragedy, according to the *Poetics*, rests on actions and not on qualities or states of mind and soul. He would understand, with a slow dawning of general illumination, that Aristotle has founded his book on the distinction between false imitation of human beings and true imitation of actions because he reckons it his first responsibility, as early as the fourth century, to oppose the inward-turning of attention and interest that goes with a stress upon *reveals*.

The gulf between our preconceptions and the express doctrine of the *Poetics* can only be bridged through the recovery of some of the lost human relevancies of action. Aristotle is assaulting the now settled habit in which we see action issuing from a solitary focus of consciousness – secret, inward, interesting – and in which the status of action must always be adjectival: action qualifies; it tells us things we want to know about the individual promoting it; the life of action is our ceaseless, animating consideration of the state of affairs 'inside' him who acts, without which action is empty and trivial, an effluvium. This movement from adjectival action to the substantive self would seem, were it conscious, not merely natural but inevitable. Were it conscious, however, we should have to admit that we are first rejecting Aristotle's injunction to make character serve action, and then replacing it with its opposite. Revealing a moral choice means, for Aristotle, declaring the moral character of an act in a situation where the act itself does not make this clear.[8] Reader and spectator are apprised of the ethical colour of the action at this point of the play. To our sense of characteristic conduct Aristotle opposes that of characterful action: the essence of conduct being that it is mine or yours; of action, that it is out there – an object for men to contemplate. . . .

Then Tragedy is the imitation of an action, and the difference now establishes itself in very broadest outline between imitating human beings and imitating an action in which humanity is effectively present. Aristotle's composing dramatist, acting out the events of his play, works himself into the pattern of the single distinct *praxis* visible to his mind's eye, struggles to get it physically and emotionally right: this is the process of translating action into plot, *praxis* into *muthos*. In the work of art, of course, his blueprint gestures and movements will be apportioned among a group of stage-figures; differentiation obviously matters, is unavoidable, and therefore falls among the subjects dealt with in Aristotle's textbook. He states the principle of differentiation thus:

Being the imitation of an action, Tragedy involves a plurality of stage-figures who do the acting. These necessarily possess certain distinctive qualities both of character and thought, since it is by virtue of these distinctive qualities that we speak of their actions also as having certain qualities. . . . [VI]

And then I think it must have struck him how difficult it is even to mention the people in the play without seeming to flout the rule against imitating human beings, because he proceeds to enunciate yet once more the leading tenet of the *Poetics*:

Tragedy is indeed the imitation of an action, and for that reason, rather than any other, it imitates the stage-figures –

this time, we note, with pointed reference to the people in the play, the stage-figures (*prattontes*, as in the earlier passage); so that his readers shall have no excuse for thinking that the place of action as tragic object is affected by anything he may say about the individuated presentation of the stage-figure. His last general pronouncement draws together the actor who includes character for the sake of action, the painter-dramatist who brings ethical colour to the service of his work of imitation, the actor-dramatist who constructs a model of his plot, the realised *praxis*, by acting out the events of his tragedy.

Differentiation turns, then, upon the distinctive qualities of which Aristotle speaks. We have already encountered these qualities, strangely overshadowed by action: 'Men owe their qualities to their characters, but it is in their actions that they are happy or the reverse' – a juxtaposition that warns us not to expect from the *Poetics* any firm repose upon mood, state of mind, consciousness. Aristotelian man cannot make a portentous gesture of 'I have that within which passes show' because he is significantly himself only in what he says and does. Instead of 'that within' – Hamlet's omnipresent consciousness – he has the qualities which he owes to his *ēthos*; these are his without being an inward possession; the self-maintained continuity of the modern ego is lacking, and the work of individual appropriation (through which we recognise the character and qualities as his) falls to the outward nexus of habit. The virtuous man – so runs the argument of the *Nicomachean Ethics* – is always one who has learned to be good through acting well: there are no natural saints.[9] And his learning to be good is not the kind of process we are likely to imagine, perhaps by picturing a growing inner resource of virtue, a reservoir upon which he draws in character-istic virtuous conduct. Learning to be good is the acquiring of a virtuous habit (*hexis*) of character through a succession of good acts. It is forming a style, and this invites comparison between Aristotle's account of the moral life and athletic stroke-play; the virtuous man is like the batsman whose full range of strokes has been so firmly grooved through practice that the bowler despairs of tempting him to make a mistake, or even of catching him momentarily in two minds.

Once again the moral philosophy sheds light on the literary essay, and again the light is wasted unless Aristotle's moral man is seen to be continuous with his tragic man, and his tragic man is acknowledged to be, for him, actual. Very suggestive is the gradual emergence of personality in a channelling of action-pattern; it directs us to the confident outward thrust and to the corresponding faintness of inner focus that separate self-definition through my habits from self-definition through my consciousness. *Hexis*, habit or bent of character, is the product of past actions; it is the present causal link between a man and his actions which enables an observer to judge whether he is being true to himself; it is the ground of the same observer's prediction as to his future actions. By the erosive flow of action the individual features are carved out, no potent shaping spirit lodges aboriginally behind the face; and thus the Aristotelian stage-figure receives his distinctive qualities.

To see how the very primordia of his identity are acquired and sustained (becoming inactive is relapsing into a state that lacks all interesting differentiation) is to recognise the fitness of that shared 'action and life' to deliver its own kind of human and tragic solitude. . . .

Aristotle's statement that Tragedy is not an imitation of human beings is balanced (and also made intelligible to us) by his confidence in the ability of tragic action, his *praxis*, to sustain all relevant human interest. He feels this confidence because he apprehends the actuality of the thing as outward and discrete and centrifugal, a continuous dying into the full life of self through the self's dissipation in action. And now, when he comes to discuss the presentation of the stage-figure, the same outward thrust is apparent in his carving of identity situationally, through status and the type: his exposition is all of a piece.

In dramatic and histrionic fact, Aristotle's stage-figure is the mask. He lays no stress on the mask in the *Poetics* because he assumes that any mature drama is bound to be masked; like the open-air theatre and the sacred character of Attic Tragedy, the mask is accepted, very much taken into account, but not discussed; for Aristotle it is simply there, a permanent feature of his dramatic universe. It is, then, a feature which we have to supply for ourselves. And in a sense we do. Great caution is needed, because nearly all the literary information about this perishable linen object is late, and the evidence of archaeology is often ambiguous: the masked figures of a vase or wall painting may or may not be actors in a play. But something can be said, and has been said. Moreover, the accounts, learned and popular, of the Greek tragic mask have most of them an important point in common, which is their emphasis on the practical advantages conferred by the mask under ancient stage conditions: the easy doubling of parts with a tiny cast; the taking of women's parts by men; the recognisability of a larger-than-life face from the back of a huge open-air theatre; the amplification of the actor's voice through a megaphone built into the mask.

And these are genuine advantages. But they are also secondary in that they do not expose the *raison d'être* of masking; no theatre, no society, assumes the masking convention because it is seen to be convenient. To the question, why mask? social anthropology does not return a single answer: the mask worn by each in succession of the Benin kings is the visible presence of kingship; the mask very commonly associated with the cult of the dead[10] is the epiphany of the departed ancestor, and its weird hooting in the night is called the voice of the dead (the root function of the so-called megaphone in the Greek dramatic mask is surely to change the voice, not to amplify it); masking flourishes in totemistic societies – the mask, like the wooden body of the totem, shows forth the psycho-physical and institutional solidarity of the descent group – and as a means whereby intricate kinship relations

may be articulated: North American shutter-masks, an inner mask
being revealed when the shutter opens, are addressed to the fact of
selfhood's simultaneous multiplicity. Masks state different truths for
different people. There is no need to generalise about these truths, but
simply to urge that the Greek tragic mask be taken seriously.

In the context of the *Poetics*, this means accepting the mask as integral
to the stage-presentation of human beings envisaged there, in fact as
more than a useful adjunct to the actor. *Prosōpon*, the Greek word for
mask, also means face, aspect, person and stage-figure (*persona*); we
should allow mask and face to draw semantically close together, and
then we should enrich the face far beyond our own conception, until it is
able to embrace (as it did for Greeks from the time of Homer) the look of
the man together with the truth about him. The face is the total aspect;
it presents the human individual, the person. Therefore to say that the
mask is a kind of face is to take it very seriously indeed; and it is also to
utter the platitude that the people of Tragedy are the people of life, as
art perceives and renders them. The ancient actor wore this object upon
which the audience could read a few simple, conventional signs
determining rank and age and sex; the artifact surpassed nature in its
lucid isolation of essentials, which was as the Greek aesthetic instinct
demanded. But mask and face were at one in their sufficiency; unlike the
modern face and the modern mask, they did not owe their interest to the
further realities lying behind them, because they declared the whole
man. They stated; they did not hint or hide. Aristotle's account of this
statement acquires its concrete point of reference when we direct his
outward self and its status-defined individuality towards the painted
surface of the mask: towards the nexus of clearly ordered type-
distinctions, and towards the face of Tragedy which has and needs
nothing behind itself.

Although he does not consider the mask, Aristotle gives an oblique
indication of its significance through the respect paid to action in the
Poetics. The work of art which begins with the dramatist contemplating
an ideal *praxis* ends with the actors executing the prescribed stage-
event. Acting is always acting for Aristotle – acting through what had to
be done in the play. The task of the actors is to support the action by
forming props on which it can be spread out for the audience to
contemplate. Further, this modest office does not call for any suppression of histrionic potential; on the contrary, it taxes the actor to his
limit because at the living heart of the tradition the actor is the mask and
the mask is an artifact-face with nothing to offer but itself. It has – more
important, it is known to have – no inside. Its being is exhausted in its
features. To think of the mask as an appendage to the human actor is to
destroy the basis of the ancient masking convention by inviting the
audience to peer behind the mask and demand of the actor that he shall

cease merely to support the action, and shall begin instead to exploit the action in the service of inwardness. The mask, as a casual survey of masking cultures makes plain, can present all manner of versions of the human self; it is almost inexhaustibly rich in its presentational modes. But it is vulnerable at one point. It cannot maintain itself against the thought that all presentational modes are inadequate to the truth. The situation in which Duncan reflects:

> There's no art
> Can find the mind's construction in the face

destroys it, for the mind's construction must be found there if it is to be found at all. And when it cannot be found there, masking becomes pointless.

The central argument of the *Poetics*, that Tragedy is an imitation not of human beings but of action and life, receives here its histrionic complement. The distinction between the composing dramatist who imitates human beings and one who imitates an action rich in human interest is paralleled by a second distinction between the actor who impersonates his mythico-historical original and the actor-mask who appropriates to that original his share of the play's action. The actor-mask is tethered to his original lightly, to ensure recognition, while his masking energies drive him on through the stage-event. The distinction again seems flimsy, since I cannot mimic the actions of Oedipus without pretending to be Oedipus: and again the distinction is important.

SOURCE: extracts from *On Aristotle and Greek Tragedy* (London, 1962), pp. 29–33, 36–8, 43–6.

NOTES

[These have been renumbered and abbreviated from the original – Ed.]

1. The answer would have to be modified if it were to embrace tragedies with wholly fictitious plots; but there is no need to do so since Aristotle assumes that the material of Tragedy is mythico-historical – in spite of a glance at Agathon's *Antheus*, a tragedy in which 'names and events are both fictitious' (51b22).

2. 50a16–22. The received text is unsatisfactory. Vahlen's view of the passage has commended itself to nearly all editors (although not to Rostagni) and I follow Vahlen here.

3. Aristotle's plain 'and forceful analogy is obscured and weakened by Castelvetro's transposition of the painter-dramatist comparison to 50a33. Castelvetro's view, favoured by most nineteenth-century editors, is now generally and rightly abandoned.

4. Bywater, note on 50a15.

5. Gerald F. Else, *Aristotle's Poetics: The Argument*, p. 253.

6. 50b7–8. Very occasionally Aristotle uses *ethos* less narrowly: at 60a11 and in chapter xv.

7. 50a28. Zeuxis's work was not always or merely photographic. Elsewhere in the *Poetics* (61b13) we hear of him improving on his models.

8. 50b7–10. I follow Rostagni's interpretation of this passage which presents difficulties of detail, none of them material to my argument.

9. 'We acquire the virtues by first exercising them. . . . We become just by doing just acts, temperate by doing temperate acts, brave by doing brave acts' (*Nicomachean Ethics*, ii 1 1103a31).

10. Sir William Ridgeway made almost no use of the mask in his world-wide search for material to support his theory that Tragedy originated in the worship of the dead. This neglect is typical of the learned tradition as a whole.

PART TWO

From Chaucer to Strindberg

Geoffrey Chaucer (c. 1393–1400)

The Monk's View of Tragedy

Tragedie is to seyn a certeyn storie,
As olde bookes maken us memorie,
Of hym that stood in greet prosperitee,
And is yfallen out of heigh degree
Into myserie, and endeth wrecchedly.
And they ben versified communely
Of six feet, which men clepen *exametron*.
In prose eek been endited many oon,
And eek in meetre, in many a sondry wyse.
. . .
I wol biwaille, in manere of tragedie,
The harm of hem that stoode in heigh degree,
And fillen so that there nas no remedie
To brynge hem out of hir adversitee.
For certein, what that Fortune list to flee,
Ther may no man the cours of hire withholde.
Lat no man truste on blynd prosperitee;
Be war by thise ensamples trewe and olde.

SOURCE: extracts from 'Prologue to The Monk's Tale' and 'The Monkes Tale De Casibus Virorum Illustrium' in *The Canterbury Tales*: F. N. Robinson (ed.), *The Works of Geoffrey Chaucer* (Boston, Mass., 1933; London, 1966).

Sir Philip Sidney (1580–81)

'High and Excellent Tragedy' and the Absurdity of Elizabethan Tragedies

. . . the right use of Comedy will (I thinke) by no body be blamed, and much lesse of the high and excellent Tragedy, that openeth the greatest wounds, and sheweth forth the Ulcers that are covered with Tissue; that maketh Kinges feare to be Tyrants, and Tyrants manifest their tirannicall humors; that, with sturring the affects of admiration and commiseration, teacheth the uncertainety of this world, and upon how weake foundations guilden roofes are builded; that maketh us knowe,

Qui sceptra saevus duro imperio regit,
Timet timentes, metus in auctorem redit.[1]

But how much it can moove, *Plutarch* yeeldeth a notable testimonie of the abhominable Tyrant *Alexander Pheraeus*; from whose eyes a Tragedy, wel made and represented, drewe aboundance of teares, who, without all pitty, had murthered infinite nombers, and some of his owne blood. So as he, that was not ashamed to make matters for Tragedies, yet coulde not resist the sweet violence of a Tragedie. And if it wrought no further good in him, it was that he, in despight of himselfe, withdrewe himselfe from harkening to that which might mollifie his hardened heart.

But it is not the Tragedy they doe mislike: For it were too absurd to cast out so excellent a representation of whatsoever is most worthy to be learned. . . .

Our Tragedies and Comedies (not without cause cried out against), observing rules neyther of honest civilitie nor of skilfull Poetrie, excepting *Gorboduck* (againe, I say, of those that I have seene), which notwithstanding, as it is full of stately speeches and well sounding Phrases, clyming to the height of *Seneca* his stile, and as full of notable moralitie, which it doth most delightfully teach, and so obtayne the very end of Poesie, yet in troth it is very defectious in the circumstaunces, which greeveth mee, because it might not remaine as an exact model of all Tragedies. For it is faulty both in place and time, the two necessary companions of all corporall actions. For where the stage should alwaies represent but one place, and the uttermost time presupposed in it should be, both by *Aristotles* precept and common reason, but one day, there is both many dayes, and many places, inartificially imagined. But if it be so in *Gorboduck*, how much more in al the rest? where you shal have *Asia* of the one side, and *Affrick* of the other, and so many other under-kingdoms, that the Player, when he commeth in, must ever begin with telling where he is, or els the tale will not be conceived. Now ye shal have three Ladies walke to gather flowers, and then we must beleeve the stage to be a Garden. By and by, we heare newes of shipwracke in the same place, and then wee are to blame if we accept it not for a Rock. Upon the backe of that, comes out a hidious Monster, with fire and smoke, and then the miserable beholders are bounde to take it for a Cave. While in the meantime two Armies flye in, represented with foure swords and bucklers, and then what harde heart will not receive it for a pitched fielde? Now, of time they are much more liberall, for ordinary it is that two young Princes fall in love. After many traverces, she is got with childe, delivered of a faire boy; he is lost, groweth a man, falls in love, and is ready to get another child; and all this in two hours space: which how absurd it is in sence even sence may imagine, and Arte hath taught, and all auncient examples iustified, and, at this day, the ordinary Players in Italie wil not erre in. Yet wil some bring in an example of *Eunuchus* in *Terence*, that containeth matter of two dayes, yet far short of twenty yeeres. True it is, and so was it to be playd in two daies, and so fitted to the time it set forth. And though *Plautus* hath in one place done amisse, let us hit with him, and not misse with him. But they wil say, how then shal we set forth a story, which containeth both many places and many times? And doe they not knowe that a Tragedie is tied to the lawes of Poesie, and not of Historie? not bound to follow the storie, but, having liberty, either to faine a quite newe matter, or to frame the history to the most tragicall conveniencie. Againe, many things may be told which cannot be shewed, if they knowe the difference betwixt reporting and representing. As, for example, I may speake (though I am heere) of *Peru*, and in speech digresse from that to the description of *Calicut*; but in action I cannot represent it without *Pacolets* horse: and so was the manner the Auncients tooke, by some *Nuncius*, to recount thinges done in former time or other place. Lastly, if they wil represent an history, they must not (as *Horace* saith) beginne *Ab ovo*, but they must come to the principall poynt of that one action which they wil represent. By example this wil be best expressed. I have a story of young *Polidorus*, delivered for safeties sake, with great riches, by his Father *Priamus*, to *Polimnestor*, king of *Thrace*, in the Troyan war time. Hee after some yeeres, hearing the over-throwe of *Priamus*, for to make the treasure his owne, murthereth the child; the body of the child is taken up by *Hecuba*; shee the same day findeth a slight to bee revenged most cruelly of the Tyrant: where nowe would one of our Tragedy writers begin, but with the delivery of the childe? Then should he sayle over into *Thrace*, and so spend I know not how many yeeres, and travaile numbers of places. But where dooth *Euripides*? Even with the finding of the body, leaving the rest to be tolde by the spirit of *Polidorus*. This need no further to be inlarged; the dullest wit may conceive it.

But besides these grosse absurdities, how all theyr Playes be neither right Tragedies, nor right Comedies; mingling Kings and Clownes, not because the matter so carrieth it, but thrust in Clownes by head and shoulders, to play a part in maiesticall matters, with neither decencie nor discretion: So as neither the admiration and commiseration, nor the right sportfulnes, is by their mungrell Tragy-comedie obtained. I know *Apuleius* did some-what so, but that is a thing recounted with space of time, not represented in one moment: and I knowe the Auncients have

one or two examples of Tragy-comedies, as *Plautus* hath *Amphitrio*. But,
if we marke them well, we shall find, that they never, or very daintily,
match Horn-pypes and Funeralls. So falleth it out that, having indeed
no right Comedy, in that comicall part of our Tragedy we have nothing
but scurrility, unwoorthy of any chast eares, or some extreame shew of
doltishnes, indeed fit to lift up a loude laughter, and nothing els: where
the whole tract of a Comedy shoulde be full of delight, as the Tragedy
should be still maintained in a well raised admiration.

SOURCE: extract from *An Apologie for Poetrie* (1580–81, published
1595); reprinted in C. Gregory Smith (ed.), *Elizabethan Critical Essays*
(London, 1904), I, pp. 197–99

NOTE

1. 'He who barbarously tyrannises over his kingdom, fears those who fear
him; fear rebounds on its author's own head.'

George Puttenham   (1589)

Tragedy and the Falls of Princes

. . . Besides those Poets *Comick* there were other who served also the
stage, but medled not with so base matters, for they set forth the dolefull
falles of infortunate & afflicted Princes, & were called Poets *Tragicall*:
such were *Euripides* and *Sophocles* with the Greeks, *Seneca* among the
Latines. . . .

. . . after that some men among the moe became mighty and famous
in the world, soveraignetie and dominion having learned them all
maner of lusts and licentiousnes of life, by which occasions also their
high estates and felicities fell many times into most lowe and lamentable
fortunes: whereas before in their great prosperities they were both
feared and reverenced in the highest degree, after their deathes, when
the posteritie stood no more in dread of them, their infamous life and
tyrannies were layd open to all the world, their wickedness reproched,
their follies and extreme insolencies derided, and their miserable ends
painted out in playes and pageants, to shew the mutabilitie of fortune,
and the iust punishment of God in revenge of a vicious and evill life.

These matters were also handled by the Poets, and represented by action as that of the *Comedies*: but because the matter was higher then that of the *Comedies*, the Poets stile was also higher and more loftie, the provision greater, the place more magnificent; for which purpose also the players garments were made more rich & costly and solemne, and every other thing apperteining, according to that rate. . . . These matters of great Princes were played upon lofty stages, & the actors thereof ware upon their legges buskins of leather called *Cothurni*, and other solemne habits, & for a speciall preheminence did walke upon those high corked shoes or pantofles, which now they call in Spaine and Italy *Shoppini*. And because those buskins and high shoes were commonly made of goats skinnes very finely tanned, and dyed into colours, or for that, as some say, the best players reward was a goate to be given him, or for that, as other thinke, a goate was the peculiar sacrifice of the god *Pan*, king of all the gods of the woodes – forasmuch as a goate in Greeke is called *Tragos*, therfore these stately playes were called *Tragedies*.

SOURCE: extracts from *The Arte of English Poesie* (1589); reprinted in C. Gregory Smith (ed.), *Elizabethan Critical Essays* (London, 1904), II, pp. 27–36.

Jean Racine   (1668, 1670, 1677)

The Imperfect Hero: First Preface to *Andromaque* (1668)

. . . the public has shown me too much favour for me to be upset by the annoyance expressed by two or three particular people who would like to see all the heroes of ancient times reformed and made into perfect heroes. I am sure they mean well in wanting to see only flawless characters on the stage. But I implore them to remember that it is not for me to change the rules of the drama. Horace recommends us to give Achilles the grim, remorseless and ferocious character that he had in real life, and that his son [Pyrrhus] is usually given. And Aristotle, far from asking us for perfect heroes, insists, on the contrary, that the tragic protagonists, i.e. those whose misfortune constitutes the tragic catastrophe, should be neither wholly good nor wholly bad. He does not want them to be paragons of virtue, because the punishment of a good man would excite indignation rather than pity in the hearts of the spectators; nor does he want them to be unduly wicked, because a villain would altogether fail to arouse pity. The tragic protagonists should therefore have qualities which are midway between these two extremes, that is to say, they should be virtuous, but capable of weakness, and they should fall into misfortune as the result of a fault which causes them to be pitied, but not detested.

The Virtues of Simplicity: Preface to *Bérénice* (1670)

Titus reginam Berenicem, cui etiam nuptias pollicitus ferebatur, statim ab Urbe dimisit invitus invitam.[1]

That is to say that 'Titus, who loved Berenice passionately, and who had even, it was thought, promised to marry her, sent her away from Rome, against his own will and against hers, in the first days of his rule'. This is a very famous event in history; and it seemed to me highly suitable dramatic material because of the strength of feeling which it could arouse on the stage. Indeed, there is nothing more moving in the whole of poetry than the separation of Dido and Aeneas in Virgil. And who can doubt that what was able to provide enough material for an entire book of an epic poem [*Aeneid* IV], the action of which lasts several days, is adequate as the subject for a tragedy, the duration of which should be no more than a few hours? It is true that I have not made Berenice commit suicide like Dido, but this is because Berenice, unlike Dido with Aeneas, did not make the final surrender of her honour to Titus and so was not obliged, as Dido was, to surrender her life. Putting that on one side, the scene of Berenice's last farewell to Titus, in which she makes such efforts to part from him, is by no means the least tragic in the play, and I dare assert that it is effective in arousing once more that emotion which the earlier scenes had stirred in the hearts of the audience. Bloodshed and death are not absolutely indispensable to a tragedy. It is enough if the action is impressive, if the characters are heroic, if the passions are aroused, and if everything is charged with that feeling of majestic sadness which constitutes the true pleasure of tragedy.

I thought that I could find all these elements in my subject. But what pleased me even more was that I found it an extremely simple one. For a long time I had wanted to see if I could write a tragedy which would have that simplicity of action so much admired by the ancients. For it is one of the principal lessons which they have taught us. 'Whatever you do', says Horace, 'should always be simple and a whole.'[2] They admired the *Ajax* of Sophocles, even though it consists of no more than Ajax's killing himself because of the madness which afflicts him after being

refused the arms of Achilles. They admired the *Philoctetes*, the whole
subject of which is that Ulysses comes with the intention of stealing the
arrows of Hercules by surprise. The *Oedipus* itself, though full of
'discoveries' [in the Aristotelian sense], has less matter than the simplest
tragedy of our days. . . .

And it is not to be thought that this rule is merely based on the
imaginations of those who invented it. It is only truth to life that makes a
tragedy moving. And what truth to life is there when a whole host of
events, which could scarcely happen in several weeks, is crowded into a
single day? Some people think that this simplicity is evidence of a lack of
invention. They seem quite unaware that, on the contrary, the secret of
invention consists in making something out of nothing, and that the
inclusion of a large number of incidents has always been the recourse of
poets who sense that their genius is not rich enough, or powerful
enough, to hold the attention of the audience for five whole acts by
means of a simple action which is sustained by depth of passion, beauty
of feeling, and elegance of style. Far be it from me to claim that all these
things are to be found in my work; but neither can I believe that the
public is altogether ungrateful that I have presented them with a
tragedy which has been honoured with so many tears, and the thirtieth
performance of which has been as well received as the first.

There have not been wanting people who have criticised me for this
very simplicity which I had taken so much trouble to achieve. They
have maintained that a tragedy which has so little plot-complication
could not be in accordance with the rules of the drama. I inquired if
they were complaining of being bored. I was told that they all
acknowledged that they were not bored, indeed that several
passages of the play moved them, and that they would gladly see it
again. What more do they want? I beg them to have a high enough
opinion of themselves to believe that a play which moves them and gives
them pleasure cannot be absolutely contrary to the rules. The chief rule
is to please and to move the feelings of the audience. All the others are
made only to bring about the achievement of this primary purpose. But
all these rules are elaborately detailed, and my advice to the audience is
not to be bothered with them. The spectators have more important
business to attend to. Let them leave the task of interpreting difficulties
in Aristotle's *Poetics* to us, while they reserve to themselves the pleasure
of weeping and being deeply moved; and allow me to say to them what a
musician said to King Philip of Macedonia, when he objected that a
song was not composed according to the rules: 'God forbid, sire, that
you should ever be so unfortunate as to know these things better than I
do!'

The Moral Dignity of Tragedy: Preface to *Phèdre* (1677)

Here is another tragedy the subject of which is taken from Euripides. Although I have followed a slightly different route from him with regard to the conduct of the action, I have not failed to enrich my play with whatever seemed to me particularly remarkable in his. Even though I were indebted to Euripides for nothing more than the idea of Phèdre's character, I could still say that I owe to him what is perhaps the most rationally constructed play that I have given to the theatre. I am not at all surprised that this character should have had so great a success in Euripides's time, or that it should have been even more acclaimed in ours, since it has all the qualities which Aristotle requires in the hero of a tragedy, and which are necessary for exciting pity and terror. Indeed, Phèdre is neither completely guilty nor completely innocent. Her fate and the anger of the gods involve her in an illicit passion which she is the first to regard with horror. She makes every effort to overcome it. She prefers to die rather than tell anyone about it. And when she is forced to reveal it, she speaks of it with such shame that we are bound to recognise that her crime is less an act of her own free will than a punishment inflicted on her by the gods.

I have even taken care to make her somewhat less odious than she is in the tragedies of the ancients, where she decides to accuse Hippolytus herself. It seemed to me that calumny was something too wicked and degrading to be put in the mouth of a princess whose feelings are otherwise so pure and noble. Such low behaviour seemed to me more appropriate to a nurse, who could be regarded as having more servile tendencies, but who, even so, only ventures on such false accusation to save the life and honour of her mistress. Phèdre falls in with it only because she is in such distress, and she comes in soon after with the intention of showing the innocence of the accused and revealing the truth. . . .

As for the rest, I dare not yet affirm that this is indeed the best of all my tragedies. I leave it to time and my readers to decide how much it is worth. What I can affirm is that in none of my tragedies have I made virtue so much the focus of attention. Here the slightest faults are severely punished. The mere thought of crime is regarded with as much horror as crime itself. The weaknesses associated with love are shown to be real weaknesses. The passions are exhibited on the stage only to make their destructive effects apparent; and everywhere vice is painted in colours which make the audience both recognise and detest its ugliness. That is the true aim which every man who works for the public should keep before him. And it is what the first writers of tragedy had in mind above all else. Their theatre was a school in which virtue was no less well taught than in the academies of the philosophers. Thus Aristotle was ready to set out the rules for a dramatic poem; and the wisest of the philosophers, Socrates, did not disdain to lend a hand with the tragedies of Euripides. It would be desirable for the works of our own time to be as substantial and as full of useful moral lessons as are the works of those poets. This would perhaps be a means of making tragedy more acceptable to a number of people well known for their piety and their doctrine who have condemned it of late, but who would no doubt judge it more favourably if writers thought as much about instructing as about entertaining their audiences, as they would do if they observed the true end of tragedy.

SOURCE: extracts from the Prefaces in Raymond Picard (ed.), *Racine: Oeuvres Complètes* (Paris, 1950), pp. 260, 483–5, 763–5; translated for this Casebook by R. P. Draper.

NOTES

1. Racine begins the Preface with his own translation of this passage from Suetonius (Titus, VII). Literally, it means: 'Titus at once sent Queen Berenice, to whom, it was said, he had even promised marriage, away from the City, against both his will and hers.'

2. denique sit quodvis, simplex dumtaxat et unum: *De Arte Poetica*, 23. ('In short, let the work be what you will, provided it is a single and uniform whole' – trans. W. S. Watt.)

John Milton   (1671)

Of that sort of Dramatic Poem which is call'd Tragedy

Tragedy, as it was antiently compos'd, hath been ever held the gravest, moralest, and most profitable of all other Poems: therefore said by *Aristotle* to be of power by raising pity and fear, or terror, to purge the mind of those and such like passions, that is to temper and reduce them to just measure with a kind of delight, stirr'd up by reading or seeing those passions well imitated. Nor is Nature wanting in her own effects to make good his assertion: for so in Physic things of melancholic hue and quality are us'd against melancholy, sowr against sowr, salt to remove salt humours. Hence Philosophers and other gravest Writers, as *Cicero*, *Plutarch* and others, frequently cite out of Tragic Poets, both to adorn and illustrate thir discourse. The Apostle *Paul* himself thought it not unworthy to insert a verse of *Euripides* into the Text of Holy Scripture, 1 *Cor.* 15.33; and *Parœus* commenting on the *Revelation*, divides the whole book as a Tragedy, into Acts distinguisht each by a Chorus of Heavenly Harpings and Song between. Heretofore Men in highest dignity have labour'd not a little to be thought able to compose a Tragedy. Of that honour *Dionysius* the elder was no less ambitious, then before of his attaining to the Tyranny. *Augustus Caesar* also had begun his *Ajax*, but unable to please his own judgment with what he had begun, left it unfinisht. *Seneca* the Philosopher is by some thought the Author of those Tragedies (at lest the best of them) that go under that name. *Gregory Nazianzen*, a Father of the Church, thought it not unbeseeming the sanctity of his person to write a Tragedy, which he entitl'd, *Christ suffering*. This is mention'd to vindicate Tragedy from the small esteem, or rather infamy, which in the account of many it undergoes at this day with other common Interludes; hap'ning through the Poets error of intermixing Comic stuff with Tragic sadness and gravity; or introducing trivial and vulgar persons, which by all judicious hath bin counted absurd; and brought in without discretion, corruptly to gratifie the people. And though antient Tragedy use no Prologue, yet using sometimes, in case of self defence, or explanation, that which *Martial* calls an Epistle; in behalf of this Tragedy coming forth after the antient manner, much different from what among us passes for best, thus much before hand may be Epistl'd; that *Chorus* is here introduc'd after the Greek manner, not antient only but modern, and still in use among the *Italians*. In the modelling therefore of this Poem, with good reason, the Antients and *Italians* are rather follow'd, as of much more authority and fame. The measure of Verse us'd in the Chorus is of all sorts, call'd by the Greeks *Monostrophic*, or rather *Apolelymenon*, without regard had to *Strophe, Antistrophe* or *Epod*, which were a kind of Stanza's fram'd only for the Music, then us'd with the Chorus that sung; not essential to the Poem, and therefore not material; or being divided into Stanza's or Pauses, they may be call'd *Allœostropha*. Division into Act and Scene referring chiefly to the Stage (to which this work never was intended) is here omitted.

It suffices if the whole Drama be found not produc't beyond the fift Act, of the style and uniformitie, and that commonly call'd the Plot, whether intricate or explicit, which is nothing indeed but such œconomy, or disposition of the fable as may stand best with verisimilitude and decorum; they only will best judge who are not unacquainted with *Aeschulus, Sophocles,* and *Euripides,* the three Tragic Poets unequall'd yet by any, and the best rule to all who endeavour to write Tragedy. The circumscription of time wherein the whole Drama begins and ends, is according to antient rule, and best example, within the space of 24 hours.

SOURCE: Preface to *Samson Agonistes* (1671); in H. C. Beeching (ed.), *Poetical Works of John Milton* (London, 1904), pp. 505–6.

John Dryden (1679)

The Grounds of Criticism in Tragedy

Tragedy is thus defined by Aristotle (omitting what I thought unnecessary in his definition). It is an imitation of one entire, great, and probable action; not told, but represented; which, by moving in us fear and pity, is conducing to the purging of those two passions in our minds. More largely thus: Tragedy describes or paints an action, which action must have all the proprieties above named. First, it must be one or single; that is, it must not be a history of one man's life, suppose of Alexander the Great, or Julius Caesar, but one single action of theirs. This condemns all Shakespeare's historical plays, which are rather chronicles represented, than tragedies; and all double action of plays. As, to avoid a satire upon others, I will make bold with my own *Marriage à la Mode*, where there are manifestly two actions, not depending on one another; but in *Oedipus* there cannot properly be said to be two actions, because the love of Adrastus and Eurydice has a necessary dependence on the principal design into which it is woven. The natural reason of this rule is plain; for two different independent actions distract the attention and concernment of the audience, and consequently destroy the intention of the poet; if his business be to move terror and pity, and one of his actions be comical, the other tragical, the former will divert the people, and utterly make void his greater purpose. Therefore, as in perspective, so in Tragedy, there must be a point of sight in which all the lines terminate; otherwise the eye wanders, and the work is false. This was the practice of the Grecian stage. But Terence made an innovation in the Roman: all his plays have double actions; for it was his custom to translate two Greek comedies, and to weave them into one of his, yet so, that both their actions were comical, and one was principal, the other but secondary or subservient. And this has obtained on the English stage, to give us the pleasure of variety.

As the action ought to be one, it ought, as such, to have order in it;

that is, to have a natural beginning, a middle, and an end. A natural beginning, says Aristotle, is that which could not necessarily have been placed after another thing; and so of the rest. . . .

The following properties of the action are so easy, that they need not my explaining. It ought to be great, and to consist of great persons, to distinguish it from Comedy, where the action is trivial, and the persons of inferior rank. The last quality of the action is, that it ought to be probable, as well as admirable and great. 'Tis not necessary that there should be historical truth in it; but always necessary that there should be a likeness of truth, something that is more than barely possible; *probable* being that which succeeds, or happens, oftener than it misses. To invent therefore a probability, and to make it wonderful, is the most difficult undertaking in the art of Poetry; for that which is not wonderful is not great; and that which is not probable will not delight a reasonable audience. This action, thus described, must be represented and not told, to distinguish Dramatic Poetry from Epic: but I hasten to the end or scope of Tragedy, which is, to rectify or purge our passions, fear and pity.

To instruct delightfully is the general end of all poetry. Philosophy instructs, but it performs its work by precept; which is not delightful, or not so delightful as example. To purge the passions by example, is therefore the particular instruction which belongs to Tragedy. Rapin, a judicious critic, has observed from Aristotle, that pride and want of commiseration are the most predominant vices in mankind; therefore, to cure us of these two, the inventors of Tragedy have chosen to work upon two other passions, which are fear and pity. We are wrought to fear by their setting before our eyes some terrible example of misfortune, which happened to persons of the highest quality; for such an action demonstrates to us that no condition is privileged from the turns of fortune; this must of necessity cause terror in us, and consequently abate our pride. But when we see that the most virtuous, as well as the greatest, are not exempt from such misfortunes, that consideration moves pity in us, and insensibly works us to be helpful to, and tender over, the distressed; which is the noblest and most god-like of moral virtues. Here it is observable, that it is absolutely necessary to make a man virtuous, if we desire he should be pitied: we lament not, but detest, a wicked man; we are glad when we behold his crimes are punished, and that poetical justice is done upon him. Euripides was censured by the critics of his time for making his chief characters too wicked; for example, Phædra, though she loved her son-in-law with reluctancy, and that it was a curse upon her family for offending Venus, yet was thought too ill a pattern for the stage. Shall we therefore banish all characters of villany? I confess I am not of that opinion; but it is necessary that the hero of the play be not a villain; that is, the characters, which should move our pity, ought to have virtuous inclinations, and degrees of moral goodness in them. As for a perfect character of virtue, it never was in Nature, and therefore there can be no imitation of it; but there are alloys of frailty to be allowed for the chief persons, yet so that the good which is in them shall outweigh the bad, and consequently leave room for punishment on the one side, and pity on the other.

After all, if any one will ask me, whether a tragedy cannot be made upon any other grounds than those of exciting pity and terror in us – Bossu, the best of modern critics, answers thus in general: That all excellent arts, and particularly that of poetry, have been invented and brought to perfection by men of a transcendent genius; and that, therefore, they, who practise afterwards the same arts, are obliged to tread in their footsteps, and to search in their writings the foundation of them; for it is not just that new rules should destroy the authority of the old. But Rapin writes more particularly thus, that no passions in a story are so proper to move our concernment as fear and pity; and that it is from our concernment we receive our pleasure, is undoubted; when the soul becomes agitated with fear for one character, or hope for another, then it is that we are pleased in Tragedy, by the interest which we take in their adventures.

Here, therefore, the general answer may be given to the first question, how far we ought to imitate Shakespeare and Fletcher in their plots; namely, that we ought to follow them so far only as they have copied the excellencies of those who invented and brought to perfection Dramatic Poetry; those things only excepted, which religion, custom of countries, idioms of languages, etc., have altered in the superstructures, but not in the foundation of the design. . . .

After the plot, which is the foundation of the play, the next thing to which we ought to apply our judgment, is the manners; for now the poet comes to work above ground. The groundwork, indeed, is that which is most necessary, as that upon which depends the firmness of the whole fabric; yet it strikes not the eye so much, as the beauties or imperfections of the manners, the thoughts, and the expressions.

The first rule which Bossu prescribes to the writer of an Heroic Poem, and which holds too by the same reason in all Dramatic Poetry, is to make the moral of the work; that is, to lay down to yourself what that precept of morality shall be, which you would insinuate into the people; as, namely, Homer's (which I have copied in my *Conquest of Granada*), was, that union preserves a commonwealth, and discord destroys it; Sophocles, in his *Oedipus*, that no man is to be accounted happy before his death. 'Tis the moral that directs the whole action of the play to one centre; and that action or fable is the example built upon the moral which confirms the truth of it to our experience: when the fable is designed, then, and not before, the persons are to be introduced, with their manners, characters, and passions.

The manners, in a poem, are understood to be those inclinations, whether natural or acquired, which move and carry us to actions, good, bad, or indifferent, in a play; or which incline the persons to such or such actions. I have anticipated part of this discourse already, in declaring that a poet ought not to make the manners perfectly good in his best persons; but neither are they to be more wicked in any of his characters than necessity requires. To produce a villain, without other reason than a natural inclination to villany, is, in Poetry, to produce an effect without a cause; and to make him more a villain than he has just reason to be, is to make an effect which is stronger than the cause.

The manners arise from many causes; and are either distinguished by complexion, as choleric and phlegmatic, or by the differences of age or sex, of climates, or quality of the persons, or their present condition. They are likewise to be gathered from the several virtues, vices, or passions, and many other commonplaces, which a poet must be supposed to have learned from natural Philosophy, Ethics, and History; of all which, whosoever is ignorant, does not deserve the name of poet.

But as the manners are useful in this art, they may be all comprised under these general heads: first, they must be apparent; that is, in every character of the play, some inclinations of the person must appear; and these are shown in the actions and discourse. Secondly, the manners must be suitable, or agreeing to the persons; that is, to the age, sex, dignity, and the other general heads of manners: thus, when a poet has given the dignity of a king to one of his persons, in all his actions and speeches, that person must discover majesty, magnanimity, and jealousy of power, because these are suitable to the general manners of a king. The third property of manners is resemblance; and this is founded upon the particular characters of men, as we have them delivered to us by relation or history; that is, when a poet has the known character of this or that man before him, he is bound to represent him such, at least not contrary to that which fame has reported him to have been. Thus, it is not a poet's choice to make Ulysses choleric, or Achilles patient, because Homer has described 'em quite otherwise. Yet this is a rock on which ignorant writers daily split; and the absurdity is as monstrous as if a painter should draw a coward running from a battle, and tell us it was the picture of Alexander the Great.

The last property of manners is, that they be constant and equal, that is, maintained the same through the whole design: thus, then Virgil had once given the name of *pious* to Æneas, he was bound to show him such, in all his words and actions, through the whole poem. . . .

From the manners, the characters of persons are derived; for, indeed, the characters are no other than the inclinations, as they appear in the several persons of the poem; a character being thus defined – that which distinguishes one man from another. Not to repeat the same things over again, which have been said of the manners, I will only add what is necessary here. A character, or that which distinguishes one man from all others, cannot be supposed to consist of one particular virtue, or vice, or passion only; but 'tis a composition of qualities which are not contrary to one another in the same person; thus, the same man may be liberal and valiant, but not liberal and covetous; so in a comical character, or humour (which is an inclination to this or that particular folly), Falstaff is a liar, and a coward, a glutton, and a buffoon, because all these qualities may agree in the same man; yet it is still to be observed, that one virtue, vice, and passion, ought to be shown in every man, as predominant over all the rest; as covetousness in Crassus, love of his country in Brutus; and the same in characters which are feigned.

The chief character or hero in a tragedy, as I have already shown, ought in prudence to be such a man who has so much more of virtue in him than of vice, that he may be left amiable to the audience, which otherwise cannot have any concernment for his sufferings; and it is on this one character, that the pity and terror must be principally, if not wholly, founded: a rule which is extremely necessary, and which none of the critics, that I know, have fully enough discovered to us. For terror and compassion work but weakly when they are divided into many persons. If Creon had been the chief character in *Oedipus*, there had neither been terror nor compassion moved; but only detestation of the man, and joy for his punishment; if Adrastus and Eurydice had been made more appearing characters, then the pity had been divided, and lessened on the part of Oedipus: but making Oedipus the best and bravest person, and even Jocasta but an underpart to him, his virtues, and the punishment of his fatal crime, drew both the pity and the terror to himself.

By what has been said of the manners, it will be easy for a reasonable man to judge whether the characters be truly or falsely drawn in a tragedy; for if there be no manners appearing in the characters, no concernment for the persons can be raised; no pity or horror can be moved, but by vice or virtue; therefore, without them, no person can have any business in the play. If the inclinations be obscure, it is a sign the poet is in the dark, and knows not what manner of man he presents to you; and consequently you can have no idea, or very imperfect, of that man; nor can judge what resolutions he ought to take; or what words or actions are proper for him. Most comedies made up of accidents or adventures are liable to fall into this error; and tragedies with many turns are subject to it; for the manners can never be evident, where the surprises of fortune take up all the business of the stage; and where the poet is more in pain to tell you what happened to such a man, than what he was. 'Tis one of the excellencies of Shakespeare, that the manners of his persons are generally apparent, and you see their bent and inclinations. Fletcher comes far short of him in this, as indeed he does almost in everything. . . . But of all poets, this commendation is to be given to Ben Jonson, that the manners, even of the most inconsiderable persons in his plays, are everywhere apparent.

By considering the second quality of manners, which is, that they be suitable to the age, quality, country, dignity, etc., of the character, we may likewise judge whether a poet has followed Nature. In this kind, Sophocles and Euripides have more excelled among the Greeks than Aeschylus; and Terence more than Plautus, among the Romans. Thus, Sophocles gives to Oedipus the true qualities of a king, in both those plays which bear his name; but in the latter, which is the *Oedipus Colonaeus*, he lets fall on purpose his tragic style; his hero speaks not in the arbitrary tone; but remembers, in the softness of his complaints, that he is an unfortunate blind old man; that he is banished from his country, and persecuted by his next relations. The present French poets are generally accused, that wheresoever they lay the scene, or in whatsoever age, the manners of their heroes are wholly French. Racine's Bajazet is bred at Constantinople; but his civilities are conveyed to him, by some secret passage, from Versailles into the Seraglio. But our Shakespeare, having ascribed to Henry the Fourth the character of a king and of a father, gives him the perfect manners of each relation, when either he transacts with his son or with his subjects. Fletcher, on the other side, gives neither to Arbaces, nor to his king, in the *Maid's Tragedy*, the qualities which are suitable to a monarch; though he may be excused a little in the latter, for the king there is not uppermost in the character; 'tis the lover of Evadne, who is king only in a second consideration; and though he be unjust, and has other faults which shall be nameless, yet he is not the hero of the play. 'Tis true, we find him a lawful prince (though I never heard of any king that was in Rhodes), and therefore Mr Rymer's criticism stands good; that he should not be shown in so vicious a character. Sophocles has been more judicious in his *Antigona*; for, though he represents in Creon a bloody prince, yet he makes him not a lawful king, but an usurper, and Antigona herself is the heroine of the tragedy: but when Philaster wounds Arethusa and the boy; and Perigot his mistress, in the *Faithful Shepherdess*, both these are contrary to the character of manhood. . . .

Under this general head of manners, the passions are naturally included as belonging to the characters. I speak not of pity and of terror, which are to be moved in the audience by the plot; but of anger, hatred, love, ambition, jealousy, revenge, etc., as they are shown in this or that person of the play. To describe these naturally, and to move them artfully, is one of the greatest commendations which can be given to a poet: to write pathetically, says Longinus, cannot proceed but from a lofty genius. A poet must be born with this quality: yet, unless he help himself by an acquired knowledge of the passions, what they are in their own nature, and by what springs they are to be moved, he will be subject either to raise them where they ought not to be raised, or not to raise them by the just degrees of nature, or to amplify them beyond the natural bounds, or not to observe the crisis and turns of them, in their cooling and decay; all which errors proceed from want of judgment in the poet, and from being unskilled in the principles of Moral Philosophy. Nothing is more frequent in a fanciful writer, than to foil himself by not managing his strength; therefore, as in a wrestler, there is first required some measure of force, a well-knit body and active limbs, without which all instruction would be vain; yet, these being granted, if he want the skill which is necessary to a wrestler, he shall make but small advantage of his natural robustuousness: so, in a poet, his inborn vehemence and force of spirit will only run him out of breath the sooner, if it be not supported by the help of Art. The roar of passion, indeed, may please an audience, three parts of which are ignorant enough to think all is moving which is noise, and it may stretch the lungs of an ambitious actor, who will die upon the spot for a thundering clap; but it will move no other passion than indignation and contempt from judicious men. Longinus, whom I have hitherto followed, continues thus: *If the passions be artfully employed, the discourse becomes vehement and lofty: if otherwise, there is nothing more ridiculous than a great passion out of season*: and to this purpose he animadverts severely upon Aeschylus, who writ nothing in cold blood, but was always in a rapture, and in fury with his audience: the inspiration was still upon him, he was ever tearing it upon the tripos; or (to run off as madly as he does, from one similitude to another) he was always at high-flood of passion, even in the dead ebb and lowest water-mark of the scene. He who would raise the passion of a judicious audience, says a learned critic, must be sure to take his hearers along with him; if they be in a calm, 'tis in vain for him to be in a huff; he must move them by degrees, and kindle with 'em; otherwise he will be in danger of setting his own heap of stubble on fire, and of burning out by himself, without warming the company that stand about him. . . .

 If Shakespeare be allowed, as I think he must, to have made his characters distinct, it will easily be inferred that he understood the nature of the passions: because it has been proved already that confused passions make undistinguishable characters: yet I cannot deny that he has his failings; but they are not so much in the passions themselves, as in his manner of expression: he often obscures his meaning by his words, and sometimes makes it unintelligible. I will not say of so great a poet, that he distinguished not the blown puffy style from true sublimity; but I may venture to maintain, that the fury of his fancy often transported him beyond the bounds of judgment, either in coining of new words and phrases, or racking words which were in use, into the violence of a catachresis. It is not that I would explode the use of metaphors from passion, for Longinus thinks 'em necessary to raise it: but to use 'em at every word, to say nothing without a metaphor, a simile, an image, or description, is, I doubt, to smell a little too strongly of the buskin. . . .

To speak justly of this whole matter: 'tis neither height of thought that is discommended, nor pathetic vehemence, nor any nobleness of expression in its proper place; but 'tis a false measure of all these, something which is like them, and is not them; 'tis the Bristol-stone, which appears like a diamond; 'tis an extravagant thought, instead of a sublime one; 'tis roaring madness, instead of vehemence; and a sound of words, instead of sense. If Shakespeare were stripped of all the bombasts in his passions, and dressed in the most vulgar words, we should find the beauties of his thoughts remaining; if his embroideries were burnt down, there would still be silver at the bottom of the melting-pot: but I fear (at least let me fear it for myself) that we, who ape his sounding words, have nothing of his thought, but are all outside; there is not so much as a dwarf within our giant's clothes. Therefore, let not Shakespeare suffer for our sakes; 'tis our fault, who succeed him in an age which is more refined, if we imitate him so ill, that we copy his failings only, and make a virtue of that in our writings which in his was an imperfection. . . .

SOURCE: extracts from 'Preface to *Troilus and Cressida*, containing the Grounds of Criticism in Tragedy' (1679); in W. P. Ker (ed.), *Essays of John Dryden* (Oxford, 1926), I, pp. 207–8, 209–11, 213–18, 220–1, 224, 227.

Joseph Addison   (1711, 1712)

'The Noblest Production of Human Nature' (1711)

As a perfect Tragedy is the Noblest Production of Human Nature, so it is capable of giving the Mind one of the most delightful and most improving Entertainments. A Virtuous Man (says *Seneca*) struling with Misfortunes, is such a Spectacle as Gods might look upon with Pleasure. And such a Pleasure it is which one meets with in the Representation of a well-written Tragedy. Diversions of this kind wear out of our

Thoughts every thing that is mean and little. They cherish and cultivate that Humanity which is the Ornament of our Nature. They soften Insolence, sooth Affliction, and subdue the Mind to the Dispensations of Providence. . . .

The 'Ridiculous Doctrine' of Poetic Justice (1711)

The English Writers of Tragedy are possessed with a Notion, that when they represent a virtuous or innocent Person in Distress, they ought not to leave him till they have delivered him from out of his Troubles, or made him triumph over his Enemies. This Errour they have been led into by a ridiculous Doctrine in modern Criticism, that they are obliged to an equal Distribution of Rewards and Punishments, and to an impartial Execution of poetical Justice. Who were the first that established this Rule I know not; but I am sure it has no Foundation in Nature, in Reason, or in the Practice of the Ancients. We find that Good and Evil happen alike to all Men on this Side the Grave; and as the principal Design of Tragedy is to raise Commiseration and Terrour in the Minds of the Audience, we shall defeat this great End, if we always make Virtue and Innocence happy and successful. Whatever Crosses and Disappointments a good Man suffers in the Body of the Tragedy, they will make but small Impression on our Minds, when we know that in the last Act he is to arrive at the End of his Wishes and Desires. When we see him engaged in the Depth of his Afflictions, we are apt to comfort ourselves, because we are sure he will find his Way out of them; and that his Grief, how great soever it may be at present, will soon terminate in Gladness. For this Reason the ancient Writers of Tragedy treated Men in their Plays, as they are dealt with in the World, by making Virtue sometimes happy and sometimes miserable, as they found it in the Fable which they made choice of, or as it might affect their Audience in the most agreeable Manner. *Aristotle* considers the Tragedies that were written in either of these Kinds, and observes, That those which ended unhappily, had always pleased the People, and carried away the Prize in the publick Disputes of the Stage, from those that ended happily. Terrour and Commiseration leave a pleasing Anguish in the Mind; and fix the Audience in such a serious Composure of Thought, as is much more lasting and delightful than any little transient Starts of Joy and Satisfaction. Accordingly we find, that more of our *English* Tragedies have succeeded, in which the Favourites of the Audience sink under their Calamities, than those in which they recover themselves out of them. The best Plays of this Kind are the *Orphan, Venice preserv'd, Alexander the Great, Theodosius, All for Love, Oedipus, Oroonoko, Othello, & c.*

King Lear is an admirable Tragedy of the same Kind, as *Shakespear* wrote it; but as it is reformed according to the chymerical Notion of poetical Justice, in my humble Opinion it has lost half its Beauty. At the same time I must allow, that there are very noble Tragedies which have been framed upon the other Plan, and have ended happily; as indeed most of the good Tragedies, which have been written since the starting of the abovementioned Criticism, have taken this Turn: As the *Mourning Bride, Tamerlane, Ulysses, Phaedra* and *Hyppolitus*, with most of Mr *Dryden*'s. I must also allow, that many of *Shakespear*'s, and several of the celebrated Tragedies of Antiquity, are cast in the same Form. I do not therefore dispute against this Way of writing Tragedies, but against the Criticism that would establish this as the only Method; and by that Means would very much cramp the *English* Tragedy, and perhaps give a wrong Bent to the Genius of our Writers. . . .

The Pleasing Pain of Tragedy (1712)

. . . The two leading passions which the more serious Parts of Poetry endeavour to stir up in us, are Terror and Pity. And here, by the way, one would wonder how it comes to pass, that such Passions as are very unpleasant at all other times, are very agreeable when excited by proper Descriptions. It is not strange, that we should take Delight in such Passages as are apt to produce Hope, Joy, Admiration, Love, or the like Emotions in us, because they never rise in the Mind without an inward Pleasure which attends them. But how comes it to pass, that we should take delight in being terrified or dejected by a Description, when we find so much Uneasiness in the Fear or Grief which we receive from any other Occasion?

If we consider, therefore, the Nature of this Pleasure, we shall find that it does not arise so properly from the Description of what is Terrible, as from the Reflection we make on our selves at the time of reading it. When we look on such hideous Objects, we are not a little pleased to think we are in no Danger of them. We consider them at the same time, as Dreadful and Harmless; so that the more frightful Appearance they make, the greater is the Pleasure we receive from the Sense of our own Safety. In short, we look upon the Terrors of a Description, with the same Curiosity and Satisfaction that we survey a dead Monster. . . . It is for the same Reason that we are delighted with the reflecting upon Dangers that are past, or in looking on a Precipice at a distance, which would fill us with a different kind of Horrour, if we saw it hanging over our Heads.

In the like manner, when we read of Torments, Wounds, Deaths, and

the like dismal Accidents, our Pleasure does not flow so properly from
the Grief which such melancholly Descriptions give us, as from the
secret Comparison which we make between our selves and the Person
who suffers. Such Representations teach us to set a just Value upon our
own Condition, and make us prize our good Fortune which exempts us
from the like Calamities. This is, however, such a kind of Pleasure as we
are not capable of receiving, when we see a Person actually lying under
the Tortures that we meet with in a Description; because, in this Case,
the Object presses too close upon our Senses, and bears so hard upon us,
that it does not give us time or leisure to reflect on our selves. Our
Thoughts are so intent upon the Miseries of the Sufferer, that we cannot
turn them upon our own Happiness. Whereas, on the contrary, we
consider the Misfortunes we read in History or Poetry, either as past, or
as fictitious, so that the Reflection upon our selves rises in us insensibly,
and over-bears the Sorrow we conceive for the Sufferings of the
Afflicted. . . .

SOURCE: extracts from *The Spectator*: No. 39 (14 April 1711); No. 40
(16 April 1711); No. 418 (30 June 1712); in Donald F. Bond (ed.),
The Spectator (Oxford, 1965), I, pp. 163–4, 168–70; III, pp. 567–9.

Edmund Burke (1757)

Tragedy and Sympathy

[XIII] . . . It is a common observation, that objects which in the reality
would shock, are in tragical, and such like representations, the source of
a very high species of pleasure. This taken as a fact, has been the cause of
much reasoning. The satisfaction has been commonly attributed, first,
to the comfort we receive in considering that so melancholy a story is no
more than a fiction; and next, to the contemplation of our own freedom
from the evils which we see represented. I am afraid it is a practice much
too common in inquiries of this nature, to attribute the cause of feelings
which merely arise from the mechanical structure of our bodies, or from
the natural frame and constitution of our minds, to certain conclusions
of the reasoning faculty on the objects presented to us; for I should
imagine, that the influence of reason in producing our passions is
nothing near so extensive as it is commonly believed.

[XIV] To examine this point concerning the effect of tragedy in a proper manner, we must previously consider, how we are affected by the feelings of our fellow creatures in circumstances of real distress. I am convinced we have a degree of delight, and that no small one, in the real misfortunes and pains of others; for let the affection be what it will in appearance, if it does not make us shun such objects, if on the contrary it induces us to approach them, if it makes us dwell upon them, in this case I conceive we must have a delight or pleasure of some species or other in contemplating objects of this kind. Do we not read the authentic histories of scenes of this nature with as much pleasure as romances or poems, where the incidents are fictitious? The prosperity of no empire, nor the grandeur of no king, can so agreeably affect in the reading, as the ruin of the state of Macedon, and the distress of its unhappy prince. Such a catastrophe touches us in history as much as the destruction of Troy does in fable. Our delight in cases of this kind is very greatly heightened, if the sufferer be some excellent person who sinks under an unworthy fortune. Scipio and Cato are both virtuous characters; but we are more deeply affected by the violent death of the one, and the ruin of the great cause he adhered to, than with the deserved triumphs and uninterrupted prosperity of the other; for terror is a passion which always produces delight when it does not press too close, and pity is a passion accompanied with pleasure, because it arises from love and social affection. Whenever we are formed by nature to any active purpose, the passion which animates us to it, is attended with delight, or a pleasure of some kind, let the subject matter be what it will; and as our Creator has designed we should be united by the bond of sympathy, he has strengthened that bond by a proportionable delight; and there most where our sympathy is most wanted, in the distresses of others. If this passion was simply painful, we would shun with the greatest care all persons and places that could excite such a passion; as, some who are so far gone in indolence as not to endure any strong impression actually do. But the case is widely different with the greater part of mankind; there is no spectacle we so eagerly pursue, as that of some uncommon and grievous calamity; so that whether the misfortune is before our eyes, or whether they are turned back to it in history, it always touches with delight. This is not an unmixed delight, but blended with no small uneasiness. The delight we have in such things, hinders us from shunning scenes of misery; and the pain we feel, prompts us to relieve ourselves in relieving those who suffer; and all this antecedent to any reasoning, by an instinct that works us to its own purposes, without our concurrence.

[xv] It is thus in real calamities. In imitated distresses the only difference is the pleasure resulting from the effects of imitation; for it is never so perfect, but we can perceive it is an imitation, and on that principle are somewhat pleased with it. And indeed in some cases we

derive as much or more pleasure from that source than from the thing itself. But then I imagine we shall be much mistaken if we attribute any considerable part of our satisfaction in tragedy to a consideration that tragedy is a deceit, and its representations no realities. The nearer it approaches the reality, and the further it removes us from all idea of fiction, the more perfect is its power. But be its power of what kind it will, it never approaches to what it represents. Chuse a day on which to represent the most sublime and affecting tragedy we have; appoint the most favourite actors; spare no cost upon the scenes and decorations; unite the greatest efforts of poetry, painting and music; and when you have collected your audience, just at the moment when their minds are erect with expectation, let it be reported that a state criminal of high rank is on the point of being executed in the adjoining square; in a moment the emptiness of the theatre would demonstrate the comparative weakness of the imitative arts, and proclaim the triumph of the real sympathy. I believe that this notion of our having a simple pain in the reality, yet a delight in the representation, arises from hence, that we do not sufficiently distinguish what we would by no means chuse to do, from what we should be eager enough to see if it was once done. We delight in seeing things, which so far from doing, our heartiest wishes would be to see redressed. This noble capital, the pride of England and of Europe, I believe no man is so strangely wicked as to desire to see destroyed by a conflagration or an earthquake, though he should be removed himself to the greatest distance from the danger. But suppose such a fatal accident to have happened, what numbers from all parts would croud to behold the ruins, and amongst them many who would have been content never to have seen London in its glory? Nor is it either in real or fictious distresses, our immunity from them which produces our delight; in my own mind I can discover nothing like it. I apprehend that this mistake is owing to a sort of sophism, by which we are frequently imposed upon; it arises from our not distinguishing between what is indeed a necessary condition to our doing or suffering any thing in general, and what is the *cause* of some particular act. If a man kills me with a sword, it is a necessary condition to this that we should have been both of us alive before the fact; and yet it would be absurd to say, that our being both living creatures was the cause of his crime and of my death. So it is certain, that it is absolutely necessary my life should be out of any imminent hazard before I can take a delight in the sufferings of others, real or imaginary, or indeed in any thing else from any cause whatsoever. But then it is a sophism to argue from thence, that this immunity is the cause of my delight either on these or on any occasions. No one can distinguish such a cause of satisfaction in his own mind I believe; nay when we do not suffer any very acute pain, nor are exposed to any imminent danger of our lives, we can feel for others, whilst we suffer ourselves; and often then most when we are softened by affliction; we see with pity even distresses which we would accept in the place of our own.

SOURCE: extracts from *A Philosophical Enquiry into the Origin of Our Ideas of the Sublime and Beautiful* (1757); modern edition, edited by J. T. Boulton (London, 1958), pp. 44–8.

David Hume   (1757)

Of Tragedy

It seems an unaccountable pleasure, which the spectators of a well-written tragedy receive from sorrow, terror, anxiety, and other passions, that are in themselves disagreeable and uneasy. The more they are touched and affected, the more are they delighted with the spectacle; and as soon as the uneasy passions cease to operate, the piece is at an end. One scene of full joy and contentment and security is the utmost, that any composition of this kind can bear; and it is sure always to be the concluding one. If, in the texture of the piece, there be interwoven any scenes of satisfaction, they afford only faint gleams of pleasure, which are thrown in by way of variety, and in order to plunge the actors into deeper distress, by means of that contrast and disappointment. The whole heart of the poet is employed, in rouzing and supporting the compassion and indignation, the anxiety and resentment of his audience. They are pleased in proportion as they are afflicted, and never are so happy as when they employ tears, sobs, and cries to give vent to their sorrow, and relieve their heart, swoln with tenderest sympathy and compassion.

The few critics who have had some tincture of philosophy, have remarked this singular phænomenon, and have endeavoured to account for it.

L'Abbé DUBOS, in his reflections on poetry and painting, asserts, that nothing is in general so disagreeable to the mind as the languid, listless state of indolence, into which it falls upon the removal of all passion and occupation. To get rid of this painful situation, it seeks every amusement and pursuit; business, gaming, shews, executions; whatever will rouze the passions, and take its attention from itself. No matter what the passion is: Let it be disagreeable, afflicting, melancholy, disordered; it is still better than that insipid languor, which arises from perfect tranquillity and repose.

It is impossible not to admit this account, as being, at least in part, satisfactory. You may observe, when there are several tables of gaming, that all the company run to those, where the deepest play is, even though they find not there the best players. The view, or, at least, imagination of high passions, arising from great loss or gain, affects the spectator by sympathy, gives him some touches of the same passions, and serves him for a momentary entertainment. It makes the time pass the easier with him, and is some relief to that oppression, under which men commonly labour, when left entirely to their own thoughts and meditations.

We find that common liars always magnify, in their narrations, all kinds of danger, pain, distress, sickness, deaths, murders, and cruelties; as well as joy, beauty, mirth, and magnificence. It is an absurd secret, which they have for pleasing their company, fixing their attention, and attaching them to such marvellous relations, by the passions and emotions, which they excite.

There is, however, a difficulty in applying to the present subject, in its full extent, this solution, however ingenious and satisfactory it may appear. It is certain, that the same object of distress, which pleases in a tragedy, were it really set before us, would give the most unfeigned uneasiness; though it be then the most effectual cure to languor and indolence. Monsieur FONTENELLE seems to have been sensible of this difficulty; and accordingly attempts another solution of the phænomenon; at least makes some addition to the theory above mentioned.

'Pleasure and pain', says he, 'which are two sentiments so different in themselves, differ not so much in their cause. From the instance of tickling, it appears, that the movement of pleasure, pushed a little too far, becomes pain; and that the movement of pain, a little moderated, becomes pleasure. Hence it proceeds, that there is such a thing as a sorrow, soft and agreeable: It is a pain weakened and diminished. The heart likes naturally to be moved and affected. Melancholy objects suit it, and even disastrous and sorrowful, provided they are softened by some circumstance. It is certain, that, on the theatre, the representation has almost the effect of reality; yet it has not altogether that effect. However we may be hurried away by the spectacle; whatever dominion the senses and imagination may usurp over the reason, there still lurks at the bottom a certain idea of falsehood in the whole of what we see. This idea, though weak and disguised, suffices to diminish the pain which we suffer from the misfortunes of those whom we love, and to reduce that affliction to such a pitch as converts it into a pleasure. We weep for the misfortune of a hero, to whom we are attached. In the same instant we comfort ourselves, by reflecting, that it is nothing but a fiction: And it is precisely that mixture of sentiments which composes an agreeable sorrow, and tears that delight us. But as that affliction, which is caused by exterior and sensible objects, is stronger than the consolation which arises from an internal reflection, they are the effects and symptoms of sorrow, that ought to predominate in the composition.'

This solution seems just and convincing; but perhaps it wants still some new addition, in order to make it answer fully the phænomenon, which we here examine. All the passions, excited by eloquence, are agreeable in the highest degree, as well as those which are moved by painting and the theatre. The epilogues of CICERO are, on this account chiefly, the delight of every reader of taste; and it is difficult to read some of them without the deepest sympathy and sorrow. His merit as an orator, no doubt, depends much on his success in this particular. When he had raised tears in his judges and all his audience, they were then the most highly delighted, and expressed the greatest satisfaction with the pleader. The pathetic description of the butchery, made by Verres of the Sicilian captains, is a masterpiece of this kind: But I believe none will affirm, that the being present at a melancholy scene of that nature would afford any entertainment. Neither is the sorrow here softened by fiction: For the audience were convinced of the reality of every circumstance. What is it then, which in this case raises a pleasure from the bosom of uneasiness, so to speak; and a pleasure, which still retains all the features and outward symptoms of distress and sorrow?

I answer: This extraordinary effect proceeds from that very eloquence, with which the melancholy scene is represented. The genius required to paint objects in a lively manner, the art employed in collecting all the pathetic circumstances, the judgment displayed in disposing them: the exercise, I say, of these noble talents, together with the force of expression, and beauty of oratorial numbers, diffuse the highest satisfaction on the audience, and excite the most delightful movements. By this means, the uneasiness of the melancholy passions is not only overpowered and effaced by something stronger of an opposite kind; but the whole impulse of those passions is converted into pleasure, and swells the delight which the eloquence raises in us. The same force of oratory, employed on an uninteresting subject, would not please half so much, or rather would appear altogether ridiculous; and the mind, being left in absolute calmness and indifference, would relish none of those beauties of imagination or expression, which, if joined to passion, give it such exquisite entertainment. The impulse or vehemence, arising from sorrow, compassion, indignation, receives a new direction from the sentiments of beauty. The latter, being the predominant emotion, seize the whole mind, and convert the former into themselves, at least tincture them so strongly as totally to alter their nature. And the soul, being, at the same time, rouzed by passion, and charmed by eloquence, feels on the whole a strong movement, which is altogether delightful.

The same principle takes place in tragedy; with this addition, that tragedy is an imitation; and imitation is always of itself agreeable. This circumstance serves still farther to smooth the motions of passion, and convert the whole feeling into one uniform and strong enjoyment. Objects of the greatest terror and distress please in painting, and please more than the most beautiful objects, that appear calm and in-different.* The affection, rouzing the mind, excites a large stock of spirit and vehemence; which is all transformed into pleasure by the force of the prevailing movement. It is thus the fiction of tragedy softens the passion, by an infusion of a new feeling, not merely by weakening or diminishing the sorrow. You may by degrees weaken a real sorrow, till it totally disappears; yet in none of its graduations will it ever give pleasure; except, perhaps, by accident, to a man sunk under lethargic indolence, whom it rouzes from that languid state.

To confirm this theory, it will be sufficient to produce other instances, where the subordinate movement is converted into the predominant, and gives force to it, though of a different, and even sometimes though of a contrary nature.

Novelty naturally rouzes the mind, and attracts our attention; and the movements, which it causes, are always converted into any passion, belonging to the object, and join their force to it. Whether an event excite joy or sorrow, pride or shame, anger or good-will, it is sure to produce a stronger affection, when new or unusual. And though novelty of itself be agreeable, it fortifies the painful, as well as agreeable passions.

Had you any intention to move a person extremely by the narration of any event, the best method of encreasing its effect would be artfully to delay informing him of it, and first to excite his curiosity and impatience before you let him into the secret. This is the artifice practised by Iago in the famous scene of SHAKESPEARE; and every spectator is sensible, that Othello's jealousy acquires additional force from his preceding im-patience, and that the subordinate passion is here readily transformed into the predominant one.

Difficulties encrease passions of every kind; and by rouzing our

---

* Painters make no scruple of representing distress and sorrow as well as any other passion. But they seem not to dwell so much on these melancholy affections as the poets, who, tho' they copy every emotion of the human breast, yet pass very quickly over the agreeable sentiments. A painter represents only one instant; and if that be passionate enough, it is sure to affect and delight the spectator. But nothing can furnish to the poet a variety of scenes and incidents and sentiments, except distress, terror, or anxiety. Compleat joy and satisfaction is attended with security, and leaves no farther room for action.

attention, and exciting our active powers, they produce an emotion, which nourishes the prevailing affection.

Parents commonly love that child most, whose sickly infirm frame of body has occasioned them the greatest pains, trouble, and anxiety in rearing him. The agreeable sentiment of affection here acquires force from sentiments of uneasiness.

Nothing endears so much a friend as sorrow for his death. The pleasure of his company has not so powerful an influence.

Jealousy is a painful passion; yet without some share of it, the agreeable affection of love has difficulty to subsist in its full force and violence. Absence is also a great source of complaint among lovers, and gives them the greatest uneasiness: Yet nothing is more favourable to their mutual passion than short intervals of that kind. And if long intervals often prove fatal, it is only because, through time, men are accustomed to them, and they cease to give uneasiness. Jealousy and absence in love compose the *dolce peccante* of the Italians, which they suppose so essential to all pleasure.

There is a fine observation of the elder PLINY, which illustrates the principle here insisted on. *It is very remarkable, says he, that the last works of celebrated artists, which they left imperfect, are always the most prized, such as the* Iris *of* ARISTIDES, *the* Tyndarides *of* NICOMACHUS, *the* Medea *of* TIMOMACHUS, *and the* Venus *of* APELLES. *These are valued even above their finished productions. The broken lineaments of the piece, and the half-formed idea of the painter are carefully studied; and our very grief for that curious hand, which had been stopped by death, is an additional encrease to our pleasure.*

These instances (and many more might be collected) are sufficient to afford us some insight into the analogy of nature, and to show us, that the pleasure, which poets, orators, and musicians give us, by exciting grief, sorrow, indignation, compassion, is not so extraordinary or paradoxical, as it may at first sight appear. The force of imagination, the energy of expression, the power of numbers, the charms of imitation; all these are naturally, of themselves, delightful to the mind: And when the object presented lays also hold of some affection, the pleasure still rises upon us, by the conversion of this subordinate movement into that which is predominant. The passion, though, perhaps, naturally, and when excited by the simple appearance of a real object, it may be painful; yet is so smoothed, and softened, and mollified, when raised by the finer arts, that it affords the highest entertainment.

To confirm this reasoning, we may observe, that if the movements of the imagination be not predominant above those of the passion, a contrary effect follows; and the former, being now subordinate, is converted into the latter, and still farther encreases the pain and affliction of the sufferer.

Who could ever think of it as a good expedient for comforting an afflicted parent, to exaggerate, with all the force of elocution, the irreparable loss, which he has met with by the death of a favourite child? The more power of imagination and expression you here employ, the more you encrease his despair and affliction.

The shame, confusion, and terror of Verres, no doubt, rose in proportion to the noble eloquence and vehemence of CICERO: So also did his pain and uneasiness. These former passions were too strong for the pleasure arising from the beauties of elocution; and operated, though from the same principle, yet in a contrary manner, to the sympathy, compassion, and indignation of the audience.

Lord CLARENDON, when he approaches towards the catastrophe of the royal party, supposes, that his narration must then become infinitely disagreeable; and he hurries over the king's death, without giving us one circumstance of it. He considers it as too horrid a scene to be contemplated with any satisfaction, or even without the utmost pain and aversion. He himself, as well as the readers of that age, were too deeply concerned in the events, and felt a pain from subjects, which an historian and a reader of another age would regard as the most pathetic and most interesting, and, by consequence, the most agreeable.

An action, represented in tragedy, may be too bloody and atrocious. It may excite such movements of horror as will not soften into pleasure; and the greatest energy of expression, bestowed on descriptions of that nature, serves only to augment our uneasiness. Such is that action represented in the *Ambitious Stepmother*, where a venerable old man, raised to the height of fury and despair, rushes against a pillar, and striking his head upon it, besmears it all over with mingled brains and gore. The English theatre abounds too much with such shocking images.

Even the common sentiments of compassion require to be softened by some agreeable affection, in order to give a thorough satisfaction to the audience. The mere suffering of plaintive virtue, under the triumphant tyranny and oppression of vice, forms a disagreeable spectacle, and is carefully avoided by all masters of the drama. In order to dismiss the audience with entire satisfaction and contentment, the virtue must either convert itself into a noble courageous despair, or the vice receive its proper punishment.

Most painters appear in this light to have been very unhappy in their subjects. As they wrought much for churches and convents, they have chiefly represented such horrible subjects as crucifixions and martyrdoms, where nothing appears but tortures, wounds, executions, and passive suffering, without any action or affection. When they turned their pencil from this ghastly mythology, they had commonly recourse to OVID, whose fictions, though passionate and agreeable, are scarcely natural or probable enough for painting.

The same inversion of that principle, which is here insisted on, displays itself in common life, as in the effects of oratory and poetry. Raise so the subordinate passion that it becomes the predominant, it swallows up that affection which it before nourished and encreased. Too much jealousy extinguishes love: Too much difficulty renders us indifferent: Too much sickness and infirmity disgusts a selfish and unkind parent.

What so disagreeable as the dismal, gloomy, disastrous stories, with which melancholy people entertain their companions? The uneasy passion being there raised alone, unaccompanied with any spirit, genius, or eloquence, conveys a pure uneasiness, and is attended with nothing that can soften it into pleasure or satisfaction.

SOURCE: essay in *Four Dissertations . . .* (1757); reprinted in T. H. Green and T. H. Grose (eds), *Essays: Moral, Political and Literary* (London, 1875), pp. 258–65.

Gotthold E. Lessing   (1767–68)

Marmontel and Domestic Tragedy

. . . 'We wrong the human heart', says Marmontel, 'we misread nature, if we believe that it requires titles to rouse and touch us. The sacred names of friend, father, lover, husband, son, mother, of mankind in general, these are far more pathetic than aught else and retain their claims for ever. What matters the rank, the surname, the genealogy of the unfortunate man whose easy good nature towards unworthy friends has involved him in gambling and who loses over this his wealth and honour and now sighs in prison distracted by shame and remorse? If asked, who is he? I reply: He was an honest man and, to add to his grief, he is a husband and a father; his wife, whom he loves and who loves him, is suffering extreme need and can only give tears to the children who clamour for bread. Show me in the history of heroes a more touching, a more moral, indeed a more tragic situation! And when at last this miserable man takes poison and then learns that Heaven had willed his release, what is absent, in this painful, terrible moment, when to the horrors of death are added the tortures of imagination, telling him how happily he could have lived – what, I say, is absent to render the situation worthy of a tragedy? The wonderful, will be replied. What! Is there not matter wonderful enough in this sudden change from honour to shame, from innocence to guilt, from sweet peace to despair; in brief, in the extreme misfortune into which mere weakness has plunged him!' . . .

On Aristotle's Pity and Fear

I

. . . It is certainly not Aristotle who has made the division so justly censured of tragic passions into terror and compassion. He has been falsely interpreted, falsely translated. He speaks of pity and *fear*, not of pity and *terror*; and his fear is by no means the fear excited in us by misfortune threatening another person. It is the fear which arises for ourselves from the similarity of our position with that of the sufferer; it is the fear that the calamities impending over the sufferers might also befall ourselves; it is the fear that we ourselves might thus become objects of pity. In a word, this fear is compassion referred back to ourselves. . . .

II

. . . When Aristotle maintains that tragedy excites pity and fear to purify pity and fear, who does not see that this comprehends far more than Dacier has deemed good to explain? For according to the different combinations of these conceptions, he who would exhaust Aristotle must prove separately: (1) How tragic pity purifies our pity; (2) How tragic fear purifies our fear; (3) How tragic pity purifies our fear; (4) How tragic fear purifies our pity. Dacier rested at the third point only, and he explained this badly and partially. For whoever has endeavoured to arrive at a just and complete conception of Aristotle's doctrine of the purification of the passions will find that each of these four points includes in it a double contingency – namely, that since (to put it briefly) this purification rests in nothing else than in the transformation of passions into virtuous habits, and since according to our philosopher each virtue has two extremes between which it rests, it follows that if tragedy is to change our pity into virtue it must also be able to purify us from the two extremes of pity, and the same is to be understood of fear. Tragic pity must not only purify the soul of him who has too much pity, but also of him who has too little; tragic fear must not simply purify the soul of him who does not fear any manner of misfortune, but also of him who is terrified by every misfortune, even the most distant and most improbable. Likewise tragic pity in regard to

fear must steer between this too much and too little, and conversely
tragic fear in regard to pity. . . .

III

. . . [discussing Weiss's play, *Richard III*]; we will give up Richard; true,
the play is called after him, but he is not on that account the hero nor the
person through whose means the purposes of tragedy are to be attained;
he is only to be the means of exciting our pity for others; do not the
queen, Elizabeth, the princes excite this pity?

To avoid all verbal disputes, I say yes. But what strange, harsh
sensation it is that has mixed itself up with my pity for these persons;
what is it that makes me wish I could spare myself this pity? I do not
generally wish this with tragic pity – I linger over it willingly and thank
the poet for this sweet torture.

Aristotle says well and truly when he speaks of a *miaron*, of something
terrible, which we experience at sight of misfortunes of wholly good,
wholly innocent persons; and are not the queen, Elizabeth, and the
princes such persons? What have they done? How have they drawn it
down upon themselves that they are in the clutches of this monster? Is it
their fault that they have a better right to the throne than he? How
·about the little moaning victims who can scarcely distinguish right from
left; who will deny that they deserve our whole sorrow? But is it sorrow,
this that causes me to think with a shudder of the destiny of these people,
with a shudder to which a murmur against Providence is added which is
followed afar by despair. Is this sorrow? I will not ask if it be pity. But
call it what we may, is it that which is meant to be excited by an
imitative art?

Let no one say history evokes it, that it is founded upon something
that really occurred. Did it really occur? Very well, granting that, it has
then its good reason in the external and infinite connection of all things.
In this connection all is wisdom and goodness which appears to us blind
fate and cruelty in the few links picked out by the poet. Out of these few
links he ought to make a whole, rounded in itself, that is fully explained
out of itself, where no difficulty arises: a solution of which is not found in
his plan and which we are therefore forced to seek outside of it in the
general plan of all things. The whole of this earthly creator should be a
mere outline of the whole of the eternal Creator, should accustom us to
the thought that, as in Him all things are resolved for the best, so also it
will be here; and the poet forgets his most noble calling when he forces
into a narrow circle the incomprehensible ways of Providence and
advisedly awakens our shudder thereat. O spare us ye that have our
hearts in your power! To what end these sad emotions? To teach us
submission? Cool reason alone could teach us this and if the teachings of

reason are to have any hold on us, if we for all our submission are to retain confidence and joyful courage, it is most necessary that we should be reminded as little as possible of the perplexing instances of such unmerited terrible fates. . . .

SOURCE: Extracts from *Hamburgische Dramaturgie*, Nos. 14, 75, 78 and 79 (1767–68); in Edward Beal (ed.), *Selected Prose Works of G. E. Lessing*, trans. E. C. Beasley and Helen Zimmern (London, 1913), pp. 267, 407, 421, 423–4.

Samuel Johnson (1776)

On Catharsis

I [Boswell] introduced Aristotle's doctrine in his 'Art of Poetry', of 'the . . . purging of the passions', as the purpose of tragedy. 'But how are the passions to be purged by terrour and pity?' (said I, with an assumed air of ignorance, to incite him to talk, for which it was often necessary to employ some address). JOHNSON: 'Why, Sir, you are to consider what is the meaning of purging in the original sense. It is to expel impurities from the human body. The mind is subject to the same imperfection. The passions are the great movers of human actions; but they are mixed with such impurities, that it is necessary they should be purged or refined by means of terrour and pity. For instance, ambition is a noble passion; but by seeing upon the stage, that a man who is so excessively ambitious as to raise himself by injustice, is punished, we are terrified at the fatal consequences of such a passion. In the same manner a certain degree of resentment is necessary; but if we see that a man carries it too far, we pity the object of it, and are taught to moderate that passion.' . . .

SOURCE: report of a conversation, dated 12 April 1776, in Boswell's *Life of Johnson* (1791); modern edition, edited by G. Birkbeck Hill (Oxford, 1934), III, p. 39.

August Wilhelm von Schlegel   (1807)

Ancient and Modern Tragedy

. . . This brings me to some general reflections on the nature and purpose of tragedy: a question which has often been considered, but rarely satisfactorily resolved, and which, indeed, is not very easy to resolve. It is somewhat surprising that such naturally compassionate beings as ourselves, beset by real misfortunes the effects of which we are helpless to remedy, should want to sadden our lives still further by the dramatic representation of imaginary calamities. Perhaps it will be suggested that we take pleasure in contrasting our own state of tranquillity with the violent upheavals caused by passion, just as a storm at sea can be watched by someone on the shore with a reassuring feeling of security. Lucretius's well-known comparison,

When stormy winds churn up the waves out on the open sea [it is pleasing to stand on the shore and watch another's tremendous struggles; not because the sufferings of others are something to rejoice in, but because it is pleasing to see from what misfortunes you yourself are free. – *De Rerum Natura*, II 1–4],

applies very well, as Lucretius intended, to a philosopher who, having reached a state of absolute conviction and certainty, can contemplate the agitations of doubt and error with perfect serenity; but it is quite unsuitable to the spectator who responds feelingly to a tragedy. If such a spectator is really involved with the tragic characters, he will not be at all concerned with himself – or if he fails to be oblivious of himself, it is a sign that he is not deeply involved, and that the tragedy is not achieving its end. Perhaps it will be said that it is our need to be roused from the apathy of ordinary life by experiencing vivid emotions, whatever their nature may be, which has brought tragedy into being. I admit that such a need does exist. It has given birth to those animal combats which are such a favourite spectacle in many countries. The Romans carried the taste for this kind of thing so far that they took pleasure in watching men fight to the death either with each other or with wild beasts; though these men were criminals or slaves who were not regarded as entitled to normal human rights. But we who are less callous than the Romans, and given to more refined forms of entertainment, only allow exalted characters to appear on the tragic stage; and would we want these heroes and demi-gods to come down into the bloody arena of tragedy, like common gladiators, simply to stimulate our jaded nerves with their suffering? No, the attraction of tragedy is not to be found in the sensational aspects of suffering, or in circus games, or even in animal combats; though in the latter one does see agility, strength and courage at work, that is to say, qualities which have some analogy with the intellectual and moral faculties of man. In my opinion, what makes us feel, when we are spectators of a good tragedy, a kind of fundamental satisfaction arising from our sympathy with the violent situations and afflictions represented on stage is either the sense of the dignity of human nature aroused in us by great examples of humanity, or the intimation of an order of things which is supernatural, imprinted, and, as it were, mysteriously revealed, in the sequence of apparently disconnected events, or the combination of these two causes.

Force, and the resistance to that force, become each a measure of the other. It is necessity which makes man show what he is capable of. At times of great misfortune a grand and powerful soul will discover deep within itself, and translate into action, that store of unconquerable resolution which the heavens seem to have put there for such occasions as these; then it will discover that, despite the limits of a transitory existence within which it seems to be confined, its reach extends to the infinite. By striking this soul, so resolutely centred on its own resources, the hammer-blows of suffering cause the spark divine to fly from it. This is why tragedy – which of all the genres is the one that most aspires towards the ideal in its characters – is, and must be, full of difficult situations, of complicated conflicts between duty and passion, or between different passions and different duties, of unexpected reverses, and of terrible catastrophes. Seneca says that a great man struggling with adversity is a sight worthy of the gods, and if at first glance this seems a hard saying, several ancient tragedies can make us realise its essential truth. Tragic poetry can depart from these sublime models in two ways. Sometimes, as a result of speeches which are coldly declamatory instead of following the accents of nature, it gives only a superficial rendering of suffering, which thus seizes only lightly on the characters without penetrating to the very centre of existence, and stifles the immediacy of expression by an extravagant heroism which is then only capable of striking dismay in the heart of a chimerical enemy. Sometimes it attempts to produce an effeminate feeling of pity, and this softens the soul instead of toughening and strengthening it. The first fault is often to be found in Corneille, and nearly always in Alfieri. The most ancient examples of the second are to be found in Euripides; Metastasio is full of them; and, as a rule, modern poets are especially prone to this second fault because of the general inclination of their age.

But the aspect of the art of tragedy which modern poets have most seriously neglected is the overall purpose which ought to emerge from the work as a whole, and this is because they lack any clear and precise ideas about the aim of tragedy. They have looked for the distinctive characteristics of this genre in features which are merely accidental, such as the tragic dénouement or the royal dignity of the protagonists. The most widely accepted definition is that tragedy is the serious representation, in speech which has an elevated style, of a single and complete action capable of exciting terror and pity. The action is held to be complete when the drama can be found to have reached its conclusion in a point of rest, despite the fact that this point of rest is often imaginatively or emotionally somewhat precarious. As for unity of action, this is a very vague term. The tragic action is necessarily made up of a number of actions which are in themselves incomplete, and it can therefore be concentrated or expanded at will. For a sequence of causally connected actions, no matter how extended it may be, will always be capable of being subordinated to a single point of view and designated by a single name. But without further insisting on that point, let me observe that a dramatic character does not act alone, but that he in his turn is influenced by the actions of others, without those actions being dependent on him. From this point of view what happens in a tragedy can be considered just as much a sequence of events as a sequence of actions. In a word, tragedy represents not only human characters, but human destiny. And what, in the tragic poet's fiction, is to be the regulating principle behind this destiny? Should it be chance, that is to say, no regulating principle at all? It is only too apparent that a good many tragedies are constructed on this basis. It would be very difficult to find any tendency in them which is inherent in the nature of the thing itself, or any other aim than simply excitement of emotions which are frequently at odds with each other. But in my opinion the progression of events must be linked to a single idea: that is what constitutes the essential unity of a tragedy. This is not at all a theory plucked out of the air, but something based on the example of the Greeks. In their tragedies one generally finds a single, clearly articulated idea, which is so much the dominant feature that it is, so to speak, the very soul and spirit of the whole genre.

This hidden principle, this fundamental motivating idea behind Greek tragedy, is fate. It was already implicit in ancient religious belief, which led men to expect favour or hostility from the gods according to whether the gods had been propitiated or angered. But these finite, albeit powerful, beings were not the sovereign arbiters of human destiny; they were themselves bound to obey a destiny which was both inevitable and incomprehensible, and they were often no more than the blind agents of its decrees. A doctrine which offers so little consolation as this, since it affords the virtuous man no assurance that he is under the special protection of the gods, can reduce the faint-hearted to a state of total dejection; but it gives new impetus to men of greater fortitude because it throws them back upon themselves and makes them rely solely on their own inner resources. It inspires them with the firm resolution to endure as best they can that which is without remedy, and to face the blows of fate with a pure conscience and inflexible courage. It is to the influence of this doctrine that we must attribute the superlatively tragic genius of the Greek poets in a period when the ordered structure of society had reached maturity, but religious belief was still in its full vigour. . . .

The idea of fate is directly opposed to our religious belief; Christianity has replaced it with the idea of providence. It is therefore to be doubted whether a Christian poet who intended to express in his work a point of view which was compatible with his religion, would not find it impossible to compose a true tragedy, and whether tragic poetry – the work of man when he is driven back on his own resources – would not disappear, along with the rest of those spectres of the dark produced by a superstitious imagination, before the dawn of revealed religion. We would certainly have to think so, if religion taught us that in this life providence always makes the good prosper and always punishes the wicked; but the ways of providence are inscrutable, and only the inspiration of the saint can trace its steps. All we know is that for the religious man eternal bliss is the compensation for his sufferings; that in the great fight between good and evil, which goes on ceaselessly in this world, good must ultimately triumph; and that all must in the end redound to the glory of God. Such an order of things allows for an infinite number of situations in which the heroism of the religious man, though of a different kind from that of the naked courage of the natural man, can display itself in all its strength. It allows for events of the deepest pathos, which, however, when seen as a whole, and, as it were, in a more elevated perspective, make us conceive the idea of a spiritual consolation.

The tragic system of the Greeks is based on a moral development which is almost entirely independent of religion. In it the dignity of man is maintained almost in spite of the supernatural order; moral liberty contends with necessity and fate, which are supposed to rule the world, for possession of the inner sanctuary of the soul, and when human nature is too weak to win a complete victory in this struggle, at least an honourable retreat is secured for it. The notion of providence has only become a generally held opinion since the arrival of Christianity; but the most enlightened among the ancients had some glimmerings of it, as of several other truths of revealed religion. The tragedies of Aeschylus are dominated by terror, and fate broods over mortal men in all its sinister splendour. However, the *Agamemnon*, the *Choephori* and the *Eumenides* – the three plays of Aeschylus which make up a *trilogy* (i.e. a series of tragedies designed to be performed together) – although each conforms exactly, when considered individually, to the system of fate, when taken as a whole reveal something which is very like providence. In the first play Agamemnon is killed by Clytemnestra. This is an act of revenge for the sacrifice of Iphigenia, which, in its turn, had been imposed on Agamemnon because he had involuntarily offended Diana. In the second, Orestes avenges his father by murdering his mother. This sequence of revenges, which are at once justified and abominable, might go on for ever, were it not that, in the third play, divine wisdom, in the shape of Minerva, puts an end to it, and restores the moral balance by causing Orestes, after he has expiated his offence against nature through his long persecution by the Furies, to be absolved of his crime by a court of justice. In *Prometheus Bound* we see a divine being, benefactor of the human race, oppressed by the tyranny of fate; but it is probable that Aeschylus's second tragedy on this subject, *Prometheus Unbound*, served to mitigate somewhat the terrible impression left by the first.

In the various plays of Sophocles there are even more remarkable gradations with regard to the severity of the rule of fate. His tragedy *Oedipus Rex* seems to have been written with the express purpose of inculcating this doctrine, and of making people realise, by means of a most elaborate and striking example, what the meaning of fate is. A man is destined to commit the most appalling crimes: all the precautions taken by his parents at his birth, and those which he takes himself later on, only serve to bring about the fulfilment of the oracles. The very same fate drags him at last to the discovery of those crimes of which he has been ignorant for so long, and, in consequence, he is plunged irretrievably from the heights of a glorious and seemingly spotless life to the depths of infamy and horrible despair. But in *Oedipus at Colonus* we see this same man – now old and blind, impoverished, banished, a vagabond on the face of the earth – finding at last a place of rest, where he is delivered from the divine curse under which he has laboured for so long. We see him in his last moments exercising his paternal authority over an unnatural son, surrounded by the tenderness of his daughters, protected and honoured by a hero of great renown, and finally sanctified by a miraculous and solemn death. And, despite the fact that during his life he was man from whom people averted their eyes in horror, his tomb becomes a blessing to the country which harbours it. The gods, who chose this innocent man to stand as an example of the blindness of mortal beings, owe him, and grant him, this restitution of honour in the eyes of the world. It is still fate, but fate which has doffed its mask of terror to show itself fair and just – fate in the guise of providence. In general, though his work is characterised by the grandeur, beauty and simplicity of the ancients, Sophocles is perhaps of all the Greek poets the one who expresses feelings which are most akin to the spirit of our religion.

In the work of Euripides one can see an author who has two different personalities: there is the dramatist who reveals a profound religious dedication, and who, because he enjoys its protection, is bound in return to show reverence towards religion; and there is the sophist with philosophical pretensions who has to draw the subject-matter of his plays from religion, but who tries to slip in his own free-thinking doubts and opinions among the wonders and miraculous events connected with it. At this period tragic poetry, perhaps because of a general relaxation in the moral climate, perhaps because of the influence of philosophical doctrines, began to deteriorate somewhat. Scenes are often to be found in Euripides which come very close to bourgeois drama, or even to high comedy. He introduces the moral standards of contemporary social life into his portrayal of heroic life; quite often he prefers a quality of effeminate tenderness to the true masculine tragic pity; and he cultivates sensational effects, and sacrifices the whole to the part.

Since the moderns, by virtue of their religion, see the destiny of man and his moral relationships in a totally different way from the ancients, it is not surprising that in their desire to imitate classical tragedy they have paid more attention to form than to the foundation on which that splendid construction rests. Whereas in Euripides we find only a certain amount of wavering, the moderns are often completely lacking in any general sense of direction. They have no compass to guide them as they sail over the vast sea represented by the many combinations which tragedy has to offer. In dealing with mythological subjects which have been handed down to us in a form modified by the ancient poets' interpretation of fate, the moderns have sometimes allowed this interpretation to penetrate their own work, without intending to do so, and possibly without even realising that it was happening. At other times a suggestion of retribution, or even of providence, will appear in their work, but superficially and in isolation from, rather than as an integral part of, the whole. But most often they think they have accomplished their task when they have found a story, or some historic event, which seems to offer them situations full of pathos and a striking catastrophe, and when they have managed to fit it into the usual five-act structure, and to observe the unities of time and place and other dramatic conventions. They do not concern themselves with any further aim.

Christianity can, however, provide a basis for tragedy which is just as sublime as that which the ancients derived from their religion, and which is capable of offering a much more profound sense of consolation. Attempts have been made at such tragedy: for example, a number of Christian plays have been written by Spanish poets. Calderon, above

all, whose inspiration was completely religious, has given us some
masterpieces of this kind, though to appreciate them properly it is
necessary to understand the conventions which are accepted as part of
Spanish drama. Christian tragedy is not unknown in the French theatre
either. Apart from *Polyeucte*, *Esther* and *Athalie*, which belong to this class
by virtue of their subject-matter, it seems to me that *Alzire* also deserves
to be called a Christian tragedy. . . .

To my mind there is also a third type of tragedy, examplified solely in
the work of Shakespeare: a poet whose work has profound meaning, but
who has been curiously misrepresented as a wild, untutored genius
blindly producing works which are artistically incoherent. I would call
Hamlet a philosophical tragedy, or, rather, a tragedy of scepticism. It
was the product of deep meditation on the nature of human destiny, and
in its turn it provokes further meditation on this subject. The mind
which is unable to achieve any kind of settled conviction strives in vain
to escape from its labyrinth by any other path than that suggested by the
idea of eternal nothingness. The deliberately slow, complicated, and
even at times retrograde, development of the action is symbolic of the
intellectual uncertainty which is the essence of the play. It is a
meditation without conclusion, and incapable of being concluded, on
the meaning of life itself, a meditation of which the gordian knot is at
last severed by death. This is perhaps the darkest form of tragedy. For
man needs the firm support of some kind of faith; he cannot tolerate
uncertainty, and only if his moral sense has been gravely weakened can
he be satisfied with an apathetic scepticism regarding the fundamental
truths which ought to concern him most of all. The tragedy of *Lear* has
much in common with that of *Hamlet*; it is even more emphatically cast
in the same mould. What is expressed in this work is no longer merely
doubt, but utter despair of ever being able to find the least trace of
consolation in the paths of this dark world. This huge canvas paints for
us a world in which moral values have been so completely overthrown
that the return of chaos seems to be imminent; it is not a tragedy of the
individual, but of the whole human race. *Macbeth*, on the other hand,
despite its great difference of form, is founded on the same principles as
classical tragedy. Fate is the dominant power; we even find there those
same prophecies which act as the instigators of the events which they
predict: treacherous oracles which, in the very process of being carried
out to the letter, betray the hopes of the man who puts his trust in them.

SOURCE: *Comparaison entre la Phèdre de Racine et celle d'Euripide* (Paris,
1807; reprinted A. L. Pollard (Old Marston, Oxford, 1962)), pp. 75–
92; translated for this Casebook by R. P. and I. F. Draper.

Arthur Schopenhauer (1819)

Tragedy and the 'Will to Live'

. . . Our pleasure in tragedy belongs, not to the sense of the beautiful, but to that of the sublime; nay, it is the highest grade of this feeling. For, as at the sight of the sublime in nature we turn away from the interests of the will, in order to be purely perceptive, so in the tragic catastrophe we turn away even from the will to live. In tragedy the terrible side of life is presented to us, the wail of humanity, the reign of chance and error, the fall of the just, the triumph of the wicked; thus the aspect of the world which directly strives against our will is brought before our eyes. At this sight we feel ourselves challenged to turn away our will from life, no longer to will it or love it. But just in this way we become conscious that then there still remains something over to us, which we absolutely cannot know positively, but only negatively, as that which does not will life. As the chord of the seventh demands the fundamental chord; as the colour red demands green, and even produces it in the eye; so every tragedy demands an entirely different kind of existence, another world, the knowledge of which can only be given us indirectly just as here by such a demand. In the moment of the tragic catastrophe the conviction becomes more distinct to us than ever that life is a bad dream from which we have to awake. So far the effect of the tragedy is analogous to that of the dynamical sublime, for like this it lifts us above the will and its interests, and puts us in such a mood that we find pleasure in the sight of what tends directly against it. What gives to all tragedy, in whatever form it may appear, the peculiar tendency towards the sublime is the awakening of the knowledge that the world, life, can afford us no true pleasure, and consequently is not worthy of our attachment. In this consists the tragic spirit: it therefore leads to resignation.

I admit that in ancient tragedy this spirit of resignation seldom appears and is expressed directly. Oedipus Colonus certainly dies resigned and willing; yet he is comforted by the revenge on his country. Iphigenia at Aulis is very willing to die; yet it is the thought of the welfare of Greece that comforts her, and occasions the change of her mind, on account of which she willingly accepts the death which at first she sought to avoid by any means. Cassandra, in the Agamemnon of the great Aeschylus, dies willingly . . . but she also is comforted by the thought of revenge. Hercules, in the Trachiniæ, submits to necessity, and dies composed, but not resigned. So also the Hippolytus of

Euripides, in whose case it surprises us that Artemis, who appears to comfort him, promises him temples and fame, but never points him to an existence beyond life, and leaves him in death, as all gods forsake the dying:—in Christianity they come to him; and so also in Brahmanism and Buddhism, although in the latter the gods are really exotic. Thus Hippolytus, like almost all the tragic heroes of the ancients, shows submission to inevitable fate and the inflexible will of the gods, but no surrender of the will to live itself. As the Stoic equanimity is fundamentally distinguished from Christian resignation by the fact that it teaches only patient endurance and composed expectation of unalterably necessary evil, while Christianity teaches renunciation, surrender of the will; so also the tragic heroes of the ancients show resolute subjection under the unavoidable blows of fate, while Christian tragedy, on the contrary, shows the surrender of the whole will to live, joyful forsaking of the world in the consciousness of its worthlessness and vanity. But I am also entirely of opinion that modern tragedy stands higher than that of the ancients. Shakespeare is much greater than Sophocles; in comparison with Goethe's Iphigenia one might find that of Euripides almost crude and vulgar. The Bacchæ of Euripides is a revolting composition in favour of the heathen priests. Many ancient pieces have no tragic tendency at all, like the Alcestis and Iphigenia in Tauris of Euripides; some have disgreeable, or even disgusting motives, like the Antigone and Philoctetes. Almost all show the human race under the fearful rule of chance and error, but not the resignation which is occasioned by it, and delivers from it. All because the ancients had not yet attained to the summit and goal of tragedy, or indeed of the view of life itself.

Although, then, the ancients displayed little of the spirit of re-signation, the turning away of the will from life, in their tragic heroes themselves, as their frame of mind, yet the peculiar tendency and effect of tragedy remains the awakening of that spirit in the beholder, the calling up of that frame of mind, even though only temporarily. The horrors upon the stage hold up to him the bitterness and worthlessness of life, thus the vanity of all its struggle. The effect of this impression must be that he becomes conscious, if only in obscure feeling, that it is better to tear his heart free from life, to turn his will from it, to love not the world nor life; whereby then, in his deepest soul, the consciousness is aroused that for another kind of willing there must also be another existence. For if this were not so, then the tendency of tragedy would not be this rising above all the ends and good things of life, this turning away from it and its seductions, and the turning towards another kind of existence, which already lies in this, although an existence which is for us quite inconceivable. How would it, then, in general, be possible that the exhibition of the most terrible side of life, brought before our eyes in the most glaring light, could act upon us beneficently, and afford us a lofty satisfaction? Fear and sympathy, in the excitement of which Aristotle places the ultimate end of tragedy, certainly do not in themselves belong to the agreeable sensations: therefore they cannot be the end, but only the means. Thus the summons to turn away the will from life remains the true tendency of tragedy, the ultimate end of the intentional exhibition of the suffering of humanity, and is so accordingly even where this resigned exaltation of the mind is not shown in the hero himself, but is merely excited in the spectator by the sight of great, unmerited, nay, even merited suffering. Many of the moderns also are, like the ancients, satisfied with throwing the spectator into the mood which has been described, by the objective representation of human misfortune as a whole; while others exhibit this through the change of the frame of mind of the hero himself, effected by suffering. The former give, as it were, only the premises, and leave the conclusion to the spectator; while the latter give the conclusion, or the moral of the fable, also, as the change of the frame of mind of the hero, and even also as reflection, in the mouth of the chorus, as, for example, Schiller in *The Bride of Messina*: 'Life is not the highest good.' Let me remark here that the genuine tragic effect of the catastrophe, thus the resignation and exaltation of the mind of the hero which is brought about by it, seldom appears so purely motived and so distinctly expressed as in the opera of *Norma*, where it comes in the duet, 'Qual cor tradisti, qual cor perdesti', in which the change of the will is distinctly indicated by the quietness which is suddenly introduced into the music. In general, this piece – regarded apart altogether from its excellent music, and also from the diction which can only be that of a libretto, and considered only according to its motives and its inner economy – is a highly perfect tragedy, a true pattern of tragic disposition of the motives, tragic progress of the action, and tragic development, together with the effect of these upon the frame of mind of the hero, raising it above the world, and which is then also communicated to the spectator; indeed the effect attained here is the less delusive and the more indicative of the true nature of tragedy that no Christians, nor even Christian ideas, appear in it. . . .

The Greeks have taken for their heroes only royal persons; and so also for the most part have the moderns. Certainly not because the rank gives more worth to him who is acting or suffering; and since the whole thing is just to set human passions in play, the relative value of the objects by which this happens is indifferent, and peasant huts achieve as much as kingdoms. Moreover, civic tragedy is by no means to be unconditionally rejected. Persons of great power and consideration are yet the best adapted for tragedy on this account, that the misfortune in which we ought to recognise the fate of humanity must have a sufficient

magnitude to appear terrible to the spectator, whoever he may be. . . .
Now the circumstances which plunge a citizen family into want and
despair are in the eyes of the great or rich, for the most part, very
insignificant, and capable of being removed by human assistance, nay,
sometimes even by a trifle: such spectators, therefore, cannot be
tragically affected by them. On the other hand, the misfortunes of the
great and powerful are unconditionally terrible, and also accessible to
no help from without; for kings must help themselves by their own
power, or fall. To this we have to add that the fall is greatest from a
height. Accordingly persons of the rank of citizens lack height to fall
from. . . .

SOURCE: extracts from ch. xxxvii of *Die Welt als Wille und Vorstellung*
(1819); English trans. by R. B. Haldane and J. Kemp, *The World as
Will and Idea* (London, 1886), iii, pp. 212–16, 217–18.

G. W. F. Hegel   (c. 1820)

'The Collision of Equally Justified Powers'

. . . In Greek tragedy, as I have said more than once, the occasion for
collision is produced by the moral justification of a specific act, and not
at all by an evil will, a crime, or infamy, or by mere misfortune,
blindness, and the like. For evil in the abstract has no truth in itself and
is of no interest. But, on the other hand, it must not look as if moral traits
of character have been assigned to individuals merely by [the
dramatist's] *intention*, for on the contrary their justification must be
shown to lie in them *essentially*. Criminal types, like those of today, good-
for-nothings, or even so-called 'morally noble' criminals with their
empty chatter about fate, we therefore do not find in Greek tragedy any
more than a decision or a deed resting on purely private interest and
personal character, on thirst for power, lust, honour, or other passions,
the right of which can be rooted only in an individual's private
inclination and personality. But an individual's decision, justified by
the object he aims at, is carried out in a one-sided and particular way,
and therefore in specific circumstances, which already carry in
themselves the real possibility of conflicts, he injures another and
equally moral sphere of the human will. To this sphere another person

clings as his own actual 'pathos' and in carrying out his aim opposes and reacts against the former individual. In this way the collision of equally justified powers and individuals is completely set afoot.

The range of the subject-matter here may be variously particularised but its essence is not very extensive. The chief conflict treated most beautifully by Sophocles, with Aeschylus as his predecessor, is that between the state, i.e. ethical life in its *spiritual* universality, and the family, i.e. *natural* ethical life. These are the clearest powers that are presented in tragedy, because the full reality of ethical existence consists in harmony between these two spheres and in absence of discord between what an agent has actually to do in one and what he has to do in the other. In this connection I need refer only to Aeschylus's *Seven against Thebes* and, still more appositely, Sophocles's *Antigone*. Antigone honours the bond of kinship, the gods of the underworld, while Creon honours Zeus alone, the dominating power over public life and social welfare. In Euripides's *Iphigenia in Aulis*, in Aeschlyus's *Agamemnon*, *Choephori*, and *Eumenides*, and in Sophocles's *Electra* we find a similar conflict. Agamemnon, as King and commander of the army, sacrifices his daughter in the interest of the Greeks and the Trojan expedition; thereby he snaps the bond of love for his daughter and his wife. This bond Clytemnestra, his wife and Iphigenia's mother, retains in the depths of her heart, and in revenge she prepares a shameful death for her home-coming husband. Orestes, her son and the King's son, honours his mother but he has to defend the right of his father, the King, and he slays the womb that bore him.

This is a subject valid for every epoch and therefore this presentation of it, despite all national differences, continues to excite our lively human and artistic sympathy.

A second main type of collision is less concrete. The Greek tragedians are fond of portraying it especially in the fate of Oedipus. The most perfect example of this has been left to us by Sophocles in his *Oedipus Tyrannus* and *Oedipus Coloneus*. What is at issue here is the right of the wide awake consciousness, the justification of what the man has self-consciously willed and knowingly done, as contrasted with what he was fated by the gods to do and actually did unconsciously and without having willed it. Oedipus has killed his father; he has married his mother and begotten children in this incestuous alliance; and yet he has been involved in these most evil crimes without either knowing or willing them. The right of our deeper consciousness today would consist in recognising that since he had neither intended nor known these crimes himself, they were not to be regarded as his own deeds. But the Greek, with his plasticity of consciousness, takes responsibility for what he has done as an individual and does not cut his purely subjective self-consciousness apart from what is objectively the case.

Lastly, there are other collisions depending partly on special circumstances and partly on the general relation between an individual's action and the Greek μοῖρα [fate]. For our purpose, these are of less importance.

But in considering all these tragic conflicts we must above all reject the false idea that they have anything to do with guilt or innocence. The tragic heroes are just as much innocent as guilty. On the presupposition that a man is only guilty if alternatives are open to him and he decides arbitrarily on what he does, the Greek plastic figures are innocent: they act out of this character of theirs, on *this* 'pathos', because this character, this 'pathos' is precisely what they are: their act is not preceded by either hesitation or choice. It is just the strength of the great characters that they do not choose but throughout, from start to finish, *are* what they will and accomplish. They are what they are, and never anything else, and this is their greatness. For weakness in action consists only in a cleavage between the individual and his object, in which case character, will, and aim do not appear as having grown into an absolute unity; and since no fixed aim is alive in the individual's soul as the substance of his own individuality, as the 'pathos' and power animating his whole will, he may swither irresolutely from this to that and let caprice decide. From this swithering the Greek plastic figures are exempt; for them the bond between the subject and what he wills as his object remains indissoluble. What drives them to act is precisely an ethically justified 'pathos' which they assert against one another with the eloquence of their 'pathos' not in sentimental and personal rhetoric or in the sophistries of passion, but in solid and cultivated objective language. (Sophocles above everyone else was a master in the depth, measure, and plastic and living beauty of language of this kind.) At the same time, however, their 'pathos' is pregnant with collisions and it leads them to injurious and guilty acts. But they do not claim to be innocent of these at all. On the contrary, what they did, and actually had to do, is their glory. No worse insult could be given to such a hero than to say that he had acted innocently. It is the honour of these great characters to be culpable. They do not want to arouse sympathy or pity, for what arouses pity is not anything substantive, but subjective grief, the subjective depth of personality. But their firm and strong character is one with its essential 'pathos', and what excites our admiration is this indestructible harmony and not the pity and emotion that Euripides alone has slipped into expressing.

The tragic complication leads finally to no other result or dénouement but this: the two sides that are in conflict with one another preserve the justification which both have, but what each upholds is one-sided, and this one-sidedness is stripped away and the inner, undisturbed harmony returns in the attitude of the chorus which clearly assigns equal honour to all the gods. The true development of the action consists solely in the cancellation of conflicts *as conflicts*, in the reconciliation of the powers animating action which struggled to destroy one another in their mutual conflict. Only in that case does finality lie not in misfortune and suffering but in the satisfaction of the spirit, because only with such a conclusion can the necessity of what happens to the individuals appear as absolute rationality, and only then can our hearts be morally at peace: shattered by the fate of the heroes but reconciled fundamentally. Only by adherence to this view can Greek tragedy be understood.

Therefore we should not interpret such a conclusion as a purely moral outcome where evil is punished and virtue rewarded. . . . Here there is no question at all of an introverted personality's subjective reflection and its good and evil, but, when the collision was complete, of the vision of an affirmative reconciliation and the equal validity of both the powers that were in conflict. Neither is the necessity of the outcome a blind fate, a purely irrational and unintelligible destiny which many people call 'classical', but a rational one, although the rationality here does not appear as a self-conscious Providence whose divine end and aim become manifest to itself and others in the world and individuals. On the contrary, the rationality consists in the fact that the power supreme over individual gods and men cannot allow persistence either to one-sided powers that make themselves independent and thereby overstep the limits of their authority, or to the conflicts that follow in consequence. Fate drives individuality back within its limits and destroys it if these are crossed. But an irrational compulsion and innocent suffering would inevitably produce in the soul of the spectator mere indignation instead of moral peace and satisfaction. . . . [Hegel discusses 'epic justice', 'epic reconciliation', which – as exhibited in the *Iliad* – have no strong moral connotation, in comparison with] the more profound tragic reconciliation . . . [which] depends on the advance of specific ethical substantive powers out of their opposition to their true harmony. But the ways in which this harmony can be brought about are very different, and I will therefore bring to your notice only the chief features at issue in this connection.

First, it needs special emphasis that if the one-sidedness of a 'pathos' is the real ground of the collisions, this can only mean that it is carried out into actually living action, and the one-sided 'pathos' has become the one and only 'pathos' of a specific individual. Now if the one-sidedness is to be cancelled, it is the individual, since he has acted solely as this *one* 'pathos', who must be got rid of and sacrificed. For the individual is only this *one* life and, if this is not to prevail on its own account as this *one*, then the individual is shattered.

This sort of development is most complete when the individuals who are at variance appear each of them in their concrete existence as a totality, so that in themselves they are in the power of what they are fighting, and therefore they violate what, if they were true to their own nature, they should be honouring. For example, Antigone lives under the political authority of Creon (the present King); she is herself the daughter of a King (Oedipus) and the fiancée of Haemon (Creon's son), so that she ought to pay obedience to the royal command. But Creon too, as father and husband, should have respected the sacred tie of blood and not ordered anything against its pious observance. So there is immanent in both Antigone and Creon something that in their own way they attack, so that they are gripped and shattered by something intrinsic to their own actual being. Antigone suffers death before enjoying the bridal dance, but Creon too is punished by the voluntary deaths of his son and his wife, incurred, the one on account of Antigone's fate, the other because of Haemon's death. Of all the masterpieces of the classical and the modern world – and I know nearly all of them and you should and can – the *Antigone* seems to me to be the most magnificent and satisfying work of art of this kind.

But the tragic dénouement need not every time require the downfall of the participating individuals in order to obliterate the one-sidedness of both sides and their equal meed of honour. We all know that the *Eumenides* of Aeschylus does not end with the death of Orestes or the discomfiture of the Eumenides. (These were the Furies, the avengers of a mother's blood, and the violation of family piety, against Apollo who means to maintain the dignity and veneration of the King and the head of the family, and who provoked Orestes to kill his mother.) On the contrary, Orestes is excused punishment and both the gods are honoured. But at the same time we see clearly in this decisive conclusion what their gods meant to the Greeks when they brought them before their eyes in a combat between one another as particular individuals. To the contemporary Athenians they were only elements which were bound together into the entire harmony of ethical life. The votes of the Areopagus were equal; it is Athene, the goddess representing the whole substance of living Athenian life, who inserts the white stone which liberates Orestes, but she promises altars and worship to the Eumenides and Apollo equally.

Secondly, in contrast to this objective reconciliation, the assuaging of conflict may be of a subjective kind when the individual agent gives up the one-sidedness of his aim. But in this desertion of a substantive 'pathos' of his own he would appear as lacking in character, and this contradicts the solidity of the Greek plastic figures. In this case, therefore, the individual can only put himself at the mercy of a higher power and its advice and command, so that while he persists on his own account in his 'pathos', his obstinate will is broken by a god. In such a case the knots cannot be untied but, as in the *Philoctetes*, for example, are cut by a *deus ex machina*.

Finally, more beautiful than this rather external sort of dénouement is an inner reconciliation which, because of its subjective character, already borders on our modern treatment. The most perfect classical example of this that we have before us is the eternally marvellous *Oedipus Coloneus*. Oedipus has murdered his father, taken the Theban throne, and mounted the marriage-bed with his mother. These unconsciously committed crimes do not make him unhappy; but of old he had solved a riddle and now he forcibly extracts [from the oracle] a knowledge of his own dark fate and acquires the dreadful realisation that it has been accomplished in himself. With this solution of the riddle in his own person he has lost his happiness as Adam did when he came to the knowledge of good and evil [Genesis, 3]. The seer now, he blinds himself, resigns the throne, exiles himself from Thebes, just as Adam and Eve were driven from Paradise, and wanders away a helpless old man. In Colonus, sore afflicted, instead of listening to his son's request that he might return, he invokes on him his own Furies [or curse]; he expunges all his own inner discord and is purified within. Then a god himself calls him [i.e. to death]; his blind eyes are transfigured and clear; his bones become a salvation and safeguard of the state that received him as friend and guest. This transfiguration in death is for us, as for him, a visible reconciliation within his own self and personality. Attempts have been made to find a Christian tone here: the vision of a sinner whom God pardons and a fate endured in life but compensated with bliss in death. But the Christian religious reconciliation is a transfiguration of the soul which, bathed in the spring of eternal salvation, is lifted above its deeds and existence in the real world, because it makes the heart itself into the grave of the heart (yes, the spirit can do this), pays the imputations of earthly guilt with its own earthly individuality and now holds itself secure against those imputations in the certainty of its own eternal and purely spiritual bliss. On the other hand, the transfiguration of Oedipus always still remains the Greek transfer of consciousness from the strife of ethical powers, and the violations involved, into the unity and harmony of the entire ethical order itself. . . .

The Subjectivity of Modern Tragedy

. . . In modern tragedy it is generally the case that individuals do not act for the sake of the *substantial* nature of their end, nor is it that nature which proves to be their motive in their passion; on the contrary, what presses for satisfaction is the *subjectivity* of their heart and mind and the privacy of their own character. . . .

In order to exhibit in more detail the difference in this respect between Greek and modern tragedy, I will direct attention only to Shakespeare's Hamlet. His character is rooted in a collision similar to that treated by Aeschylus in the *Choephori* and Sophocles in the *Electra*. For in Hamlet's case too his father, the King, is murdered and his mother has married the murderer. But whereas in the Greek poets the King's death does have an ethical justification, in Shakespeare it is simply and solely an atrocious crime and Hamlet's mother is guiltless of it. Consequently the son has to wreak his revenge only on the fratricide King in whom he sees nothing really worthy of respect. Therefore the collision turns strictly here not on a son's pursuing an ethically justified revenge and being forced in the process to violate the ethical order, but on Hamlet's personal character. His noble soul is not made for this kind of energetic activity; and, full of disgust with the world and life, what with decision, proof, arrangements for carrying out his resolve, and being bandied from pillar to post, he eventually perishes owing to his own hesitation and a complication of external circumstances.

If we turn now, in the second place, to that aspect which is of more outstanding importance in modern tragedy, to the characters, namely, and their conflict, the first thing that we can take as a starting-point is, in brief summary, the following:

The heroes of Greek classical tragedy are confronted by circumstances in which, after firmly identifying themselves with the one ethical 'pathos' which alone corresponds to their own already established nature, they necessarily come into conflict with the opposite but equally justified ethical power. The romantic dramatis personae, on the other hand, are from the beginning in the midst of a wide field of more or less accidental circumstances and conditions within which it is possible to act either in this way or in that. Consequently the conflict, for which the external circumstances do of course provide the occasion, lies essentially in the character to which the individuals adhere in their passion, not because of any substantial justification but because they are what they are once and for all. The Greek heroes too do act in their individual capacity, but, as I have said, when Greek tragedy is at its height their individuality is itself of necessity an inherently ethical 'pathos', whereas in modern tragedy it remains a matter of chance whether the individual's character is gripped by something intrinsically justified or whether he is led into crime and wrong, and in either case he makes his decision according to his own wishes and needs, or owing to external influences, etc. It is true, therefore, that character and an ethical end *may* coincide, but since aims, passions, and the subjective inner life are all particular [and not universal], this coincidence is not the *essential* foundation and objective condition of the depth and beauty of a [modern] tragedy. . . .

SOURCE: extracts from *Aesthetics: Lectures on Fine Art* (c. 1820); trans. T. M. Knox (Oxford, 1975), II, pp. 1212–16, 1217–20, 1225–6.

P. B. Shelley (1821)

Tragedy at its Peak in the Drama of Athens

. . . Homer and the cyclic poets were followed at a certain interval by the dramatic and lyrical poets of Athens, who flourished contemporaneously with all that is most perfect in the kindred expressions of the poetical faculty: architecture, painting, music, the dance, sculpture, philosophy and, we may add, the forms of civil life. . . .

It was at the period here adverted to, that the drama had its birth; and however a succeeding writer may have equalled or surpassed those few great specimens of the Athenian drama which have been preserved to us, it is indisputable that the art itself never was understood or practised according to the true philosophy of it, as at Athens. For the Athenians employed language, action, music, painting, the dance, and religious institutions, to produce a common effect in the representation of the highest idealisms of passion and of power; each division in the art was made perfect in its kind by artists of the most consummate skill, and was disciplined into a beautiful proportion and unity one towards the other. On the modern stage a few only of the elements capable of expressing the image of the poet's conception are employed at once. We have tragedy without music and dancing; and music and dancing without the highest impersonations of which they are the fit accompaniment, and both without religion and solemnity. Religious institution has indeed been usually banished from the stage. Our system of divesting the actor's face of a mask, on which the many expressions appropriated to his dramatic character might be moulded into one permanent and unchanging expression, is favourable only to a partial and inharmonious effect; it is fit for nothing but a monologue, where all the attention may be directed to some great master of ideal mimicry. The modern practice of blending comedy with tragedy, though liable to great abuse in point of practice, is undoubtedly an extension of the dramatic circle; but the comedy should be as in *King Lear*, universal, ideal, and sublime. It is perhaps the intervention of this principle which determines the balance in favour of *King Lear* against the *Oedipus Tyrannus* or the *Agamemnon*, or, if you will, the trilogies with which they are connected; unless the intense power of the choral poetry, especially that of the latter, should be considered as restoring the equilibrium. *King Lear*, if it can sustain this comparison, may be judged to be the most perfect specimen of the dramatic art existing in the world; in spite of the narrow conditions to which the poet was subjected by the ignorance of the philosophy of the drama which has prevailed in modern Europe. Calderon, in his religious *Autos*, has attempted to fulfil some of the high conditions of dramatic representation neglected by Shakespeare; such as the establishing a relation between the drama and religion, and the accommodating them to music and dancing; but he omits the observation of conditions still more important, and more is lost than gained by the substitution of the rigidly-defined and ever-repeated idealisms of a distorted superstition for the living impersonations of the truth of human passion.

But I digress. The connection of scenic exhibitions with the improvement or corruption of the manners of men, has been universally recognised: in other words, the presence or absence of poetry in its most perfect and universal form, has been found to be connected with good and evil in conduct or habit. The corruption which has been imputed to the drama as an effect, begins, when the poetry employed in its constitution ends: I appeal to the history of manners whether the periods of the growth of the one and the decline of the other have not corresponded with an exactness equal to any example of moral cause and effect.

The drama at Athens, or wheresoever else it may have approached to its perfection, ever co-existed with the moral and intellectual greatness of the age. The tragedies of the Athenian poets are as mirrors in which the spectator beholds himself, under a thin disguise of circumstance, stript of all but that ideal perfection and energy which every one feels to be the internal type of all that he loves, admires, and would become. The imagination is enlarged by a sympathy with pains and passions so mighty, that they distend in their conception the capacity of that by which they are conceived; the good affections are strengthened by pity, indignation, terror, and sorrow; and an exalted calm is prolonged from the satiety of this high exercise of them into the tumult of familiar life: even crime is disarmed of half its horror and all its contagion by being represented as the fatal consequence of the unfathomable agencies of nature; error is thus divested of its wilfulness; men can no longer cherish it as the creation of their choice. In a drama of the highest order there is little food for censure or hatred; it teaches rather self-knowledge and self-respect. Neither the eye nor the mind can see itself, unless reflected upon that which it resembles. The drama, so long as it continues to express poetry, is as a prismatic and many-sided mirror, which collects the brightest rays of human nature and divides and reproduces them from the simplicity of these elementary forms, and touches them with majesty and beauty, and multiplies all that it reflects, and endows it with the power of propagating its like wherever it may fall.

But in periods of the decay of social life, the drama sympathises with that decay. Tragedy becomes a cold imitation of the form of the great masterpieces of antiquity, divested of all harmonious accompaniment of the kindred arts; and often the very form misunderstood, or a weak attempt to teach certain doctrines, which the writer considers as moral truths; and which are usually no more than specious flatteries of some gross vice or weakness, with which the author, in common with his auditors, are infected. Hence what has been called the classical and domestic drama. Addison's *Cato* is a specimen of the one; and would it were not superfluous to cite examples of the other! To such purposes poetry cannot be made subservient. Poetry is a sword of lightning, ever unsheathed, which consumes the scabbard that would contain it. And thus we observe that all dramatic writings of this nature are unimaginative in a singular degree; they affect sentiment and passion, which, divested of imagination, are other names for caprice and appetite. The period in our own history of the grossest degradation of the drama is the reign of Charles II, when all forms in which poetry had been accustomed to be expressed became hymns to the triumph of kingly power over liberty and virtue. Milton stood alone illuminating an age unworthy of him. . . .

The drama being that form under which a greater number of modes of expression of poetry are susceptible of being combined than any other, the connection of poetry and social good is more observable in the drama than in whatever other form. And it is indisputable that the highest perfection of human society has ever corresponded with the highest dramatic excellence; and that the corruption or the extinction of the drama in a nation where it has once flourished, is a mark of a corruption of manners, and an extinction of the energies which sustain the soul of social life. . . .

SOURCE: extracts from *A Defence of Poetry* (1821; published 1840); in John Shawcross (ed.), *Shelley's Literary and Philosophical Criticism* (London, 1909), pp. 132, 133–6, 137.

George Eliot   (1856)

The *Antigone* and its Moral

'Lo! here a little volume but great Book' – a volume small enough to slip into your breast pocket, but containing in fine print one of the finest tragedies of the single dramatic poet who can be said to stand on a level with Shakespeare. Sophocles is the crown and flower of the classic tragedy as Shakespeare is of the romantic: to borrow Schlegel's comparison, which cannot be improved upon, they are related to each other as the Parthenon to Strasburg Cathedral.

The opinion which decried all enthusiasm for Greek literature as 'humbug', was put to an excellent test some years ago by the production of the *Antigone* at Drury Lane. The translation then adopted was among the feeblest by which a great poet has ever been misrepresented; yet so completely did the poet triumph over the disadvantages of his medium and of a dramatic motive foreign to modern sympathies, that the Pit was electrified, and Sophocles, over a chasm of two thousand years, once more swayed the emotions of a popular audience. And no wonder. The *Antigone* has every quality of a fine tragedy, and fine tragedies can never become mere mummies for Hermanns and Böckhs to dispute about: they must appeal to perennial human nature, and even the ingenious dulness of translators cannot exhaust them of their passion and their poetry.

E'en in their ashes live their wonted fires.

We said that the dramatic motive of the *Antigone* was foreign to modern sympathies, but it is only superficially so. It is true we no longer believe that a brother, if left unburied, is condemned to wander a hundred years without repose on the banks of the Styx; we no longer believe that to neglect funeral rites is to violate the claims of the infernal deities. But these beliefs are the accidents and not the substance of the poet's conception. The turning point of the tragedy is not, as it is stated to be in the argument prefixed to this edition, ' reverence for the dead and the importance of the sacred rites of burial', but the *conflict* between these and obedience to the State. Here lies the dramatic collision: the impulse of sisterly piety which allies itself with reverence for the Gods, clashes with the duties of citizenship; two principles, both having their validity, are at war with each. [The plot is outlined– Ed.] . .˙.

It is a very superficial criticism which interprets the character of Creon as that of a hypocritical tyrant, and regards Antigone as a blameless victim. Coarse contrasts like this are not the materials handled by great dramatists. The exquisite art of Sophocles is shown in the touches by which he makes us feel that Creon, as well as Antigone, is contending for what he believes to be the right, while both are also conscious that, in following out one principle, they are laying themselves open to just blame for transgressing another; and it is this consciousness which secretly heightens the exasperation of Creon and the defiant hardness of Antigone. The best critics have agreed with Böckh in recognising this balance of principles, this antagonism between valid claims; they generally regard it, however, as dependent entirely on the Greek point of view, as springing simply from the polytheistic conception, according to which the requirements of the Gods often clashed with the duties of man to man.

But, is it the fact that this antagonism of valid principles is peculiar to polytheism? Is it not rather that the struggle between Antigone and Creon represents that struggle between elemental tendencies and established laws by which the outer life of man is gradually and painfully being brought into harmony with his inward needs. Until this harmony is perfected, we shall never be able to attain a great right without also doing a wrong. Reformers, martyrs, revolutionists, are never fighting against evil only; they are also placing themselves in opposition to a good – to a valid principle which cannot be infringed without harm. Resist the payment of ship-money, you bring on civil war; preach against false doctrines, you disturb feeble minds and send them adrift on a sea of doubt; make a new road, and you annihilate vested interests; cultivate a new region of the earth, and you exterminate a race of men. Wherever the strength of a man's intellect, or moral sense, or affection brings him into opposition with the rules which society has sanctioned, *there* is renewed the conflict between Antigone and Creon; such a man must not only dare to be right, he must also dare to be wrong – to shake faith, to wound friendship, perhaps, to hem in his own powers. Like Antigone, he may fall a victim to the struggle, and yet he can never earn the name of a blameless martyr any more than the society – the Creon he has defied – can be branded as a hypocritical tyrant.

Perhaps the best moral we can draw is that to which the Chorus points: that our protest for the right should be seasoned with moderation and reverence, and that lofty words . . . are not becoming to mortals.

SOURCE: review article in *The Leader*, VII (29 March 1856); reprinted in Thomas Pinney (ed.), *Essays of George Eliot* (London, 1963), pp. 261–3, 264–5.

F. W. Nietzsche   (1872)

The Origin of Greek Tragedy

. . . I do not think I am unreasonable in saying that the problem of this origin has as yet not even been seriously posed, to say nothing of solved, however often the ragged tatters of ancient tradition have been sewn together in various combinations and torn apart again. This tradition tells us quite unequivocally *that tragedy arose from the tragic chorus*, and was originally only chorus and nothing but chorus. Hence we consider it our duty to look into the heart of this tragic chorus as the real proto-drama, without resting satisfied with such arty clichés as that the chorus is the 'ideal spectator' or that it represents the people in contrast to the aristocratic region of the scene. This latter explanation has a sublime sound to many a politician – as if the immutable moral law had been embodied by the democratic Athenians in the popular chorus, which always won out over the passionate excesses and extravagances of kings. This theory may be ever so forcibly suggested by one of Aristotle's observations; still, it has no influence on the original formation of tragedy, inasmuch as the whole opposition of prince and people – indeed the whole politico-social sphere – was excluded from the purely religious origins of tragedy. But even regarding the classical form of the chorus in Aeschylus and Sophocles, which is known to us, we should deem it blasphemy to speak here of intimations of 'constitutional popular representation'. From this blasphemy, however, others have not shrunk. Ancient constitutions knew of no constitutional representation of the people in *praxi*, and it is to be hoped that they did not even 'have intimations' of it in tragedy.

Much more famous than this political interpretation of the chorus is the idea of A. W. Schlegel, who advises us to regard the chorus somehow as the essence and extract of the crowd of spectators – as the 'ideal spectator'. This view, when compared with the historical tradition that originally tragedy was only chorus, reveals itself for what it is: a crude, unscientific, yet brilliant claim that owes its brilliancy only to its concentrated form of expression, to the typically Germanic bias in favour of anything called 'ideal', and to our momentary astonishment. For we are certainly astonished the moment we compare our familiar theatrical public with this chorus, and ask ourselves whether it could ever be possible to idealise from such a public something analogous to the Greek tragic chorus. We tacitly deny this, and now wonder as much at the boldness of Schlegel's claim as at the totally different nature of the Greek public. For we had always believed that the right spectator, whoever he might be, must always remain conscious that he was viewing a work of art and not an empirical reality. But the tragic chorus of the Greeks is forced to recognise real beings in the figures on the stage. The chorus of the Oceanides really believes that it sees before it the Titan Prometheus, and it considers itself as real as the god of the scene. But could the highest and purest type of spectator regard Prometheus as bodily present and real, as the Oceanides do? Is it characteristic of the ideal spectator to run onto the stage and free the god from his torments? We had always believed in an aesthetic public and considered the individual spectator the better qualified the more he was capable of viewing a work of art as art, that is, aesthetically. But now Schlegel tells us that the perfect, ideal spectator does not at all allow the world of the drama to act on him aesthetically, but corporally and empirically. Oh, these Greeks! we sigh; they upset all our aesthetics! But once accustomed to this, we repeated Schlegel's saying whenever the chorus came up for discussion.

Now the tradition, which is quite explicit, speaks against Schlegel. The chorus as such, without the stage – the primitive form of tragedy – and the chorus of ideal spectators do not go together. What kind of artistic genre could possibly be extracted from the concept of the spectator, and find its true form in the 'spectator as such'? The spectator without the spectacle is an absurd notion. We fear that the birth of tragedy is to be explained neither by any high esteem for the moral intelligence of the masses nor by the concept of the spectator without a spectacle; and we consider the problem too deep to be even touched by such superficial considerations.

An infinitely more valuable insight into the significance of the chorus was displayed by Schiller in the celebrated Preface to his *Bride of Messina*, where he regards the chorus as a living wall that tragedy constructs around itself in order to close itself off from the world of reality and to preserve its ideal domain and its poetical freedom.

With this, his chief weapon, Schiller combats the ordinary conception of the natural, the illusion usually demanded in dramatic poetry. Although the stage day is merely artificial, the architecture only symbolical, and the metrical language ideal in character, nevertheless an erroneous view still prevails in the main, as he points out: it is not sufficient that one merely tolerates as poetic license what is actually the essence of all poetry. The introduction of the chorus, says Schiller, is the decisive step by which war is declared openly and honourably against all naturalism in art.

It would seem that to denigrate this view of the matter our would-be superior age has coined the disdainful catchword 'pseudo-idealism'. I

fear, however, that we, on the other hand, with our present adoration of
the natural and the real, have reached the opposite pole of all idealism,
namely, the region of wax-work cabinets. There is an art in these, too, as
there is in certain novels much in vogue at present; but we really should
not be plagued with the claim that such art has overcome the 'pseudo-
idealism' of Goethe and Schiller.

It is indeed an 'ideal' domain, as Schiller correctly perceived, in
which the Greek satyr chorus, the chorus of primitive tragedy, was wont
to dwell. It is a domain raised high above the actual paths of mortals.
For this chorus the Greek built up the scaffolding of a fictitious *natural
state* and on it placed fictitious *natural beings*. On this foundation tragedy
developed and so, of course, it could dispense from the beginning with a
painstaking portrayal of reality. Yet it is no arbitrary world placed by
whim between heaven and earth; rather it is a world with the same
reality and credibility that Olympus with its inhabitants possessed for
the believing Hellene. The satyr, as the Dionysian chorist, lives in a
religiously acknowledged reality under the sanction of myth and cult.
That tragedy should begin with him, that he should be the voice of the
Dionysian wisdom of tragedy, is just as strange a phenomenon for us as
the general derivation of tragedy from the chorus.

Perhaps we shall have a point of departure for our inquiry if I put
forward the proposition that the satyr, the fictitious natural being, bears
the same relation to the man of culture that Dionysian music bears to
civilisation. Concerning the latter, Richard Wagner says that it is
nullified by music just as lamplight is nullified by the light of day.
Similarly, I believe, the Greek man of culture felt himself nullified in the
presence of the satyric chorus; and this is the most immediate effect of
the Dionysian tragedy, that the state and society and, quite generally,
the gulfs between man and man give way to an overwhelming feeling of
unity leading back to the very heart of nature. The metaphysical
comfort – with which, I am suggesting even now, every true tragedy
leaves us – that life is at the bottom of things, despite all the changes of
appearances, indestructibly powerful and pleasurable: this comfort
appears in incarnate clarity in the chorus of satyrs, a chorus of natural
beings who live ineradicably, as it were, behind all civilisation and
remain eternally the same, despite the changes of generations and of the
history of nations.

With this chorus the profound Hellene, uniquely susceptible to the
tenderest and deepest suffering, comforts himself, having looked boldly
right into the terrible destructiveness of so-called world history as well as
the cruelty of nature, and being in danger of longing for a Buddhistic
negation of the will. Art saves him, and through art – life.

For the rapture of the Dionysian state with its annihilation of the
ordinary bounds and limits of existence contains, while it lasts, a *lethargic*

element in which all personal experiences of the past become immersed. This chasm of oblivion separates the worlds of everyday reality and of Dionysian reality. But as soon as this everyday reality re-enters consciousness, it is experienced as such, with nausea: an ascetic, will-negating mood is the fruit of these states.

In this sense the Dionysian man resembles Hamlet: both have once looked truly into the essence of things, they have *gained knowledge*, and nausea inhibits action; for their action could not change anything in the eternal nature of things; they feel it to be ridiculous or humiliating that they should be asked to set right a world that is out of joint. Knowledge kills action; action requires the veils of illusion: that is the doctrine of Hamlet, not that cheap wisdom of Jack the Dreamer who reflects too much and, as it were, from an excess of possibilities does not get around to action. Not reflection, no – true knowledge, an insight into the horrible truth, outweighs any motive for action, both in Hamlet and in the Dionysian man.

Now no comfort avails any more; longing transcends a world after death, even the gods; existence is negated along with its glittering reflection in the gods or in an immortal beyond. Conscious of the truth he has once seen, man now sees everywhere only the horror or absurdity of existence; now he understands what is symbolic in Ophelia's fate; now he understands the wisdom of the sylvan god, Silenus: he is nauseated.

Here, when the danger to his will is greatest, *art* approaches as a saving sorceress, expert at healing. She alone knows how to turn these nauseous thoughts about the horror or absurdity of existence into notions with which one can live: these are the *sublime* as the artistic taming of the horrible, and the *comic* as the artistic discharge of the nausea of absurdity. The satyr chorus of the dithyramb is the saving deed of Greek art; faced with the intermediary world of these Dionysian companions, the feelings described here exhausted themselves. . . .

. . . The tradition is undisputed that Greek tragedy in its earliest form had for its sole theme the sufferings of Dionysus and that for a long time the only stage hero was Dionysus himself. But it may be claimed with equal confidence that until Euripides, Dionysus never ceased to be the tragic hero; that all the celebrated figures of the Greek stage – Prometheus, Oedipus, etc. – are mere masks of this original hero, Dionysus. That behind all these masks there is a deity, that is one essential reason for the typical 'ideality' of these famous figures which has caused so much astonishment. Somebody, I do not know who, has claimed that all individuals, taken as individuals, are comic and hence untragic – from which it would follow that the Greeks simply *could* not suffer individuals on the tragic stage. In fact, this is what they seem to have felt; and the Platonic distinction and evaluation of the 'idea' and the 'idol', the mere image, is very deeply rooted in the Hellenic character.

Using Plato's terms we should have to speak of the tragic figures of the Hellenic stage somewhat as follows: the one truly real Dionysus appears in a variety of forms, in the mask of a fighting hero, and entangled, as it were, in the net of the individual will. The god who appears talks and acts so as to resemble an erring, striving, suffering individual. That he *appears* at all with such epic precision and clarity is the work of the dream-interpreter, Apollo, who through this symbolic appearance interprets to the chorus its Dionysian state. In truth, however, the hero is the suffering Dionysus of the Mysteries, the god experiencing in himself the agonies of individuation, of whom wonderful myths tell that as a boy he was torn to pieces by the Titans and now is worshiped in this state as Zagreus. Thus it is intimated that this dismemberment, the properly Dionysian *suffering*, is like a transformation into air, water, earth, and fire, that we are therefore to regard the state of individuation as the origin and primal cause of all suffering, as something objectionable in itself. From the smile of this Dionysus sprang the Olympian gods, from his tears sprang man. In this existence as a dismembered god, Dionysus possesses the dual nature of a cruel, barbarised demon and a mild, gentle ruler. But the hope of the epopts [initiates in the mysteries of the cult – Ed.] looked toward a rebirth of Dionysus, which we must now dimly conceive as the end of individuation. It was for this coming third Dionysus that the epopts' roaring hymns of joy resounded. And it is this hope alone that casts a gleam of joy upon the features of a world torn asunder and shattered into individuals; this is symbolised in the myth of Demeter, sunk in eternal sorrow, who *rejoices* again for the first time when told that she may *once more* give birth to Dionysus. This view of things already provides us with all the elements of a profound and pessimistic view of the world, together with the *mystery doctrine of tragedy*: the fundamental knowledge of the oneness of everything existent, the conception of individuation as the primal cause of evil, and of art as the joyous hope that the spell of individuation may be broken in augury of a restored oneness.

We have already suggested that the Homeric epos is the poem of Olympian culture, in which this culture has sung its own song of victory over the terrors of the war of the Titans. Under the predominating influence of tragic poetry, these Homeric myths are now born anew; and this metempsychosis reveals that in the meantime the Olympian culture also has been conquered by a still more profound view of the world. The defiant Titan Prometheus has announced to his Olympian tormentor that some day the greatest danger will menace his rule, unless Zeus should enter into an alliance with him in time. In Aeschylus we recognise how the terrified Zeus, fearful of his end, allies himself with the Titan. Thus the former age of the Titans is once more recovered from Tartarus and brought to the light.

The philosophy of wild and naked nature beholds with the frank, undissembling gaze of truth the myths of the Homeric world as they dance past: they turn pale, they tremble under the piercing glance of this goddess [Truth] – till the powerful fist of the Dionysian artist forces them into the service of the new deity. Dionysian truth takes over the entire domain of myth as the symbolism of *its* knowledge which it makes known partly in the public cult of tragedy and partly in the secret celebrations of dramatic mysteries, but always in the old mythical garb.

What power was it that freed Prometheus from his vultures and transformed the myth into a vehicle of Dionysian wisdom? It is the Heracleian power of music: having reached its highest manifestation in tragedy, it can invest myths with a new and most profound significance. This we have already characterised as the most powerful function of music. For it is the fate of every myth to creep by degrees into the narrow limits of some alleged historical reality, and to be treated by some later generation as a unique fact with historical claims: and the Greeks were already fairly on the way toward restamping the whole of their mythical juvenile dream sagaciously and arbitrarily into a historico-pragmatical *juvenile history*. For this is the way in which religions are wont to die out: under the stern, intelligent eyes of an orthodox dogmatism, the mythical premises of a religion are systematised as a sum total of historical events; one begins apprehensively to defend the credibility of the myths, while at the same time one opposes any continuation of their natural vitality and growth; the feeling for myth perishes, and its place is taken by the claim of religion to historical foundations. This dying myth was now seized by the new-born genius of Dionysian music; and in these hands it flourished once more with colours such as it had never yet displayed, with a fragrance that awakened a longing anticipation of a metaphysical world. After this final effulgence it collapses, its leaves wither, and soon the mocking Lucians of antiquity catch at the discoloured and faded flowers carried away by the four winds. Through tragedy the myth attains its most profound content, its most expressive form; it rises once more like a wounded hero, and its whole excess of strength, together with the philosophic calm of the dying, burns in its eyes with a last powerful gleam.

What did you want, sacrilegious Euripides, when you sought to compel this dying myth to serve you once more? It died under your violent hands – and then you needed a copied, masked myth that, like the ape of Heracles, merely knew how to deck itself out in the ancient pomp. And just as the myth died on you, the genius of music died on you, too. Though with greedy hands you plundered all the gardens of music, you still managed only copied, masked music. And because you had abandoned Dionysus, Apollo abandoned you: rouse all the passions from their resting places and conjure them into your circle, sharpen and whet a sophistical dialectic for the speeches of your heroes – your heroes, too, have only copied, masked passions and speak only copied, masked speeches. . . .

. . . Dionysus had already been scared from the tragic stage, by a demonic power speaking through Euripides. Even Euripides was, in a sense, only a mask: the deity that spoke through him was neither Dionysus nor Apollo, but an altogether newborn demon, called *Socrates*.

This is the new opposition: the Dionysian and the Socratic – and the art of Greek tragedy was wrecked on this. Though Euripides may seek to comfort us by his recantation, he does not succeed: the most magnificent temple lies in ruins. What does the lamentation of the destroyer profit us, or his confession that it was the most beautiful of all temples? And even if Euripides has been punished by being changed into a dragon by the art critics of all ages – who could be content with so miserable a compensation?

Let us now approach this *Socratic* tendency with which Euripides combated and vanquished Aeschylean tragedy.

We must now ask ourselves, what could be the aim of the Euripidean design, which, in its most ideal form, would wish to base drama exclusively on the un-Dionysian? What form of drama still remained, if it was not to be born of the womb of music, in the mysterious twilight of the Dionysian? Only *the dramatised epos* – but in this Apollinian domain of art the *tragic* effect is certainly unattainable. The subject matter of the events represented is not decisive; indeed, I suggest that it would have been impossible for Goethe in his projected *Nausikaa* to have rendered tragically effective the suicide of this idyllic being, which was to have completed the fifth act. So extraordinary is the power of the epic-Apollinian that before our eyes it transforms the most terrible things by the joy in mere appearance and in redemption through mere appearance. The poet of the dramatised epos cannot blend completely with his images any more than the epic rhapsodist can. He is still that calm, unmoved contemplation which sees the images *before* its wide-open eyes. The actor in this dramatised epos still remains fundamentally a rhapsodist: the consecration of the inner dream lies on all his actions, so that he is never wholly an actor.

How, then, is the Euripidean play related to this ideal of the Appollinian drama? Just as the younger rhapsodist is related to the solemn rhapsodist of old times. In the Platonic *Ion*, the younger rhapsodist describes his own nature as follows: 'When I am saying anything sad, my eyes fill with tears; and when I am saying something awful and terrible, then my hair stands on end with fright and my heart beats quickly.' Here we no longer remark anything of the epic absorption in mere appearance, or of the dispassionate coolness of the true actor, who precisely in his highest activity is wholly mere appearance and joy in mere appearance. Euripides is the actor whose heart beats, whose hair stands on end; as Socratic thinker he designs the plan, as passionate actor he executes it. Neither in the designing nor in the execution is he a pure artist. Thus the Euripidean drama is a thing both cool and fiery, equally capable of freezing and burning. It is impossible for it to attain the Apollinian effect of the epos, while, on the other hand, it has alienated itself as much as possible from Dionysian elements. Now, in order to be effective at all, it requires new stimulants, which can no longer lie within the sphere of the only two art-impulses, the Apollinian and the Dionysian. These stimulants are cool, paradoxical thoughts, replacing Apollinian contemplation – and fiery *affects*, replacing Dionysian ecstasies; and, it may be added, thoughts and affects copied very realistically and in no sense dipped into the ether of art.

So we see that Euripides did not succeed in basing the drama exclusively on the Apollinian, and his un-Dionysian tendency actually went astray and became naturalistic and inartistic. Now we should be able to come closer to the character of *aesthetic Socratism*, whose supreme law reads roughly as follows, 'To be beautiful everything must be intelligible', as the counterpart to the Socratic dictum, 'Knowledge is virtue'. With this canon in his hands, Euripides measured all the separate elements of the drama – language, characters, dramaturgic structure, and choric music – and corrected them according to this principle.

The poetic deficiency and degeneration, which are so often imputed to Euripides in comparison with Sophocles, are for the most part products of this penetrating critical process, this audacious reasonableness. . . .

. . . What aesthetic effect results when the essentially separate art-forms, the Apollinian and the Dionysian, enter into simultaneous activity? Or more briefly: how is music related to image and concept? Schopenhauer, whom Richard Wagner, with special reference to this point, praises for an unsurpassable clearness and clarity of exposition, expresses himself most thoroughly on the subject in the following passage which I shall cite here at full length (*Welt als Wille und Vorstellung*, i, p. 309):[1]

According to all this, we may regard the phenomenal world, or nature, and music as two different expressions of the same thing [the will] which is therefore itself the only medium of their analogy, so that a knowledge of it is demanded in order to understand that analogy. Music, therefore, if regarded as an expression of the world, is in the highest degree a universal language, which is related indeed to the universality of concepts, much as they are related to the particular things. Its universality, however, is by no means that empty universality of abstraction, but of quite a different kind, and is united with thorough and distinct definiteness. In this respect it resembles geometrical figures and numbers, which are the universal forms of all possible objects of experience and applicable to them all *a priori*, and yet are not abstract but perceptible and thoroughly determinate. All possible efforts, excitements, and manifestations of will, all that goes on in the heart of man and that reason includes in the wide, negative concept of feeling, may be expressed by the infinite number of possible melodies, but always in the universal, in the mere form, without the material, always according to the thing-in-itself, not the phenomenon, the inmost soul, as it were, of the phenomenon without the body. This deep relation which music has to the true nature of all things also explains the fact that suitable music played to any scene, action, event, or surrounding seems to disclose to us its most secret meaning, and appears as the most accurate and distinct commentary upon it. This is so truly the case that whoever gives himself up entirely to the impression of a symphony, seems to see all the possible events of life and the world take place in himself; yet if he reflects, he can find no likeness between the music and the things that passed before his mind. For, as we have said, music is distinguished from all the other arts by the fact that it is not a copy of the phenomenon, or, more accurately, of the adequate objectivity of the will, but an immediate copy of the will itself, and therefore complements everything physical in the world and every phenomenon by representing what is metaphysical, the thing in itself. We might, therefore, just as well call the world embodied music as embodied will; and this is the reason why music makes every painting, and indeed every scene of real life and of the world, at once appear with higher significance, certainly all the more, in proportion as its melody is analogous to the inner spirit of the given phenomenon. Therefore we are able to set a poem to music as a song, or a visible representation as a pantomime, or both as an opera. Such particular pictures of human life, set to the universal language of music, are never bound to it or correspond to it with stringent necessity; but they stand to it only in the relation of an example chosen at will to a general concept. In the determinateness of the real, they represent that which music expresses in the universality of mere form. For melodies are to a certain extent, like general concepts, an abstraction from the actual. This actual world, then, the world of particular things, affords the object of perception, the special and individual, the particular case, both to the universality of the concepts and to the universality of the melodies. But these two universalities are in a certain respect opposed to each other; for the concepts contain particulars only as the first forms abstracted from perception, as it were, the separated shell of things; thus they are, strictly speaking, *abstracta*: music, on the other hand, gives the inmost kernel which precedes all forms, or the heart of things. This relation may be very well expressed in the language of the schoolmen, by saying, the concepts are the *universalia post rem*, but music gives the *universalia ante rem*, and the real world the *universalia in re*. But that in general a relation is possible between a composition and a visible representation rests, as we have said, upon the fact that both are simply different expressions of the same inner being of the world.

When now, in the particular case, such a relation is actually given, that is to say, when the composer has been able to express in the universal language of music the stirrings of will which constitute the heart of an event, then the melody of the song, the music of the opera, is expressive. But the analogy discovered by the composer between the two must have proceeded from the direct knowledge of the nature of the world unknown to his reason, and must not be an imitation produced with conscious intention by means of concepts, otherwise the music does not express the inner nature, the will itself, but merely gives an inadequate imitation of its phenomenon. All truly imitative music does this.

According to the doctrine of Schopenhauer, therefore, we understand music as the immediate language of the will, and we feel our fancy stimulated to give form to this invisible and yet so actively stirred spirit-world which speaks to us, and we feel prompted to embody it in an analogous example. On the other hand, image and concept, under the influence of a truly corresponding music, acquire a higher significance. Dionysian art therefore is wont to exercise two kinds of influences on the Apollinian art faculty: music incites to the *symbolic intuition* of Dionysian universality, and music allows the symbolic image to emerge *in its highest significance*. From these facts, intelligible in themselves and not inaccessible to a more penetrating examination, I infer the capacity of music to give birth to *myth* (the most significant example), and particularly the *tragic* myth: the myth which expresses Dionysian knowledge in symbols. In the phenomenon of the lyrist, I have shown how music strives to express its nature in Apollinian images. If now we reflect that music at its highest stage must seek to attain also to its highest objectification in images, we must deem it possible that it also knows how to find the symbolic expression for its unique Dionysian wisdom; and where shall we seek for this expression if not in tragedy and, in general, in the conception of the tragic?

From the nature of art as it is usually conceived according to the single category of appearance and beauty, the tragic cannot honestly be deduced at all; it is only through the spirit of music that we can understand the joy involved in the annihilation of the individual. For it is only in particular examples of such annihilation that we see clearly the eternal phenomenon of Dionysian art, which gives expression to the will in its omnipotence, as it were, behind the *principium individuationis*, the eternal life beyond all phenomena, and despite all annihilation. The metaphysical joy in the tragic is a translation of the instinctive unconscious Dionysian wisdom into the language of images: the hero, the highest manifestation of the will, is negated for our pleasure, because he is only phenomenon, and because the eternal life of the will is not affected by his annihilation. 'We believe in eternal life', exclaims tragedy; while music is the immediate idea of this life. Plastic art has an altogether different aim: here Apollo overcomes the suffering of the individual by the radiant glorification of the *eternity of the phenomenon*: here beauty triumphs over the suffering inherent in life; pain is obliterated by lies from the features of nature. In Dionysian art and its tragic symbolism the same nature cries to us with its true, undissembled voice: 'Be as I am! Amid the ceaseless flux of phenomena I am the eternally creative primordial mother, eternally impelling to existence, eternally finding satisfaction in this change of phenomena!' . . .

. . . The content of the tragic myth is, first of all, an epic event and the glorification of the fighting hero. But what is the origin of this enigmatic trait that the suffering and the fate of the hero, the most painful triumphs, the most agonising oppositions of motives, in short, the exemplification of this wisdom of Silenus, or, to put it aesthetically, that which is ugly and disharmonic, is represented ever anew in such countless forms and with such a distinct preference – and precisely in the most fruitful and youthful period of a people? Surely a higher pleasure must be perceived in all this.

That life is really so tragic would least of all explain the origin of an art form – assuming that art is not merely imitation of the reality of nature but rather a metaphysical supplement of the reality of nature, placed beside it for its overcoming. The tragic myth, too, insofar as it belongs to art at all, participates fully in this metaphysical intention of art to transfigure. But what does it transfigure when it presents the world of appearance in the image of the suffering hero? Least of all the 'reality' of this world of appearance, for it says to us: 'Look there! Look closely! This is your life, this is the hand on the clock of your existence.'

And the myth should show us this life in order to thus transfigure it for us? But if not, in what then lies the aesthetic pleasure with which we let these images, too, pass before us? I ask about the aesthetic pleasure, though I know full well that many of these images also produce at times a moral delight, for example, under the form of pity or moral triumph. But those who would derive the effect of the tragic solely from these moral sources – which, to be sure, has been the custom in aesthetics all too long – should least of all believe that they have thus accomplished something for art, which above all must demand purity in its sphere. If you would explain the tragic myth, the first requirement is to seek the pleasure that is peculiar to it in the purely aesthetic sphere, without transgressing into the region of pity, fear, or the morally sublime. How can the ugly and the disharmonic, the content of the tragic myth, stimulate aesthetic pleasure?

Here it becomes necessary to take a bold running start and leap into a metaphysics of art, by repeating . . . that existence and the world seem justified only as an aesthetic phenomenon. In this sense, it is precisely the tragic myth that has to convince us that even the ugly and disharmonic are part of an artistic game that the will in the eternal amplitude of its pleasure plays with itself. But this primordial phenomenon of Dionysian art is difficult to grasp, and there is only one direct way to make it intelligible and grasp it immediately: through the wonderful significance of *musical dissonance*. Quite generally, only music, placed beside the world, can give us an idea of what is meant by the justification of the world as an aesthetic phenomenon. The joy aroused by the tragic myth has the same origin as the joyous sensation of dissonance in music. The Dionysian, with its primordial joy experienced even in pain, is the common source of music and tragic myth. . . .

SOURCE: extracts from *The Birth of Tragedy* (1872); in *Basic Writings of Nietzsche*, trans. Walter Kaufmann (New York, 1968), pp. 56–60, 73–6, 82–4, 101–4, 140–1.

NOTE

1. Translator's note: The reference is Nietzsche's own. I have used the R. B. Haldane and J. Kemp translation of this long passage (*World as Will and Idea*, 1907 printing, I, p. 239) but have revised a number of inaccuracies.

August Strindberg (1888)

A Naturalistic Tragedy

The theatre, and indeed art in general, has long seemed to me a *Biblia pauperum*, a Bible in pictures for the benefit of the illiterate; with the dramatist as a lay preacher hawking contemporary ideas in a popular form, popular enough for the middle classes, who comprise the bulk of playgoers, to be able to grasp without too much effort what the minority is arguing about. The theatre has always been a primary school for the young, the semi-educated, and women, all of whom retain the humble faculty of being able to deceive themselves and let themselves be deceived – in other words, to accept the illusion, and react to the suggestion, of the author. Nowadays the primitive process of intuition is giving way to reflection, investigation and analysis, and I feel that the theatre, like religion, is on the way to being discarded as a dying form which we lack the necessary conditions to enjoy. This hypothesis is evidenced by the theatrical crisis now dominating the whole of Europe; and, not least, by the fact that in those cultural strongholds which have nurtured the greatest thinkers of our age, namely England and Germany, the art of writing plays is, like most of the other fine arts, dead.

In other countries, men have tried to create a new drama by pouring new ideas into the old forms. But this has failed, partly because the new thinkers have not yet had time to become popularised and thus educate the public to understand the issues involved; partly because polemical differences have so inflamed emotions that dispassionate appreciation has become impossible – the cheers and whistles of the majority exercise a pressure that upsets one's instinctive reaction – and partly also because we have not succeeded in adapting the old form to the new content, so that the new wine has burst the old bottles.

In my previous plays, I have not tried to do anything new – for that one can never do – but merely to modernise the form so as to meet the demands which I supposed that the new men and women of today would make of this art. To this end I chose, or let myself be caught up by, a theme [that of *Miss Julie* – Ed.] which may be said to lie outside current party conflicts. For the problem of social ascent and decline, of higher or lower, better or worse, man or woman, is, has been and will be of permanent interest. When I took this theme from an actual incident which I heard about some years ago, and which at the time made a deep impression on me, it seemed to me suitable matter for tragedy; for it is still tragic to see one on whom fortune has smiled go under, much more to see a line die out. But the time may come when we shall have become so developed and enlightened that we shall be able to observe with indifference the harsh, cynical and heartless drama that life presents – when we shall have discarded those inferior and unreliable thought-mechanisms called feelings, which will become superfluous and harmful once our powers of judgement reach maturity. The fact that the heroine arouses our sympathy is merely due to our weakness in not being able to resist a feeling of fear lest the same fate should befall us. Even so, the hyper-sensitive spectator may possibly even feel that sympathy is not enough, while the politically-minded will doubtless demand positive measures to remedy the evil – some kind of 'programme'. But there is no such thing as absolute evil, since the death of a family is good luck for some other family that will be able to take its place, and social change constitutes one of the main pleasures of life, happiness being dependent on comparison. As for the political planner, who wishes to remedy the regrettable fact that the bird of prey eats the dove, and the louse eats the bird of prey, I would ask him: 'Why should this state of affairs be remedied?' Life is not so foolishly and mathematically arranged that the great always devour the small. It happens equally often that a bee kills a lion, or at any rate drives it mad.

If my tragedy makes a tragic impression on people, they have only themselves to blame. When we become as strong as the first French revolutionaries, we shall feel uninhibited pleasure and relief at seeing our national forests thinned out by the removal of decayed and superannuated trees which have too long obstructed the growth of others with an equal right to live and fertilise their age – a relief such as one feels when one sees an incurable invalid at last allowed to die.

Recently, people complained of my tragedy *The Father* that it was too tragic – as though tragedies ought to be jolly. One hears pretentious talk about 'the joy of life', and theatrical managers feverishly commission farces, as though joy consisted in behaving idiotically and portraying the world as though it were peopled by lunatics with an insatiable passion for dancing. I find 'the joy of life' in life's cruel and mighty conflicts; I delight in knowledge and discovery. And that is why I have chosen a case that is unusual but from which one can learn much – an exception, if you like, but an important exception which proves the rule – though I dare say it will offend those people who love only what is commonplace. Another thing that will offend simple souls is the fact that the motivation of my play is not simple, and that life is seen from more than one viewpoint. An incident in real life (and this is quite a new discovery!) is usually the outcome of a whole series of deep-buried motives, but the spectator commonly settles for the one that he finds easiest to understand, or that he finds most flattering to his powers of judgement. Someone commits suicide. 'Bad business!', says the business man. 'Unrequited love!', say the ladies. 'Bodily illness!', says the invalid. 'Shattered hopes!', says the man who is a failure. But it may be that the motive lay quite elsewhere, or nowhere, and that the dead man concealed his true motive by suggesting another more likely to do credit to his memory!

I have suggested many possible motivations for Miss Julie's unhappy fate. The passionate character of her mother; the upbringing mis-guidedly inflicted on her by her father; her own character; and the suggestive effect of her fiancé upon her weak and degenerate brain. Also, more immediately, the festive atmosphere of Midsummer Night; her father's absence; her menstruation; her association with animals; the intoxicating effect of the dance; the midsummer twilight; the powerfully aphrodisiac influence of the flowers; and, finally, the chance that drove these two people together into a private room – plus of course the passion of the sexually inflamed man.

I have therefore not suggested that the motivation was purely physiological, nor that it was exclusively psychological. I have not attributed her fate solely to her heritage, nor thrown the entire blame on to her menstruation, or her lack of morals. I have not set out to preach morality. This, in the absence of a priest, I have left to a cook.

This multiplicity of motives is, I like to think, typical of our times. And if others have done this before me, then I congratulate myself in not being alone in my belief in these 'paradoxes' (the word always used to describe new discoveries). . . .

SOURCE: extract from Preface to *Miss Julie: A Naturalistic Tragedy* (1888); in '*The Father*', '*Miss Julie*' and '*The Ghost Sonata*', trans. by Michael Meyer (London, 1964; reprint 1976), pp. 91–4.

PART THREE

Twentieth-Century Views

W. B. Yeats   The Tragic Theatre (1910)

... In poetical drama there is, it is held, an antithesis between character and lyric poetry, for lyric poetry – however much it move you when you read out of a book – can, as these critics think, but encumber the action. Yet when we go back a few centuries and enter the great periods of drama, character grows less and sometimes disappears, and there is much lyric feeling, and at times a lyric measure will be wrought into the dialogue, a flowing measure that had well befitted music, or that more lumbering one of the sonnet. Suddenly it strikes us that character is continuously present in comedy alone, and that there is much tragedy, that of Corneille, that of Racine, that of Greece and Rome, where its place is taken by passions and motives, one person being jealous, another full of love or remorse or pride or anger. In writers of tragi-comedy (and Shakespeare is always a writer of tragi-comedy) there is indeed character, but we notice that it is in the moments of comedy that character is defined, in Hamlet's gaiety, let us say; while amid the great moments, when Timon orders his tomb, when Hamlet cries to Horatio 'Absent thee from felicity awhile', when Antony names 'Of many thousand kisses the poor last', all is lyricism, unmixed passion, 'the integrity of fire'. Nor does character ever attain to complete definition in these lamps ready for the taper, no matter how circumstantial and gradual the opening of events, as it does in Falstaff, who has no passionate purpose to fulfil, or as it does in Henry v, whose poetry, never touched by lyric heat, is oratorical; nor when the tragic reverie is at its height do we say, 'How well that man is realised! I should know him were I to meet him in the street', for it is always ourselves that we see upon the stage, and should it be a tragedy of love, we renew, it may be, some loyalty of our youth, and go from the theatre with our eyes dim for an old love's sake.

I think it was while rehearsing a translation of *Les Fourberies de Scapin* in Dublin, and noticing how passionless it all was, that I saw what should have been plain from the first line I had written, that tragedy must always be a drowning and breaking of the dykes that separate man from man, and that it is upon these dykes comedy keeps house. But I was not certain of the site of that house (one always hesitates when there is no testimony but one's own) till somebody told me of a certain letter of Congreve's. He describes the external and superficial expressions of 'humour' on which farce is founded and then defines 'humour' itself – the foundation of comedy – as a 'singular and unavoidable way of doing anything peculiar to one man only, by which his speech and actions are distinguished from all other men', and adds to it that 'passions are too powerful in the sex to let humour have its course', or, as I would rather put it, that you can find but little of what we call character in unspoiled youth, whatever be the sex, for, as he indeed shows in another sentence, it grows with time like the ash of a burning stick, and strengthens towards middle life till there is little else at seventy years.

Since then I have discovered an antagonism between all the old art and our new art of comedy and understand why I hated at nineteen years Thackeray's novels and the new French painting. A big picture of *cocottes* sitting at little tables outside a café, by some follower of Manet, was exhibited at the Royal Hibernian Academy while I was a student at a life class there, and I was miserable for days. I found no desirable place, no man I could have wished to be, no woman I could have loved, no Golden Age, no lure for secret hope, no adventure with myself for theme out of that endless tale I told myself all day long. Years after, I saw the *Olympia* of Manet at the Luxembourg and watched it without hostility indeed, but as I might some incomparable talker whose precision of gesture gave me pleasure, though I did not understand his language. I returned to it again and again at intervals of years, saying to myself, 'Some day I will understand'; and yet it was not until Sir Hugh Lane brought the *Eva Gonzales* to Dublin, and I had said to myself, 'How perfectly that woman is realised as distinct from all other women that have lived or shall live', that I understood I was carrying on in my own mind that quarrel between a tragedian and a comedian which the Devil on Two Sticks in Le Sage showed to the young man who had climbed through the window.

There is an art of the flood, the art of Titian when his *Ariosto*, and his *Bacchus and Ariadne*, give new images to the dreams of youth, and of Shakespeare when he shows us Hamlet broken away from life by the passionate hesitations of his reverie. And we call this art poetical, because we must bring more to it than our daily mood if we would take our pleasure; and because it takes delight in the moment of exaltation, of excitement, of dreaming (or in the capacity for it, as in that still face of Ariosto's that is like some vessel soon to be full of wine). And there is an art that we call real, because character can only express itself perfectly in a real world, being that world's creature, and because we understand it best through a delicate discrimination of the senses which is but entire wakefulness, the daily mood grown cold and crystalline.

We may not find either mood in its purity, but in mainly tragic art one distinguishes devices to exclude or lessen character, to diminish the power of that daily mood, to cheat or blind its too clear perception. If the real world is not altogether rejected, it is but touched here and there, and into the places we have left empty we summon rhythm, balance, pattern, images that remind us of vast passions, the vagueness of past times, all the chimeras that haunt the edge of trance; and if we are painters, we shall express personal emotion through ideal form, a symbolism handled by the generations, a mask from whose eyes the disembodied looks, a style that remembers many masters that it may escape contemporary suggestion; or we shall leave out some element of reality as in Byzantine painting, where there is no mass, nothing in relief; and so it is that in the supreme moment of tragic art there comes upon one that strange sensation as though the hair of one's head stood up. And when we love, if it be in the excitement of youth, do we not also, that the flood may find no stone to convulse, no wall to narrow it, exclude character or the signs of it by choosing that beauty which seems unearthly because the individual woman is lost amid the labyrinth of its lines as though life were trembling into stillness and silence, or at last folding itself away? Some little irrelevance of line, some promise of character to come, may indeed put us at our ease, 'give more interest' as the humour of the old man with the basket does to Cleopatra's dying; but should it come, as we had dreamed in love's frenzy, to our dying for that woman's sake, we would find that the discord had its value from the tune. Nor have we chosen illusion in choosing the outward sign of that moral genius that lives among the subtlety of the passions, and can for her moment make her of the one mind with great artists and poets. In the studio we may indeed say to one another, 'Character is the only beauty', but when we choose a wife, as when we go to the gymnasium to be shaped for woman's eyes, we remember academic form, even though we enlarge a little the point of interest and choose 'a painter's beauty', finding it the more easy to believe in the fire because it has made ashes.

When we look at the faces of the old tragic paintings, whether it is in Titian or in some painter of mediaeval China, we find there sadness and gravity, a certain emptiness even, as of a mind that waited the supreme crisis (and indeed it seems at times as if the graphic art, unlike poetry which sings the crisis itself, were the celebration of waiting). Whereas in modern art, whether in Japan or Europe, 'vitality' (is not that the great word of the studios?), the energy, that is to say, which is under the command of our common moments, sings, laughs, chatters or looks its busy thoughts.

Certainly we have here the Tree of Life and that of the Knowledge of Good and Evil which is rooted in our interests, and if we have forgotten their differing virtues it is surely because we have taken delight in a confusion of crossing branches. Tragic art, passionate art, the drowner of dykes, the confounder of understanding, moves us by setting us to reverie, by alluring us almost to the intensity of trance. The persons upon the stage, let us say, greaten till they are humanity itself. We feel our minds expand convulsively or spread out slowly like some moon-

brightened image-crowded sea. That which is before our eyes per-
petually vanishes and returns again in the midst of the excitement it
creates, and the more enthralling it is, the more do we forget it.

SOURCE: extract from essay in *The Cutting of An Agate* (London,
1910); reprinted in *Essays and Introductions* (London, 1961), pp. 240–5.

James Joyce   'Stephen Dedalus on Pity and Terror' (1916)

. . . They lit their cigarettes and turned to the right. After a pause
Stephen began:
–Aristotle has not defined pity and terror. I have, I say –
  Lynch halted and said bluntly:
–Stop! I won't listen! I am sick. I was out last night on a yellow drunk
with Horan and Goggins.
  Stephen went on:
– Pity is the feeling which arrests the mind in the presence of whatsoever
is grave and constant in human sufferings and unites it with the human
sufferer. Terror is the feeling which arrests the mind in the presence of
whatsoever is grave and constant in human sufferings and unites it with
the secret cause.
– Repeat, said Lynch.
  Stephen repeated the definitions slowly.
– A girl got into a hansom a few days ago, he went on, in London. She
was on her way to meet her mother whom she had not seen for many
years. At the corner of a street the shaft of a lorry shivered the window of
the hansom in the shape of a star. A long fine needle of the shivered glass
pierced her heart. She died on the instant. The reporter called it a tragic
death. It is not. It is remote from terror and pity according to the terms
of my definitions.
– The tragic emotion, in fact, is a face looking two ways, towards terror
and towards pity, both of which are phases of it. You see I use the word
arrest. I mean that the tragic emotion is static. Or rather the dramatic
emotion is. The feelings excited by improper art are kinetic, desire or
loathing. Desire urges us to possess, to go to something; loathing urges us
to abandon, to go from something. The arts which excite them,
pornographical or didactic, are therefore improper arts. The esthetic

emotion (I used the general term) is therefore static. The mind is arrested and raised above desire and loathing. . . .

SOURCE: extract from *A Portrait of the Artist as a Young Man* (1916); paperback edn (Harmondsworth, 1960), pp. 204–5.

I. A. Richards · 'The Balance or Reconciliation of Opposite and Discordant Qualities' (1924)

. . . We have suggested, but only by accident, that imagination characteristically produces effects similar to those which accompany great and sudden crises in experience. This would be misleading. What is true is that those imaginative syntheses which most nearly approach to these climaxes, Tragedy for example, are the most easy to analyse. What clearer instance of the 'balance or reconciliation of opposite and discordant qualities' can be found than Tragedy? Pity, the impulse to approach, and Terror, the impulse to retreat, are brought in Tragedy to a reconciliation which they find nowhere else, and with them who knows what other allied groups of equally discordant impulses. Their union in an ordered single response is the *catharsis* by which Tragedy is recognised, whether Aristotle meant anything of this kind or not. This is the explanation of that sense of release, of repose in the midst of stress, of balance and composure, given by Tragedy, for there is no other way in which such impulses, once awakened, can be set at rest without suppression.

It is essential to recognise that in the full tragic experience there is no suppression. The mind does not shy away from anything, it does not protect itself with any illusion, it stands uncomforted, unintimidated, alone and self-reliant. The test of its success is whether it can face what is before it and respond to it without any of the innumerable subterfuges by which it ordinarily dodges the full development of experience. Suppressions and sublimations alike are devices by which we endeavour to avoid issues which might bewilder us. The essence of Tragedy is that it forces us to live for a moment without them. When we succeed we find, as usual, that there is no difficulty; the difficulty came from the suppressions and sublimations. The joy which is so strangely the heart of the experience is not an indication that 'all's right with the world' or that 'somewhere, somehow, there is Justice'; it is an indication that all is right here and now in the nervous system. Because Tragedy is the experience which most invites these subterfuges, it is the greatest and the rarest thing in literature, for the vast majority of works which pass by that name are of a different order. Tragedy is only possible to a mind which is for the moment agnostic or Manichean. The least touch of any theology which has a compensating Heaven to offer the tragic hero is fatal. That is why *Romeo and Juliet* is not a Tragedy in the sense in which *King Lear* is.

But there is more in Tragedy than unmitigated experience. Besides Terror there is Pity, and if there is substituted for either something a little different – Horror or Dread, say, for Terror; Regret or Shame for Pity; or that kind of Pity which yields the adjective 'Pitiable' in place of that which yields 'Piteous' – the whole effect is altered. It is the relation between the two sets of impulses, Pity and Terror, which gives its specific character to Tragedy, and from that relation the peculiar poise of the Tragic experience springs.

The metaphor of a balance or poise will bear consideration. For Pity and Terror are opposites in a sense in which Pity and Dread are not. Dread or Horror are nearer than Terror to Pity, for they contain attraction as well as repulsion. As in colour, tones just not in harmonic relation are peculiarly unmanageable and jarring, so it is with these more easily describable responses. The extraordinarily stable experience of Tragedy, which is capable of admitting almost any other impulses so long as the relation of the main components is exactly right, changes at once if these are altered. Even if it keeps its coherence it becomes at once a far narrower, more limited, and exclusive thing, a much more partial, restricted and specialised response. Tragedy is perhaps the most general, all-accepting, all-ordering experience known. It can take anything into its organisation, modifying it so that it finds a place. It is invulnerable; there is nothing which does not present to the tragic attitude *when fully developed* a fitting aspect and only a fitting aspect. Its sole rivals in this respect are the attitudes of Falstaff and of the Voltaire of *Candide*. But pseudo-tragedy – the greater part of Greek Tragedy as well as almost all Elizabethan Tragedy outside Shakespeare's six masterpieces comes under this head – is one of the most fragile and precarious of attitudes. Parody easily overthrows it, the ironic addition paralyses it; even a mediocre joke may make it look lopsided and extravagant. . . .

Source: extract from *Principles of Literary Criticism* (London, 1924), pp. 245–8.

Virginia Woolf 'The Stable, the Permanent, the Original Human Being' (1925)

. . . It is the climate that is impossible. If we try to think of Sophocles here, we must annihilate the smoke and the damp and the thick wet mists. We must sharpen the lines of the hills. We must imagine a beauty of stone and earth rather than of woods and greenery. With warmth and sunshine and months of brilliant, fine weather, life of course is instantly changed; it is transacted out of doors, with the result, known to all who visit Italy, that small incidents are debated in the street, not in the sitting-room, and become dramatic; make people voluble; inspire in them that sneering, laughing, nimbleness of wit and tongue peculiar to the Southern races, which has nothing in common with the slow reserve, the low half-tones, the brooding introspective melancholy of people accustomed to live more than half the year indoors.

That is the quality that first strikes us in Greek literature, the lightning-quick, sneering, out-of-doors manner. It is apparent in the most august as well as in the most trivial places. Queens and Princesses in this very tragedy by Sophocles stand at the door bandying words like village women, with a tendency, as one might expect, to rejoice in language, to split phrases into slices, to be intent on verbal victory. The humour of the people was not good-natured like that of our postmen and cab-drivers. The taunts of men lounging at the street corners had something cruel in them as well as witty. There is a cruelty in Greek tragedy which is quite unlike our English brutality. Is not Pentheus, for example, that highly respectable man, made ridiculous in the *Bacchae* before he is destroyed? In fact, of course, these Queens and Princesses were out of doors, with the bees buzzing past them, shadows crossing them, and the wind taking their draperies. They were speaking to an enormous audience rayed round them on one of those brilliant southern days when the sun is so hot and yet the air so exciting. The poet, therefore, had to bethink him, not of some theme which could be read for hours by people in privacy, but of something emphatic, familiar, brief, that would carry, instantly and directly, to an audience of seventeen thousand people perhaps, with ears and eyes eager and attentive, with bodies whose muscles would grow stiff if they sat too long without diversion. Music and dancing he would need, and naturally would choose one of those legends, like our Tristram and Iseult, which are known to everyone in outline, so that a great fund of emotion is ready prepared, but can be stressed in a new place by each new poet.

Sophocles would take the old story of Electra, for instance, but would at once impose his stamp upon it. Of that, in spite of our weakness and distortion, what remains visible to us? That his genius was of the extreme kind in the first place; that he chose a design which, if it failed, would show its failure in gashes and ruin, not in the gentle blurring of some insignificant detail; which, if it succeeded, would cut each stroke to the bone, would stamp each fingerprint in marble. His Electra stands before us like a figure so tightly bound that she can only move an inch this way, an inch that. But each movement must tell to the utmost, or, bound as she is, denied the relief of all hints, repetitions, suggestions, she will be nothing but a dummy, tightly bound. Her words in crisis are, as a matter of fact, bare; mere cries of despair, joy, hate . . . . These cries give angle and outline to the play. . . .

But it is not so easy to decide what it is that gives these cries of Electra in her anguish their power to cut and wound and excite. It is partly that we know her, that we have picked up from little turns and twists of the dialogue hints of her character, of her appearance, which, characteristically, she neglected; of something suffering in her, outraged and stimulated to its utmost stretch of capacity, yet, as she herself knows ('my behaviour is unseemly and becomes me ill'), blunted and debased by the horror of her position, an unwed girl made to witness her mother's vileness and denounce it in loud, almost vulgar, clamour to the world at large. It is partly, too, that we know in the same way that Clytemnestra is no unmitigated villainess. 'δεινὸν τὸ τίκτειν ἐστίν', she says – 'there is a strange power in motherhood'. It is no murderess, violent and unredeemed, whom Orestes kills within the house, and Electra bids him utterly destroy – 'Strike again.' No; the men and women standing out in the sunlight before the audience on the hillside were alive enough, subtle enough, not mere figures, or plaster casts of human beings.

Yet it is not because we can analyse them into feelings that they impress us. In six pages of Proust we can find more complicated and varied emotions than in the whole of the *Electra*. But in the *Electra* or in the *Antigone* we are impressed by something different, by something perhaps more impressive – by heroism itself, by fidelity itself. In spite of the labour and the difficulty it is this that draws us back and back to the Greeks; the stable, the permanent, the original human being is to be found there. Violent emotions are needed to rouse him into action, but when thus stirred by death, by betrayal, by some other primitive calamity, Antigone and Ajax and Electra behave in the way in which we should behave thus struck down; the way in which everybody has always behaved; and thus we understand them more easily and more directly than we understand the characters in the *Canterbury Tales*.

These are the originals, Chaucer's the varieties of the human species.

It is true, of course, that these types of the original man or woman, these heroic Kings, these faithful daughters, these tragic Queens who stalk through the ages always planting their feet in the same places, twitching their robes with the same gestures, from habit not from impulse, are among the greatest bores and the most demoralising companions in the world. The plays of Addison, Voltaire, and a host of others are there to prove it. But encounter them in Greek. Even in Sophocles, whose reputation for restraint and mastery has filtered down to us from the scholars, they are decided, ruthless, direct. A fragment of their speech broken off would, we feel, colour oceans and oceans of the respectable drama. Here we meet them before their emotions have been worn into uniformity. Here we listen to the nightingale whose song echoes through English literature singing in her own Greek tongue. For the first time Orpheus with his lute makes men and beasts follow him. Their voices ring out clear and sharp; we see the hairy, tawny bodies at play in the sunlight among the olive trees, not posed gracefully on granite plinths in the pale corridors of the British Museum. And then suddenly, in the midst of all this sharpness and compression, Electra, as if she swept her veil over her face and forbade us to think of her any more, speaks of that very nightingale: 'that bird distraught with grief, the messenger of Zeus. Ah, queen of sorrow, Niobe, thee I deem divine – thee; who evermore weepest in thy rocky tomb.' . . .

. . . The intolerable restrictions of the drama could be loosened . . . if a means could be found by which what was general and poetic, comment, not action, could be freed without interrupting the movement of the whole. It is this that the choruses supply; the old men or women who take no active part in the drama, the undifferentiated voices who sing like birds in the pauses of the wind; who can comment, or sum up, or allow the poet to speak himself or supply, by contrast, another side to his conception. Always in imaginative literature, where characters speak for themselves and the author has no part, the need of that voice is making itself felt. For though Shakespeare (unless we consider that his fools and madmen supply the part) dispensed with the chorus, novelists are always devising some substitute – Thackeray speaking in his own person, Fielding coming out and addressing the world before his curtain rises. So to grasp the meaning of the play the chorus is of the utmost importance. One must be able to pass easily into those ecstasies, those wild and apparently irrelevant utterances, those sometimes obvious and commonplace statements, to decide their relevance or irrelevance, and give them their relation to the play as a whole.

We must 'be able to pass easily'; but that of course is exactly what we cannot do. For the most part the choruses, with all their obscurities, must be spelt out and their symmetry mauled. But we can guess that Sophocles used them not to express something outside the action of the play, but to sing the praises of some virtue, or the beauties of some place mentioned in it. He selects what he wishes to emphasise and sings of white Colonus and its nightingale, or of love unconquered in fight. Lovely, lofty, and serene, his choruses grow naturally out of his situations, and change, not the point of view, but the mood. In Euripides, however, the situations are not contained within themselves; they give off an atmosphere of doubt, of suggestion, of questioning; but if we look to the choruses to make this plain we are often baffled rather than instructed. At once in the *Bacchae* we are in the world of psychology and doubt; the world where the mind twists facts and changes them and makes the familiar aspects of life appear new and questionable. What is Bacchus, and who are the Gods, and what is man's duty to them, and what the rights of his subtle brain? To these questions the chorus makes no reply, or replies mockingly, or speaks darkly as if the straitness of the dramatic form had tempted Euripides to violate it, in order to relieve his mind of its weight. Time is so short and I have so much to say, that unless you will allow me to place together two apparently unrelated statements and trust to you to pull them together, you must be content with a mere skeleton of the play I might have given you. Such is the argument. Euripides therefore suffers less than Sophocles and less than Aeschylus from being read privately in a room, and not seen on a hillside in the sunshine. He can be acted in the mind; he can comment upon the questions of the moment; more than the others he will vary in popularity from age to age.

If then in Sophocles the play is concentrated in the figures themselves, and in Euripides is to be retrieved from flashes of poetry and questions far flung and unanswered, Aeschylus makes these little dramas (the *Agamemnon* has 1663 lines; *Lear* about 2600) tremendous by stretching every phrase to the utmost, by sending them floating forth in metaphors, by bidding them rise up and stalk eyeless and majestic through the scene. To understand him it is not so necessary to understand Greek as to understand poetry. It is necessary to take that dangerous leap through the air without the support of words which Shakespeare also asks of us. For words, when opposed to such a blast of meaning, must give out, must be blown astray, and only by collecting in companies convey the meaning which each one separately is too weak to express. Connecting them in a rapid flight of the mind we know instantly and instinctively what they mean, but could not decant that meaning afresh into any other words. . . .

SOURCE: extracts from 'On Not Knowing Greek', in *The Common Reader* (1925); reprinted in *Collected Essays* (London, 1966), I, pp. 2–7.

Aldous Huxley   Tragedy and the Whole Truth (1931)

There were six of them, the best and bravest of the hero's companions. Turning back from his post in the bows, Odysseus was in time to see them lifted, struggling, into the air, to hear their screams, the desperate repetition of his own name. The survivors could only look on, helplessly, while Scylla 'at the mouth of her cave devoured them, still screaming, still stretching out their hands to me in the frightful struggle'. And Odysseus adds that it was the most dreadful and lamentable sight he ever saw in all his 'explorings of the passes of the sea'. We can believe it; Homer's brief description (the too poetical simile is a later interpolation) convinces us.

Later, the danger passed, Odysseus and his men went ashore for the night, and, on the Sicilian beach, prepared their supper – prepared it, says Homer, 'expertly'. The Twelfth Book of the *Odyssey* concludes with these words: 'When they had satisfied their thirst and hunger, they thought of their dear companions and wept, and in the midst of their tears sleep came gently upon them.'

The truth, the whole truth and nothing but the truth – how rarely the older literatures ever told it! Bits of the truth, yes; every good book gives us bits of the truth, would not be a good book if it did not. But the whole truth, no. Of the great writers of the past incredibly few have given us that. Homer – the Homer of the *Odyssey* – is one of those few.

'Truth?' you question. 'For example, $2 + 2 = 4$? Or Queen Victoria came to the throne in 1837? Or light travels at the rate of 187,000 miles a second?' No, obviously, you won't find much of that sort of thing in literature. The 'truth' of which I was speaking just now is in fact no more than an acceptable verisimilitude. When the experiences recorded in a piece of literature correspond fairly closely with our own actual experiences, or with what I may call our potential experiences – experiences, that is to say, which we feel (as the result of a more or less explicit process of inference from known facts) that we might have had – we say, inaccurately no doubt: 'This piece of writing is true.' But this, of course, is not the whole story. The record of a case in a text-book of psychology is scientifically true, in so far as it is an accurate account of particular events. But it might also strike the reader as being 'true' with regard to himself – that is to say, acceptable, probable, having a correspondence with his own actual or potential experiences. But a text-book of psychology is not a work of art – or only secondarily and incidentally a work of art. Mere verisimilitude, mere correspondence of experience recorded by the writer with experience remembered or imaginable by the reader, is not enough to make a work of art seem 'true'. Good art possesses a kind of super-truth – is more probable, more acceptable, more convincing than fact itself. Naturally; for the artist is endowed with a sensibility and a power of communication, a capacity to 'put things across', which events and the majority of people to whom events happen, do not possess. Experience teaches only the teachable, who are by no means as numerous as Mrs Micawber's papa's favourite proverb would lead us to suppose. Artists are eminently teachable and also eminently teachers. They receive from events much more than most men receive, and they can transmit what they have received with a peculiar penetrative force, which drives their communication deep into the reader's mind. One of our most ordinary reactions to a good piece of literary art is expressed in the formula: 'This is what I have always felt and thought, but have never been able to put clearly into words, even for myself.'

We are now in a position to explain what we mean when we say that Homer is a writer who tells the Whole Truth. We mean that the experiences he records correspond fairly closely with our own actual or potential experiences – and correspond with our experiences not on a single limited sector, but all along the line of our physical and spiritual being. And we also mean that Homer records these experiences with a penetrative artistic force that makes them seem peculiarly acceptable and convincing.

So much, then, for truth in literature. Homer's, I repeat, is the Whole Truth. Consider how almost any other of the great poets would have concluded the story of Scylla's attack on the passing ship. Six men, remember, have been taken and devoured before the eyes of their friends. In any other poem but the *Odyssey*, what would the survivors have done? They would, of course, have wept, even as Homer made them weep. But would they previously have cooked their supper, and cooked it, what's more, in a masterly fashion? Would they previously have drunk and eaten to satiety? And after weeping, or actually while weeping, would they have dropped quietly off to sleep? No, they most certainly would not have done any of these things. They would simply have wept, lamenting their own misfortune and the horrible fate of their companions, and the canto would have ended tragically on their tears.

Homer, however, preferred to tell the Whole Truth. He knew that even the most cruelly bereaved must eat; that hunger is stronger than sorrow and that its satisfaction takes precedence even of tears. He knew that experts continue to act expertly and to find satisfaction in their accomplishment, even when friends have just been eaten, even when the accomplishment is only cooking the supper. He knew that, when the belly is full (and only when the belly is full), men can afford to grieve, and that sorrow after supper is almost a luxury. And finally he knew that, even as hunger takes precedence of grief, so fatigue, supervening, cuts short its career and drowns it in a sleep all the sweeter for bringing forgetfulness of bereavement. In a word, Homer refused to treat the theme tragically. He preferred to tell the Whole Truth.

Another author who preferred to tell the Whole Truth was Fielding. *Tom Jones* is one of the very few Odyssean books written in Europe between the time of Aeschylus and the present age; Odyssean, because never tragical; never – even when painful and disastrous, even when pathetic and beautiful things are happening. For they do happen; Fielding, like Homer, admits all the facts, shirks nothing. Indeed, it is precisely because these authors shirk nothing that their books are not tragical. For among the things they don't shirk are the irrelevancies which, in actual life, always temper the situations and characters that writers of tragedy insist on keeping chemically pure. Consider, for example, the case of Sophia Western, that most charming, most nearly perfect of young women. Fielding, it is obvious, adored her (she is said to have been created in the image of his first, much-loved wife). But, in spite of his adoration, he refused to turn her into one of those chemically pure and, as it were, focused beings who do and suffer in the world of tragedy. [Cites the incident of Sophia's embarrassing exposure in falling off a horse.] . . . There is nothing intrinsically improbable about this incident, which is stamped, indeed, with all the marks of literary truth. But however true, it is an incident which could never, never have happened to a heroine of tragedy. It would never have been allowed to happen. But Fielding refused to impose the tragedian's veto; he shirked nothing – neither the intrusion of irrelevant absurdities into the midst of romance or disaster, nor any of life's no less irrelevantly painful interruptions in the course of happiness. He did not want to be a tragedian. And, sure enough, that brief and pearly gleam of Sophia's charming posterior was sufficient to scare the Muse of Tragedy out of *Tom Jones* just as, more than five and twenty centuries before, the sight of stricken men first eating, then remembering to weep, then forgetting their tears in slumber had scared her out of the *Odyssey*.

In his *Principles of Literary Criticism* Mr I. A. Richards affirms [see excerpt, above–Ed.) that good tragedy is proof against irony and irrelevance, that it can absorb anything into itself and still remain tragedy. Indeed, he seems to make of this capacity to absorb the untragical and the anti-tragical a touchstone of tragic merit. Thus tried, practically all Greek, all French and most Elizabethan tragedies are found wanting. Only the best of Shakespeare can stand the test. So, at least, says Mr Richards. Is he right? I have often had my doubts. The

tragedies of Shakespeare are veined, it is true, with irony and an often
terrifying cynicism; but the cynicism is always heroic idealism turned
neatly inside out, the irony is a kind of photographic negative of heroic
romance. Turn Troilus's white into black and all his blacks into white
and you have Thersites. Reversed, Othello and Desdemona become
Iago. White Ophelia's negative is the irony of Hamlet, is the ingenuous
bawdry of her own mad songs; just as the cynicism of mad King Lear is
the black shadow-replica of Cordelia. Now, the shadow, the photographic negative of a thing, is in no sense irrelevant to it. Shakespeare's
ironies and cynicisms serve to deepen his tragic world, but not to widen
it. If they had widened it, as the Homeric irrelevancies widened out the
universe of the *Odyssey* – why, then, the world of Shakespearean tragedy
would automatically have ceased to exist. For example, a scene showing
the bereaved Macduff eating his supper, growing melancholy, over the
whisky, with thoughts of his murdered wife and children, and then, with
lashes still wet, dropping off to sleep, would be true enough to life; but it
would not be true to tragic art. The introduction of such a scene would
change the whole quality of the play; treated in this Odyssean style,
Macbeth would cease to be a tragedy. Or take the case of Desdemona.
Iago's bestially cynical remarks about her character are in no sense, as
we have seen, irrelevant to the tragedy. They present us with negative
images of her real nature and of the feelings she has for Othello. These
negative images are always *here*, are always recognisably the property of
the heroine-victim of a tragedy. Whereas, if, springing ashore at
Cyprus, she had tumbled, as the no less exquisite Sophia was to tumble,
and revealed the inadequacies of sixteenth-century underclothing, the
play would no longer be the *Othello* we know. Iago might breed a family
of little cynics and the existing dose of bitterness and savage negation be
doubled and trebled; *Othello* would still remain fundamentally *Othello*.
But a few Fieldingesque irrelevancies would destroy it – destroy it, that
is to say, as a tragedy; for there would be nothing to prevent it from
becoming a magnificent drama of some other kind. For the fact is that
tragedy and what I have called the Whole Truth are not compatible;
where one is, the other is not. There are certain things which even the
best, even Shakespearean tragedy, cannot absorb into itself.

   To make a tragedy the artist must isolate a single element out of the
totality of human experience and use that exclusively as his material.
Tragedy is something that is separated out from the Whole Truth,
distilled from it, so to speak, as an essence is distilled from the living
flower. Tragedy is chemically pure. Hence its power to act quickly and
intensely on our feelings. All chemically pure art has this power to act
upon us quickly and intensely. Thus, chemically pure pornography (on
the rare occasions when it happens to be written convincingly, by some
one who has the gift of 'putting things across') is a quick-acting

emotional drug of incomparably greater power than the Whole Truth about sensuality, or even (for many people) than the tangible and carnal reality itself. It is because of this chemical purity that tragedy so effectively performs its function of catharsis. It refines and corrects and gives a style to our emotional life, and does so swiftly, with power. Brought into contact with tragedy, the elements of our being fall, for the moment at any rate, into an ordered and beautiful pattern, as the iron filings arrange themselves under the influence of the magnet. Through all its individual variations, this pattern is always fundamentally of the same kind. From the reading or hearing of a tragedy we rise with the feeling that

> Our friends are exultations, agonies,
> And love, and man's unconquerable mind;

with the heroic conviction that we too would be unconquerable if subjected to the agonies, that in the midst of the agonies we too should continue to love, might even learn to exult. It is because it does these things to us that tragedy is felt to be so valuable. What are the values of Wholly-Truthful art? What does it do to us that seems worth doing? Let us try to discover.

Wholly-Truthful art overflows the limits of tragedy and shows us, if only by hints and implications, what happened before the tragic story began, what will happen after it is over, what is happening simultaneously elsewhere (and 'elsewhere' includes all those parts of the minds and bodies of the protagonists not immediately engaged in the tragic struggle). Tragedy is an arbitrarily isolated eddy on the surface of a vast river that flows on majestically, irresistibly, around, beneath, and to either side of it. Wholly-Truthful art contrives to imply the existence of the entire river as well as of the eddy. It is quite different from tragedy, even though it may contain, among other constituents, all the elements from which tragedy is made. (The 'same thing', placed in different contexts, loses its identity and becomes, for the perceiving mind, a succession of different things.) In Wholly-Truthful art the agonies may be just as real, love and the unconquerable mind just as admirable, just as important, as in tragedy. Thus, Scylla's victims suffer as painfully as the monster-devoured Hippolytus in *Phèdre*; the mental anguish of Tom Jones when he thinks he has lost his Sophia, and lost her by his own fault, is hardly less than that of Othello after Desdemona's murder. (The fact that Fielding's power of 'putting things across' is by no means equal to Shakespeare's is, of course, merely an accident.) But the agonies and indomitabilities are placed by the Wholly-Truthful writer in another, wider context, with the result that they cease to be the same as the intrinsically identical agonies and indomitabilities of tragedy. Consequently, Wholly-Truthful art produces in us an effect quite different from that produced by tragedy. Our mood when we have read a Wholly-Truthful book is never one of heroic exultation; it is one of resignation, of acceptance. (Acceptance can also be heroic.) Being chemically impure, Wholly-Truthful literature cannot move us as quickly and intensely as tragedy or any other kind of chemically pure art. But I believe that its effects are more lasting. The exultations that follow the reading or hearing of a tragedy are in the nature of temporary inebriations. Our being cannot long hold the pattern imposed by tragedy. Remove the magnet and the filings tend to fall back into confusion. But the pattern of acceptance and resignation imposed on us by Wholly-Truthful literature, though perhaps less unexpectedly beautiful in design, is (for that very reason perhaps) more stable. The catharsis of tragedy is violent and apocalyptic; but the milder catharsis of Wholly-Truthful literature is lasting.

In recent times literature has become more and more acutely conscious of the Whole Truth – of the great oceans of irrelevant things, events and thoughts stretching endlessly away in every direction from whatever island point (a character, a story) the author may choose to contemplate. To impose the kind of arbitrary limitations, which must be imposed by any one who wants to write a tragedy, has become more and more difficult: is now indeed, for those who are at all sensitive to contemporaneity, almost impossible. This does not mean, of course, that the modern writer must confine himself to a merely naturalistic manner. One can imply the existence of the Whole Truth, without laboriously cataloguing every object within sight. A book can be written in terms of pure phantasy and yet, by implication, tell the Whole Truth. Of all the important works of contemporary literature not one is a pure tragedy. There is no contemporary writer of significance who does not prefer to state or imply the Whole Truth. However different one from another in style, in ethical, philosophical and artistic intention, in the scale of values accepted, contemporary writers have this in common, that they are interested in the Whole Truth. Proust, D. H. Lawrence, André Gide, Kafka, Hemingway – here are five obviously significant and important contemporary writers; five authors as remarkably unlike one another as they could well be. They are at one only in this: that none of them has written a pure tragedy, that all are concerned with the Whole Truth.

I have sometimes wondered whether tragedy, as a form of art, may not be doomed. But the fact that we are still profoundly moved by the tragic masterpieces of the past – that we can be moved, against our better judgement, even by the bad tragedies of the contemporary stage and film – makes me think that the day of chemically pure art is not over. Tragedy happens to be passing through a period of eclipse, because all the significant writers of our age are too busy exploring the newly discovered, or rediscovered, world of the Whole Truth to be able to pay any attention to it. But there is no good reason to believe that this state of things will last for ever. Tragedy is too valuable to be allowed to die. There is no reason, after all, why the two kinds of literature – the Chemically Impure and the Chemically Pure, the literature of the Whole Truth and the literature of Partial Truth – should not exist simultaneously, each in its separate sphere. The human spirit has need of both.

SOURCE: *Music at Night* (1931; paperback 1950), pp. 9–18.

Northrop Frye   'Tragic Modes' (1957)

. . . Fictions . . . may be classified . . . by the hero's power of action, which may be greater than ours, less, or roughly the same. Thus:

1. If superior in *kind* both to other men and to the environment of other men, the hero is a divine being, and the story about him will be a *myth* in the common sense of a story about a god. Such stories have an important place in literature, but are as a rule found outside the normal literary categories.

2. If superior in *degree* to other men and to his environment, the hero is the typical hero of *romance*, whose actions are marvellous but who is himself identified as a human being. The hero of romance moves in a world in which the ordinary laws of nature are slightly suspended: prodigies of courage and endurance, unnatural to us, are natural to him, and enchanted weapons, talking animals, terrifying ogres and witches, and talismans of miraculous power violate no rule of probability once the postulates of romance have been established. Here we have moved from myth, properly so called, into legend, folk tale, *märchen*, and their literary affiliates and derivatives.

3. If superior in degree to other men but not to his natural environment, the hero is a leader. He has authority, passions, and powers of expression far greater than ours, but what he does is subject both to social criticism and to the order of nature. This is the hero of the *high mimetic* mode, of most epic and tragedy, and is primarily the kind of hero that Aristotle had in mind.

4. If superior neither to other men nor to his environment, the hero is one of us: we respond to a sense of his common humanity, and demand from the poet the same canons of probability that we find in our own

experience. This gives us the hero of the *low mimetic* mode, of most comedy and of realistic fiction. 'High' and 'low' have no connotations of comparative value, but are purely diagrammatic, as they are when they refer to Biblical critics or Anglicans. On this level the difficulty in retaining the word 'hero', which has a more limited meaning among the preceding modes, occasionally strikes an author. Thackeray thus feels obliged to call *Vanity Fair* a novel without a hero.

5. If inferior in power or intelligence to ourselves, so that we have the sense of looking down on a scene of bondage, frustration, or absurdity, the hero belongs to the *ironic* mode. This is still true when the reader feels that he is or might be in the same situation, as the situation is being judged by the norms of a greater freedom. . . .

Tragic stories, when they apply to divine beings, may be called Dionysiac. These are stories of dying gods, like Hercules with his poisoned shirt and his pyre, Orpheus torn to pieces by the Bacchantes, Balder murdered by the treachery of Loki, Christ dying on the cross and marking with the words 'Why hast thou forsaken me?' a sense of his exclusion, as a divine being, from the society of the Trinity.

The association of a god's death with autumn or sunset does not, in literature, necessarily mean that he is a god 'of' vegetation or the sun, but only that he is a god capable of dying, whatever his department. But as a god is superior to nature as well as to other men, the death of a god appropriately involves what Shakespeare, in *Venus and Adonis*, calls the 'solemn sympathy' of nature, the word solemn having here some of its etymological connections with ritual. Ruskin's pathetic fallacy can hardly be a fallacy when a god is the hero of the action, as when the poet of *The Dream of the Rood* tells us that all creation wept at the death of Christ. Of course there is never any real fallacy in making a purely imaginative alignment between man and nature, but the use of 'solemn sympathy' in a piece of more realistic fiction indicates that the author is trying to give his hero some of the overtones of the mythical mode. Ruskin's example of a pathetic fallacy is 'the cruel, crawling foam' from Kingsley's ballad about a girl drowned in the tide. But the fact that the foam is so described gives to Kingsley's Mary a faint coloring of the myth of Andromeda.

The same associations with sunset and the fall of the leaf linger in romance, where the hero is still half a god. In romance the suspension of natural law and the individualising of the hero's exploits reduce nature largely to the animal and vegetable world. Much of the hero's life is spent with animals, or at any rate the animals that are incurable romantics, such as horses, dogs, and falcons, and the typical setting of romance is the forest. The hero's death or isolation thus has the effect of a spirit passing out of nature, and evokes a mood best described as elegiac. The elegiac presents a heroism unspoiled by irony. The inevitability in the death of Beowulf, the treachery in the death of Roland, the malignancy that compasses the death of the martyred saint, are of much greater emotional importance than any ironic complications of hybris and hamartia that may be involved. Hence the elegiac is often accompanied by a diffused, resigned, melancholy sense of the passing of time, of the old order changing and yielding to a new one: one thinks of Beowulf looking, while he is dying, at the great stone monuments of the eras of history that vanished before him. In a very late 'sentimental' form the same mood is well caught in Tennyson's *Passing of Arthur*.

Tragedy in the central or high mimetic sense, the fiction of the fall of a leader (he has to fall because that is the only way in which a leader can be isolated from his society), mingles the heroic with the ironic. In elegiac romance the hero's mortality is primarily a natural fact, the sign of his humanity; in high mimetic tragedy it is also a social and moral fact. The tragic hero has to be of a properly heroic size, but his fall is involved both with a sense of his relation to society and with a sense of the supremacy of natural law, both of which are ironic in reference. Tragedy belongs chiefly to the two indigenous developments of tragic drama in fifth-century Athens and seventeenth-century Europe from Shakespeare to Racine. Both belong to a period of social history in which an aristocracy is fast losing its effective power but still retains a good deal of ideological prestige.

The central position of high mimetic tragedy in the five tragic modes, balanced midway between godlike heroism and all-too-human irony, is expressed in the traditional conception of catharsis. The words pity and fear may be taken as referring to the two general directions in which emotion moves, whether towards an object or away from it. Naïve romance, being closer to the wish-fulfilment dream, tends to absorb emotion and communicate it internally to the reader. Romance, therefore, is characterised by the acceptance of pity and fear, which in ordinary life relate to pain, as forms of pleasure. It turns fear at a distance, or terror, into the adventurous; fear at contact, or horror, into the marvellous, and fear without an object, or dread (*Angst*) into a pensive melancholy. It turns pity at a distance, or concern, into the theme of chivalrous rescue; pity at contact, or tenderness, into a languid and relaxed charm, and pity without an object (which has no name but is a kind of animism, or treating everything in nature as though it had human feelings) into creative fantasy. In sophisticated romance the characteristics peculiar to the form are less obvious, especially in tragic romance, where the theme of inevitable death works against the marvellous, and often forces it into the background. In *Romeo and Juliet*, for instance, the marvellous survives only in Mercutio's speech on Queen Mab. But this play is marked as closer to romance than the later tragedies by the softening influences that work in the opposite direction from catharsis, draining off the irony, so to speak, from the main characters.

In high mimetic tragedy pity and fear become, respectively, favorable and adverse moral judgement, which are relevant to tragedy but not central to it. We pity Desdemona and fear Iago, but the central tragic figure is Othello, and our feelings about him are mixed. The particular thing called tragedy that happens to the tragic hero does not depend on his moral status. If it is causally related to something he has done, as it generally is, the tragedy is in the inevitability of the consequences of the act, not in its moral significance as an act. Hence the paradox that in tragedy pity and fear are raised and cast out. Aristotle's hamartia or 'flaw', therefore, is not necessarily wrongdoing, much less moral weakness: it may be simply a matter of being a strong character in an exposed position, like Cordelia. The exposed position is usually the place of leadership, in which a character is exceptional and isolated at the same time, giving us that curious blend of the inevitable and the incongruous which is peculiar to tragedy. The principle of the hamartia of leadership can be more clearly seen in naïve high mimetic tragedy, as we get it in *The Mirror for Magistrates* and similar collections of tales based on the theme of the wheel of fortune.

In low mimetic tragedy, pity and fear are neither purged nor absorbed into pleasures, but are communicated externally, as sensations. In fact the word 'sensational' could have a more useful meaning in criticism if it were not merely an adverse value-judgement. The best word for low mimetic or domestic tragedy is, perhaps, pathos, and pathos has a close relation to the sensational reflex of tears. Pathos presents its hero as isolated by a weakness which appeals to our sympathy because it is on our own level of experience. I speak of a hero, but the central figure of pathos is often a woman or a child (or both, as in the death-scenes of Little Eva and Little Nell), and we have a whole procession of pathetic female sacrifices in English low mimetic fiction from Clarissa Harlowe to Hardy's Tess and James's Daisy Miller. We notice that while tragedy may massacre a whole cast, pathos is usually concentrated on a single character, partly because low mimetic society is more strongly individualised.

Again, in contrast to high mimetic tragedy, pathos is increased by the inarticulateness of the victim. The death of an animal is usually pathetic, and so is the catastrophe of defective intelligence that is frequent in modern American literature. Wordsworth, who as a low mimetic artist was one of our great masters of pathos, makes his sailor's mother speak in a flat, dumpy, absurdly inadequate style about her efforts to salvage her son's clothes and 'other property' – or did before bad criticism made him spoil his poem. Pathos is a queer ghoulish emotion, and some failure of expression, real or simulated, seems to be peculiar to it. It will always leave a fluently plangent funeral elegy to go and batten on something like Swift's memoir of Stella. Highly articulate pathos is apt to become a factitious appeal to self-pity, or tear-jerking. The exploiting of fear in the low mimetic is also sensational, and is a kind of pathos in reverse. The terrible figure in this tradition, exemplified by Heathcliff, Simon Legree, and the villains of Dickens, is normally a ruthless figure strongly contrasted with some kind of delicate virtue, generally a helpless victim in his power.

The root idea of pathos is the exclusion of an individual on our own level from a social group to which he is trying to belong. Hence the central tradition of sophisticated pathos is the study of the isolated mind, the story of how someone recognisably like ourselves is broken by a conflict between the inner and outer world, between imaginative reality and the sort of reality which is established by a social consensus. Such tragedy may be concerned, as it often is in Balzac, with a mania or obsession about rising in the world, this being the central low mimetic counterpart of the fiction of the fall of the leader. Or it may deal with the conflict of inner and outer life, as in *Madame Bovary* and *Lord Jim*, or with the impact of inflexible morality on experience, as in Melville's *Pierre* and Ibsen's *Brand*. The type of character involved here we may call by the Greek word *alazon*, which means impostor, someone who pretends or tries to be something more than he is. The most popular types of *alazon* are the *miles gloriosus* and the learned crank or obsessed philosopher.

We are most familiar with such characters in comedy, where they are looked at from the outside, so that we see only the social mask. But the *alazon* may be one aspect of the tragic hero as well: the touch of *miles gloriosus* in Tamburlaine, even in Othello, is unmistakable, as is the touch of the obsessed philosopher in Faustus and Hamlet. It is very difficult to study a case of obsession, or even hypocrisy, from the inside, in a dramatic medium: even Tartuffe, as far as his dramatic function is concerned, is a study of parasitism rather than hypocrisy. The analysis of obsession belongs more naturally to prose fiction or to a semi-dramatic medium like the Browning monologue. For all the differences in technique and attitude, Conrad's Lord Jim is a lineal descendant of the *miles gloriosus*, of the same family as Shaw's Sergius or Synge's playboy, who are parallel types in a dramatic and comic setting. It is, of course, quite possible to take the *alazon* at his own valuation: this is done for instance by the creators of the inscrutable gloomy heroes in Gothic thrillers, with their wild or piercing eyes and their dark hints of interesting sins. The result as a rule is not tragedy so much as the kind of melodrama which may be defined as comedy without humor. When it rises out of this, we have a study of obsession presented in terms of fear instead of pity: that is, the obsession takes the form of an unconditioned will that drives its victim beyond the normal limits of humanity. One of the clearest examples is Heathcliff, who plunges through death itself into vampirism; but there are many others, ranging from Conrad's Kurtz to the mad scientists of popular fiction.

The conception of irony meets us in Aristotle's *Ethics*, where the *eiron* is the man who deprecates himself, as opposed to the *alazon*. Such a man makes himself invulnerable, and, though Aristotle disapproves of him, there is no question that he is a predestined artist, just as the *alazon* is one of his predestined victims. The term irony, then, indicates a technique of appearing to be less than one is, which in literature becomes most commonly a technique of saying as little and meaning as much as possible, or, in a more general way, a pattern of words that turns away from direct statement or its own obvious meaning. (I am not using the word ironic itself in any unfamiliar sense, though I am exploring some of its implications.)

The ironic fiction-writer, then, deprecates himself and, like Socrates, pretends to know nothing, even that he is ironic. Complete objectivity and suppression of all explicit moral judgements are essential to his method. Thus pity and fear are not raised in ironic art: they are reflected to the reader from the art. When we try to isolate the ironic as such, we find that it seems to be simply the attitude of the poet as such, a dispassionate construction of a literary form, with all assertive elements, implied or expressed, eliminated. Irony, as a mode, is born from the low mimetic; it takes life exactly as it finds it. But the ironist fables without moralising, and has no object but his subject. Irony is naturally a sophisticated mode, and the chief difference between sophisticated and naïve irony is that the naïve ironist calls attention to the fact that he is being ironic, whereas sophisticated irony merely states, and lets the reader add the ironic tone himself. Coleridge, noting an ironic comment in Defoe, points out how Defoe's subtlety could be made crude and obvious simply by over-punctuating the same words with italics, dashes, exclamation points, and other signs of being oneself aware of irony.

Tragic irony, then, becomes simply the study of tragic isolation as such, and it thereby drops out the element of the special case, which in some degree is in all the other modes. Its hero does not necessarily have any tragic hamartia or pathetic obsession: he is only somebody who gets isolated from his society. Thus the central principle of tragic irony is that whatever exceptional happens to the hero should be causally out of line with his character. Tragedy is intelligible, not in the sense of having any pat moral to go with it, but in the sense that Aristotle had in mind when he spoke of discovery or recognition as essential to the tragic plot. Tragedy is intelligible because its catastrophe is plausibly related to its situation. Irony isolates from the tragic situation the sense of arbitrariness, of the victim's having been unlucky, selected at random or by lot, and no more deserving of what happens to him than anyone else would be. If there is a reason for choosing him for catastrophe, it is an inadequate reason, and raises more objections than it answers.

Thus the figure of a typical or random victim begins to crystallise in domestic tragedy as it deepens in ironic tone. We may call this typical victim the *pharmakos* or scapegoat. We meet a *pharmakos* figure in Hawthorne's Hester Prynne, in Melville's Billy Budd, in Hardy's Tess, in the Septimus of *Mrs Dalloway*, in stories of persecuted Jews and Negroes, in stories of artists whose genius makes them Ishmaels of a bourgeois society. The *pharmakos* is neither innocent nor guilty. He is innocent in the sense that what happens to him is far greater than anything he has done provokes, like the mountaineer whose shout brings down an avalanche. He is guilty in the sense that he is a member of a guilty society, or living in a world where such injustices are an inescapable part of existence. The two facts do not come together; they remain ironically apart. The *pharmakos*, in short, is in the situation of Job. Job can defend himself against the charge of having done something that makes his catastrophe morally intelligible; but the success of his defense makes it morally unintelligible.

Thus the incongruous and the inevitable, which are combined in tragedy, separate into opposite poles of irony. At one pole is the inevitable irony of human life. What happens to, say, the hero of Kafka's *Trial* is not the result of what he has done, but the end of what he is, which is an 'all too human' being. The archetype of the inevitably ironic is Adam, human nature under sentence of death. At the other pole is the incongruous irony of human life, in which all attempts to transfer guilt to a victim give that victim something of the dignity of innocence. The archetype of the incongruously ironic is Christ, the perfectly innocent victim excluded from human society. Halfway between is the central figure of tragedy, who is human and yet of a heroic size which often has in it the suggestion of divinity. His archetype is Prometheus, the immortal titan rejected by the gods for befriending men. The Book of Job is not a tragedy of the Promethean type, but a tragic irony in which the dialectic of the divine and the human nature works itself out. By justifying himself as a victim of God, Job tries to make himself into a tragic Promethean figure, but he does not succeed.

These references may help to explain something that might otherwise be a puzzling fact about modern literature. Irony descends from the low mimetic: it begins in realism and dispassionate observation. But as it does so, it moves steadily towards myth, and dim outlines of sacrificial rituals and dying gods begin to reappear in it. Our five modes evidently go around in a circle. This reappearance of myth in the ironic is particularly clear in Kafka and in Joyce. In Kafka, whose work, from one point of view, may be said to form a series of commentaries on the Book of Job, the common contemporary types of tragic irony (the Jew, the artist, Everyman, and a kind of sombre Chaplin clown) are all found, and most of these elements are combined, in a comic form, in Joyce's Shem. However, ironic myth is frequent enough elsewhere, and many features of ironic literature are unintelligible without it. Henry James learned his trade mainly from the realists and naturalists of the nineteenth century, but if we were to judge, for example, the story called *The Altar of the Dead* purely by low mimetic standards, we should have to call it a tissue of improbable coincidence, inadequate motivation, and inconclusive resolution. When we look at it as ironic myth, a story of how the god of one person is the *pharmakos* of another, its structure becomes simple and logical. . . .

Source: extract from *Anatomy of Criticism* (Princeton, N.J., 1957), pp. 33–4, 35–43.

Arthur Miller   'The Tragedy of the Common Man' (1958)

. . . The play [*Death of a Salesman*] was always heroic to me, and in later years the academy's charge that Willy lacked the 'stature' for the tragic hero seemed incredible to me. I had not understood that these matters are measured by Graeco-Elizabethan paragraphs, which hold no mention of insurance payments, front porches, refrigerator fan belts, steering knuckles, Chevrolets, and visions seen not through the portals of Delphi but in the blue flame of the hot-water heater. How could 'Tragedy' make people weep, of all things?

I set out not to 'write a tragedy' in this play, but to show the truth as I saw it. However, some of the attacks upon it as a pseudo-tragedy contain ideas so misleading, and in some cases so laughable, that it might be in place here to deal with a few of them.

Aristotle having spoken of a fall from the heights, it goes without saying that someone of the common mold cannot be a fit tragic hero. It is now many centuries since Aristotle lived. There is no more reason for falling down in a faint before his *Poetics* than before Euclid's geometry, which has been amended numerous times by men with new insights;

nor, for that matter, would I choose to have my illnesses diagnosed by Hippocrates rather than the most ordinary graduate of an American medical school, despite the Greek's genius. Things do change, and even a genius is limited by his time and the nature of his society.

I would deny, on grounds of simple logic, this one of Aristotle's contentions if only because he lived in a slave society. When a vast number of people are divested of alternatives, as slaves are, it is rather inevitable that one will not be able to imagine drama, let alone tragedy, as being possible for any but the higher ranks of society. There is a legitimate question of stature here, but none of rank, which is so often confused with it. So long as the hero may be said to have had alternatives of a magnitude to have materially changed the course of his life, it seems to me that in this respect at least, he cannot be debarred from the heroic role.

The question of rank is significant to me only as it reflects the question of the social application of the hero's career. There is no doubt that if a character is shown on the stage who goes through the most ordinary actions, and is suddenly revealed to be the President of the United States, his actions immediately assume a much greater magnitude, and pose the possibilities of much greater meaning, than if he is the corner grocer. But at the same time, his stature as a hero is not so utterly dependent upon his rank that the corner grocer cannot outdistance him as a tragic figure – providing, of course, that the grocer's career engages the issues of, for instance, the survival of the race, the relationships of man to God – the questions, in short, whose answers define humanity and the right way to live so that the world is a home, instead of a battleground or a fog in which disembodied spirits pass each other in an endless twilight.

In this respect *Death of a Salesman* is a slippery play to categorise because nobody in it stops to make a speech objectively stating the great issues which I believe it embodies. If it were a worse play, less closely articulating its meanings with its actions, I think it would have more quickly satisfied a certain kind of criticism. But it was meant to be less a play than a fact; it refused admission to its author's opinions and opened itself to a revelation of process and the operations of an ethic, of social laws of action no less powerful in their effects upon individuals than any tribal law administered by gods with names. I need not claim that this play is a genuine solid gold tragedy for my opinions on tragedy to be held valid. My purpose here is simply to point out a historical fact which must be taken into account in any consideration of tragedy, and it is the sharp alteration in the meaning of rank in society between the present time and the distant past. More important to me is the fact that this particular kind of argument obscures much more relevant considerations.

One of these is the question of intensity. It matters not at all whether a modern play concerns itself with a grocer or a president if the intensity of the hero's commitment to his course is less than the maximum possible. It matters not at all whether the hero falls from a great height or a small one, whether he is highly conscious or only dimly aware of what is happening, whether his pride brings the fall or an unseen pattern written behind clouds; if the intensity, the human passion to surpass his given bounds, the fanatic insistence upon his self-conceived role – if these are not present there can only be an outline of tragedy but no living thing. I believe, for myself, that the lasting appeal of tragedy is due to our need to face the fact of death in order to strengthen ourselves for life, and that over and above this function of the tragic viewpoint there are and will be a great number of formal variations which no single definition will ever embrace.

Another issue worth considering is the so-called tragic victory, a question closely related to the consciousness of the hero. One makes nonsense of this if a 'victory' means that the hero makes us feel some certain joy when, for instance, he sacrifices himself for a 'cause', and unhappy and morose because he dies without one. To begin at the bottom, a man's death is and ought to be an essentially terrifying thing and ought to make nobody happy. But in a great variety of ways even death, the ultimate negative, can be, and appear to be, an assertion of bravery, and can serve to separate the death of man from the death of animals; and I think it is this distinction which underlies any conception of a victory in death. For a society of faith, the nature of the death can prove the existence of the spirit, and posit its immortality. For a secular society it is perhaps more difficult for such a victory to document itself and to make itself felt, but, conversely, the need to offer greater proofs of the humanity of man can make that victory more real. It goes without saying that in a society where there is basic disagreement as to the right way to live, there can hardly be agreement as to the right way to die, and both life and death must be heavily weighted with meaningless futility.

It was not out of any deference to a tragic definition that Willy Loman is filled with a joy, however broken-hearted, as he approaches his end, but simply that my sense of his character dicated his joy, and even what I felt was an exultation. In terms of his character, he has achieved a very powerful piece of knowledge, which is that he is loved by his son and has been embraced by him and forgiven. In this he is given his existence, so to speak – his fatherhood, for which he has always striven and which until now he could not achieve. That he is unable to take this victory thoroughly to his heart, that it closes the circle for him and propels him to his death, is the wage of his sin, which was to have committed himself so completely to the counterfeits of dignity and the false coinage embodied in his idea of success that he can prove his existence only by bestowing 'power' on his posterity, a power deriving from the sale of his last asset, himself, for the price of his insurance policy.

I must confess here to a miscalculation, however. I did not realise while writing the play that so many people in the world do not see as clearly, or would not admit, as I thought they must, how futile most lives are; so there could be no hope of consoling the audience for the death of this man. I did not realise either how few would be impressed by the fact that this man is actually a very brave spirit who cannot settle for half but must pursue his dream of himself to the end. Finally, I thought it must be clear, even obvious, that this was no dumb brute heading mindlessly to his catastrophe.

I have no need to be Willy's advocate before the jury which decides who is and who is not a tragic hero. I am merely noting that the lingering ponderousness of so many ancient definitions has blinded students and critics to the facts before them, and not only in regard to this play. Had Willy been unaware of his separation from values that endure he would have died contentedly while polishing his car, probably on a Sunday afternoon with the ball game coming over the radio. But he was agonised by his awareness of being in a false position, so constantly haunted by the hollowness of all he had placed his faith in, so aware, in short, that he must somehow be filled in his spirit or fly apart, that he staked his very life on the ultimate assertion. That he had not the intellectual fluency to verbalise his situation is not the same thing as saying that he lacked awareness, even an overly intensified consciousness that the life he had made was without form and inner meaning.

To be sure, had he been able to know that he was as much the victim of his beliefs as their defeated exemplar, had he known how much of guilt he ought to bear and how much to shed from his soul, he would be more conscious. But it seems to me that there is of necessity a severe limitation of self-awareness in any character, even the most knowing, which serves to define him as a character, and more, that this very limit serves to complete the tragedy and, indeed, to make it at all possible. Complete consciousness is possible only in a play about forces, like *Prometheus*, but not in a play about people. I think that the point is whether there is a sufficient awareness in the hero's career to make the audience supply the rest. Had Oedipus, for instance, been more conscious and more aware of the forces at work upon him he must surely have said that he was not really to blame for having cohabited with his mother since neither he nor anyone else knew she was his mother. He must surely decide to divorce her, provide for their children, firmly resolve to investigate the family background of his next wife, and thus deprive us of a very fine play and the name for a famous neurosis. But he is conscious only up to a point, the point at which guilt begins. Now he is inconsolable and must tear out his eyes. What is tragic about this? Why is it not even ridiculous? How can we respect a man who goes to such extremities over something he could in no way help or prevent? The answer, I think, is not that we respect the man, but that we respect the Law he has so completely broken, wittingly or not, for it is that Law which, we believe, defines us as men. The confusion of some critics viewing *Death of a Salesman* in this regard is that they do not see that Willy Loman has broken a law without whose protection life is insupportable if not incomprehensible to him and to many others; it is the law which says that a failure in society and in business has no right to live. Unlike the law against incest, the law of success is not administered by statute or church, but it is very nearly as powerful in its grip upon men. The confusion increases because, while it is a law, it is by no means a wholly agreeable one even as it is slavishly obeyed, for to fail is no longer to belong to society, in his estimate. Therefore, the path is opened for those who wish to call Willy merely a foolish man even as they themselves are living in obedience to the same law that killed him. Equally, the fact that Willy's law – the belief, in other words, which administers guilt to him – is not a civilising statute whose destruction menaces us all; it is, rather, a deeply believed and deeply suspect 'good' which, when questioned as to its value, as it is in this play, serves more to raise our anxieties than to reassure us of the existence of an unseen but humane metaphysical system in the world. My attempt in the play was to counter this anxiety with an opposing system which, so to speak, is in a race for Willy's faith, and it is the system of love which is the opposite of the law of success. It is embodied in Biff Loman, but by the time Willy can perceive his love it can serve as an ironic comment upon the life he sacrificed for power and for success and its tokens. . . .

SOURCE: extract from Introduction to *Collected Plays* (New York and London, 1958), pp. 31–6.

George Steiner 'The Romantic Evasion of Tragedy' (1961)

. . . A century apart, Hazlitt and Hardy both discern in the spirit of the modern age a prevailing nervousness, a falling away of the imaginative. Something is lacking of the superb confidence needed of a man to create a major stage character, to endow some presence within himself with the carnal mystery of gesture and dramatic speech. What remains obscure is the source of failure. Do art forms have their prescribed life cycle? Perhaps there is in poetic energy no principle of conservation. Manifestly, the Greek and the Elizabethan achievement seem to lie on the back of all later drama with a wearying weight of precedent. Or is the heart of the crisis within society? Did the dramatic poets of the nineteenth century fail to produce good plays because there were available to them neither the necessary theatres nor the requisite audience?

In the early decades of the romantic period, such queries and doubts were much in the air. But the writers themselves were in no way ready to concede the game. On the contrary, the more they dwelt on the dreary state of contemporary drama, the more certain did they become that it would be one of the tasks and glories of romanticism to restore tragedy to its former honours. The thought of such restoration preoccupied the best poets and novelists of the century. In many it grew to obsession. Consider even a partial list of the tragic plays written or planned by the English romantics.

William Blake wrote a part of an *Edward III*; Wordsworth wrote *The Borderers*; Sir Walter Scott composed four dramas; Coleridge collaborated with Southey in *The Fall of Robespierre*, then went on to write *Remorse* and *Zapolya*; Southey himself put together *Wat Tyler*. In addition to his dramatic sketches, Walter Savage Landor wrote four tragedies. Leigh Hunt published *Scenes from an Unfinished Drama* in 1820, and his *Legend of Florence* was performed at Covent Garden in 1840. Byron is the author of eight dramas. Shelley wrote *The Cenci*, *Prometheus*, and *Hellas*, and translated scenes from Goethe and Calderón. Keats placed great hopes on *Otho the Great* and began *King Stephen*. Thomas Lovell Beddoes wrote a number of strange Gothic tragedies, at least one of which is carried near mastery by its unflagging wildness and stress.

I do not set down this list in antiquarian pedantry (though such registers have a certain dusty fascination). I enumerate only to suggest the magnitude of implied aspiration and effort. Here we find some of the masters of the language producing tragedies which are, with few signal exceptions, dismally bad. . . .

Yet as the sum of failure grew, so did the ambition. We can hardly refer to a poet or novelist of the nineteenth century without finding somewhere in his actual writings or intent the mirage of drama. Browning, Dickens, Tennyson, Swinburne, George Meredith; Stendhal, Balzac, Flaubert, Zola; Dostoevsky; Henry James. In each there burnt on occasion the resolve to master the stage, the determination to add something to the literary form which had in antiquity, in the renaissance, and in the baroque marshalled the best of poetic genius. But consider the plays these writers actually turned out; the incongruity is baffling. There appears to be no relationship between the stature of the artist and the bleak conventionality or total mechanical failure of the work.

There is here some need of explanation. And the problem is not solely one of theatrical history. For only if we come nearer to the causes of the downfall of romantic drama, can we get into focus the question of what it was that had receded from western sensibility after Racine. And it was the failure of the romantics to restore to life the ideal of high tragedy which prepared the ground for the two major events in the history of the modern theatre: the separation between literature and the playhouse, and the radical change in the notion of the tragic and the comic brought on by Ibsen, Strindberg, Chekhov, and Pirandello. We cannot judge the extent of their victory without knowing something of the previous débâcle.

Romanticism and revolution are essentially related. In romanticism there is a liberation of thought from the deductive sobriety of Cartesian and Newtonian rationalism. There is a liberation of the imagination from the ferule of logic. There is, both intuitively and practically, a liberation of the individual from predetermined hierarchies of social station and caste. . . . The first romantic decades were 'a dawn', said Wordsworth, in which it was bliss to be alive. For at the heart of their liberating energy lay a conviction inherited from Rousseau. The misery and injustice of man's fate were not caused by a primal fall from grace. They were not the consequence of some tragic, immutable flaw in human nature. They arose from the absurdities and archaic inequalities built into the social fabric by generations of tyrants and exploiters. The chains of man, proclaimed Rousseau, were man-forged. They could be broken by human hammers. It was a doctrine of immense implications, signifying that the shape of man's future lay within his own moulding. If Rousseau was right (and most political systems are, to this day, heirs to his assertion), the quality of being could be radically altered and improved by changes in education and in the social and material circumstances of existence. Man stood no longer under the shadow of original corruption; he carried within him no germ of preordained failure. On the contrary, he could be led toward tremendous progress. He was, in the vocabulary of romanticism, perfectible. Hence the glow of optimism in early romantic art, the feeling of ancient gates broken open and flung wide to a luminous future. . . .

After 1820, the glow faded from the air. Reactionary forces reimposed their rule throughout Europe, and the middle class, which had been the source of radical energy, turned prosperous and conservative. The romantics experienced profound dejection (the word is decisive in Coleridge). They suffered a sense of betrayal, and Musset gave a classic account of their disillusion in the *Confession d'un enfant du siècle*. Romanticism developed qualities of autumn and afternoon: the stoicism of the late Wordsworth, the wild sadness of Byron, the autumnal, apocalyptic *tristesse* of the later Victor Hugo. There ripened in the romantic temper those elements of melancholy and nervous frustration which characterise post-romantic art. Symbolism and the Decadent movements of the later nineteenth century are a nightfall to the long decline of day.

But these darkenings were hardly perceptible in the period in which the romantics were trying to create a new dramatic tradition. And even when the light had grown lurid and uncertain, the original premise of romanticism retained much of its force. The Rousseauist belief in the perfectibility of man survived the partial defeats of liberalism in 1830 and 1848. Autocracy and *bourgeois* greed were fighting momentarily victorious rear-guard actions. But over the longer view, the human condition was one of destined progress. The city of justice lay in distant sight. Call it democracy, as did the romantic revolutionaries of the west, or the classless society as did Marx. In either case, it was the dream of progress first dreamt by Rousseau.

The Rousseauist and romantic vision had specific psychological correlatives. It implied a radical critique of the notion of guilt. In the Rousseauist mythology of conduct, a man could commit a crime either because his education had not taught him how to distinguish good and evil, or because he had been corrupted by society. Responsibility lay with his schooling or environment, for evil cannot be native to the soul. And because the individual is not wholly responsible, he cannot be wholly damned. Rousseauism closes the doors of hell. In the hour of truth, the criminal will be possessed with remorse. The crime will be undone or the error made good. Crime leads not to punishment, but to redemption. That is the *leit-motiv* in the romantic treatment of evil, from *The Ancient Mariner* to Goethe's *Faust*, from *Les Misérables* to the apotheosis of redemption in *Götterdämmerung*.

This redemptive mythology may have social and psychological merit, freeing the spirit from the black forebodings of Calvinism. But one thing is clear: such a view of the human condition is radically optimistic. It cannot engender any natural form of tragic drama. The romantic vision of life is non-tragic. In authentic tragedy, the gates of hell stand open and damnation is real. The tragic personage cannot evade responsibility. To argue that Oedipus should have been excused on grounds of ignorance, or that Phèdre was merely prey to hereditary chaos of the blood, is to diminish to absurdity the weight and meaning of the tragic action. The redeeming insight comes too late to mend the ruins or is purchased at the price of irremediable suffering. Samson goes blind to his death, and Faustus is dragged howling to perdition. Where a tragic conception of life is in force, moreover, there can be no recourse to secular or material remedies. The destiny of Lear cannot be resolved by the establishment of adequate homes for the aged. The dilemma which dooms Antigone lies deeper than any conceivable reform of the conventions that govern burial. In tragedy, the twist of the net which brings down the hero may be an accident or hazard of circumstance, but the mesh is woven into the heart of life. Tragedy would have us know that there is in the very fact of human existence a provocation or paradox; it tells us that the purposes of men sometimes run against the grain of inexplicable and destructive forces that lie 'outside' yet very close. To ask of the gods why Oedipus should have been chosen for his agony or why Macbeth should have met the Witches on his path, is to ask for reason and justification from the voiceless night. There is no answer. Why should there be? If there was, we would be dealing with just or unjust suffering, as do parables and cautionary tales, not with tragedy. And beyond the tragic, there lies no 'happy ending' in some other dimension of place or time. The wounds are not healed and the broken spirit is not mended. In the norm of tragedy, there can be no compensation. The mind, says I. A. Richards,

does not shy away from anything, it does not protect itself with any illusion, it stands uncomforted, alone and self reliant. . . . The least touch of any theology which has a compensating Heaven to offer the tragic hero is fatal. [See excerpt, above–Ed.]

But it is precisely a 'compensating Heaven' that romanticism promises to the guilt and sufferings of man. It may be a literal Heaven as in *Faust*. More often, it is a state of bliss and redemption on earth. By virtue of remorse, the tragic sufferer is restored to a condition of grace. Or the ignorance and social injustice which have brought on the tragedy are removed by reform and the awakening of conscience. In the poetics of romanticism, the Scrooges turn golden.

The theme of remorse resounds through the entire tradition of romantic drama, from Coleridge to Wagner. The fable varies, but the characteristic *clichés* are constant. The tragic hero or hero-villain has committed a terrible, perhaps nameless, crime. He is tormented by his conscience and roams the earth, hiding an inward fire which reveals itself by his feverish aspect and glittering eye. We know him as the Ancient Mariner, Cain, the Flying Dutchman, Manfred, or the Wandering Jew. Sometimes he is haunted by a pursuing double, an avenging image of himself or of his innocent victim. At the hour of mortal crisis or approaching death, the soul of the romantic hero is 'wrenched with a woeful agony'. Suddenly, there is a flowering of remorse: brought to the repentant Tannhäuser, the Papal staff puts forth leaves. Salvation descends on the bruised spirit, and the hero steps toward grace out of the shadow of damnation:

> The self-same moment I could pray;
> And from my neck so free
> The Albatross fell off, and sank
> Like lead into the sea.

The murderous villain who is responsible for the evils committed in Wordsworth's tragedy, *The Borderers*, is told at the close of the play:

> Thy office, thy ambition, be henceforth
> To feed remorse, to welcome every sting
> Of penitential anguish, yea with tears.

. . . . In Coleridge's *Remorse*, the problem of the quality of repentance is made the centre of the drama:

> Remorse is at the heart, in which it grows:
> If that be gentle, it drops balmy dews
> Of true repentance; but if proud and gloomy,
> It is a poison-tree, that pierced to the inmost
> Weeps only tears of poison!

Coleridge was far too perceptive not to realise that there is in the entire notion of redemptive remorse something fraudulent. The villain of the play, Ordonio, gets to the heart of the matter:

> ALVAR: Yet, yet thou may'st be sav'd –
> ORDONIO: Sav'd? sav'd?
> ALVAR: One pang!
>   Could I call up one pang of true remorse!
> ORDONIO: . . . . remorse! remorse!
>   Where gott'st thou that fool's word? Curse on remorse!

Can it give up the dead or recompact
A mangled body? mangled—dashed to atoms!
Not all the blessings of a host of angels
Can blow away a desolate widow's curse!
And though thou spill thy heart's blood for atonement,
It will not weigh against an orphan's tear!

A superb answer, and one that cuts to the heart of the distinction between romanticism and a tragic sense of life. But the prevailing mythology proved too strong, and the drama ends on a note of redemption. Ordonio perishes crying: 'Atonement!'

The theme of the 'poison-tree', remorse turning to venom because the mind does not accept the possibility of redemption, obsessed Byron. Manfred is wracked by

The innate tortures of that deep despair,
Which is remorse without the fear of hell.

He knows there is no future pang

Can deal that justice on the self-condemned
He deals on his own soul.

And because he has determined, in his mad pride, that his punishment must be commensurate to his mysterious crime, Manfred will not give himself absolution. He says to the avenging Spirit:

I have not been thy dupe, nor am thy prey —
But was my own destroyer, and will be
My own hereafter.

There is in this final arrogance a grim justice, and it gives to the close of *Manfred* an element of real tragedy.

But what we find in most romantic dramas and in Wagnerian opera is not tragedy. Dramas of remorse cannot be ultimately tragic. The formula is one of 'near tragedy'. Four acts of tragic violence and guilt are followed by a fifth act of redemption and innocence regained. 'Near-tragedy' is precisely the compromise of an age which did not believe in the finality of evil. It represents the desire of the romantics to enjoy the privileges of grandeur and intense feeling associated with tragic drama without paying the full price. This price is the recognition of the fact that there are in the world mysteries of injustice, disasters in excess of guilt, and realities which do constant violence to our moral expectations. The mechanism of timely remorse or redemption through love – the arch-Wagnerian theme – allows the romantic hero to partake of the excitement of evil without bearing the real cost. It carries the audience to the brink of terror only to snatch them away at the last moment into the light of forgiveness. 'Near-tragedy' is, in fact, another word for melodrama.

I have insisted on this theme of remorse because it exhibits clearly that evasion of the tragic which is central to the romantic temper. It is relevant, moreover, to more than the bad plays of poets who may, for a multitude of reasons, have been bad playwrights. The evasion of tragedy is decisive in Goethe's *Faust*. Marlowe's Faustus descends to hell-fire with a terrible, graphic awareness of his condition. He pleads: 'My God, my God, look not so fierce on me.' But it is too late. In his lucid mind, he is aware of the possibility of repentance, but he knows also that the habits of evil have grown native to his heart: 'My heart is harden'd, I cannot repent'. It is precisely because he can no longer cross the shadow line between the thought of remorse and the redemptive act, that Faustus is damned. But his awareness of the truth, his assumption of complete responsibility, make of him a tragic and heroic personage. His last contact with the secular world is to bid his disciples move away from him, 'lest you perish with me'.

Goethe's Faust, on the contrary, is saved. He is borne away amid falling rose-petals and the music of angelic choirs. The Devil is robbed of his just reward by a cunning psychological twist. Faust's intellect is corrupted by his commerce with hell, but his will has remained sanctified (this being the exact reverse of Dr Faustus who wills evil even when he retains a knowledge of the good). The supreme bliss for which Faust bargained with the infernal powers turns out to be an act of Rousseauist benevolence – the draining of marshes toward the building of a new society. It is Mephistopheles who loses the wager. The heavens stream not with blood, as in Marlowe, but with redemptive hosannas. Nor is this a concession of the aged poet to his long ripening belief in the progressive, sanctified quality of life and the world. The idea of the 'happy ending' is explicit in the first sketches of a Faust play set down by the young Goethe in the 1770s. Marlowe's *Faustus* is a tragedy; Goethe's *Faust* is sublime melodrama.

This bias toward the 'near-tragic' controls the romantic theatre even where the subject seems least susceptible to happy resolution. In Schiller's *Jungfrau von Orleans*, the lady is not for burning. Joan dies near the battlefield in an apotheosis of victory and forgiveness. The curtain falls on her jubilation:

> Hinauf – hinauf – Die Erde flieht zurück –
> Kurz ist der Schmerz, und ewig ist die Freude!
> [Aloft – aloft – The earth recoils from me –
> Pain is short-lived, and joy is everlasting!]

It is a glorious assertion. We hear it celebrated in Beethoven's setting of
Schiller's *Ode to Joy*. It has in it the music of revolution and the sunrise of
a new century. But it is a denial of the meaning of tragic drama.
Schiller, who discriminated carefully between literary genres, was
aware of the contradiction. He entitled the play *Eine romantische
Tragödie*, and this is, I believe, the first time the antithetical terms
'romanticism' and 'tragedy' were conjoined. They cannot honestly go
together. Romanticism substituted for the realness of hell which
confronts Faustus, Macbeth, or Phèdre, the saving clause of timely
redemption and the 'compensating Heaven' of Rousseau. . . .

SOURCE: extracts from *The Death of Tragedy* (London, 1961), pp.
121–2, 123–4, 124–5, 126–30, 131–5.

J. L. Styan   Tragedy and Tragicomedy (1962)

It is understandable if today we are inhibited in our diagnosis of tragedy
and comedy. The vexed question of what properly constitutes the tragic
is accentuated by our often muddled preoccupation with an appropriate dramatic formula and correct playing convention for the play. We
may too readily anticipate as the form for a tragedy what should grow
out of the content of the play and not be imposed upon it: recent efforts
to resurrect the ancient Greek tragic chorus on the modern stage, or to
find a verse pattern for the lines, or to contrive a modern equivalent for
the soliloquy and other conventional devices, or to employ a mythological framework within which to work, are symptomatic. The elements
by which we tend to identify tragedy are generally conventional ones:
verse, in preference to prose, that the diction may be suitably
'heightened'; kings, princes, heroes and their rarefied circumstances
providing the characters and their situations, that the play may be
suitably elevated in tone; the plot leading remorselessly towards
disaster, that the spectator shall be properly edified, sometimes by pity,
sometimes by fear, sometimes by both. Each of these agencies is
artistically equivocal.

Drama is not to be heightened by verbal dexterity alone – burlesque
gains some of its peculiar force by being grand with the words when the
situation or the character explicitly lacks grandeur. The words take

their substance from the action to which in turn they give rise, and prose dialogue which is functioning fully within the play may be reinforced as well by the action on the stage as verse is. The unaffected language and the exquisitely simple expression of Lear's grief in the lines,

> Why should a dog, a horse, a rat, have life,
> And thou no breath at all? Thou'lt come no more,
> Never, never, never, never, never!
> Pray you, undo this button. Thank you, sir,

gather power chiefly because of the context: it comes quietly at the end of a great rush of feeling and it marks the reversal of the King's former attitude and his complete humility. Nor could the magnificent appeal of Lear's

> O, reason not the need; our basest beggars
> Are in the poorest thing superfluous . . .

reach its intended degree of poignancy out of the mouth of the Fool or of Edgar.

The heroic character is dependent for its dignity upon the world in which it moves: Hamlet grows taller in our eyes in proportion as Ophelia, Gertrude, Claudius or Laertes by their presence raise him and in consequence grow smaller themselves. But the commonplace world can have its relative nobility too, and can be equally fearful and pitiful, just as a man can attain heroic proportions in his own circle or in his own eyes. Provided that circle is recognisable and brought close enough to us, and provided his eyes are our eyes, with our absorption in the play intense and complete, the character can be exalted for us too. For the quality of the heroic on the stage must always lie within the imagination of the audience: Nora, the child-wife of Ibsen's *A Doll's House* who defies the world of respectability, or Maurya, the fisherwife of Synge's *Riders to the Sea* who faces nature itself, can rise above her littleness to the solemnity and grandeur of a queen; Willy Loman, Arthur Miller's salesman in his tough territory, can have the temporary dramatic stature of a king on his uncertain throne. [See Miller's statement, above–Ed.] Theatrical convention dictates that the stature of the hero is relative to the setting in which he is placed, and if the dramatist is capable of passing a character into our experience, that character may also be capable of assuming tragic proportions.

A sense of 'the remorseless' in the drive of the plot towards the dethronement of man in his pride by forces beyond his control is what induces the emotion characteristic of tragedy. This remorselessness is felt by ironic implications which must lie within the structure of the play: a snare is set by the dramatist for the protagonist, and we wait breathlessly for the trap to be sprung. Yet the spectator must not feel that the trap is there by accident, that it is arbitrarily planted to rouse his excitement: his natural sense of unfairness must not betray his dramatic sense of the just subjugation of his deputy on the stage. Whether Fate, Necessity, or the Gods, or the short-sightedness of the hero himself, shall set and spring the trap, punishment must be in one sense explicable: it must be justifiable. Here too convention plays its part. If any audience is to declare, 'Yes, this outcome is fitting', it must have some moral presuppositions; by common assent there must be some scale of judgement. Thus, unless we are prepared to share imaginatively the convictions of the Greek world, we may doubt whether we can today know the catharsis of which Aristotle speaks after we witness, for example, the *Oedipus Rex* of Sophocles. Nor is the glory of Thomas à Becket's martyrdom in Eliot's *Murder in the Cathedral* likely to be fully meaningful outside Christendom. This is not to say, of course, that the pity or fear felt about our mortality, which is common to ancient Greek, modern Christian and all men alike, may not persuade us to an emotional response in the theatre satisfying in itself.

Today the ethical conventionalism of tragedy seems impossible to adopt. If an implicit moral valuation must contribute to the understanding and enjoyment of the play, the dramatist must share it with his audience, and a homogeneous theatre seems a prerequisite for successful tragedy. In his researches as a playwright since the war in plays like *The Cocktail Party*, Eliot has trusted his audience less and less: he does not deploy religious counters about his play; he merely implies a vaguely Christian reference which may be felt or not felt only after the characters have suffered a particular secular experience. Writing in France during the same period, Sartre sets up his own framework of values in order to lend moral significance to the events of his play. But the obsessive inevitability of tragedy is lost in *Men Without Shadows*, his play about men of the French Resistance who discover an existentialist meaning in their sufferings, or *Crime Passionnel*, the play which invites us to question whether its hero has acquired existentialist grace, because we are too busy questioning first premises to attend to conclusions; we think too much to be passionate. The important 'universal human predicament' may exist within Celia Coplestone of *The Cocktail Party*, the society girl who suffers a change of heart sufficient to sacrifice herself as a missionary, or within Hugo Barine of *Crime Passionnel*, the new party member who asks to be allowed to kill a traitor in order to prove himself a man; but the universal impact is dangerously softened by our asking with simple pagan sentiment whether Celia has not wasted her talents, or whether Hugo did not die a rather selfish death.

The Elizabethans had no need to ask whether Romeo and Juliet died worthwhile deaths: they defied the irrepressible powers of society to the glory of a greater cause, and a limited sexual encounter became a spiritual triumph in an age which admitted individualistic experiment. Tragedy, like any drama, should be a reflection and interpretation of life – on this it stands or falls; but it may argue from a silly philosophical standpoint even though it may have much of 'life' in it. If Eliot's philosophy is too narrow, or Sartre's incomplete, there is no reason why it may not be dramatised successfully, though this may yet not prove the value of the philosophy: it merely proves that it may be dramatised. Tragedy may escape. Both Eliot and Sartre have nevertheless done us a service by implying within the body of the play a code by which to reason and evaluate its meaning; they have shown again that it is possible to evolve a serious drama, given meaning by what may be a selected, fantastic and subjective ethic, in a play which is, however, neither tragedy nor comedy.

In these ways at least 'tragedy' is precariously balanced on variously ephemeral conventions of theatre or audience, and it is not surprising that the tragic of one age may not easily be revived in another with any assurance. Especially where the appositeness of earlier conventions is in doubt, a parochial near-tragedy is likely to follow. Thus Arthur Miller's *Death of a Salesman* is arguably a lesser creation than the *Agamemnon* of Aeschylus; but if criticism, in order to make sense of such a play as Miller's continues to employ a term associated with a set of conventions no longer in use, it invites confusion.

Perhaps the most tiresome instance in modern times has been the drama of Ibsen. Those who missed the ritualistic heroism in his mature plays found it necessary to say he was writing a solemn form of satirical domestic tragicomedy based on personal psychology but having social reference. Oh, dear. We see more clearly now that the movement towards realism of subject and manner in the nineteenth century was one which simply modified the conventions of classical tragedy and produced another kind of play. The tragic individual superseded the tragic hero, but had the power to be no less moving and no less significant. Ibsen was raising important issues for drama: What are the near limits of the tragic world? May the spectator's intelligence be used with his emotions to help rationalise his interest and yet allow the flow of the play to be preserved? Dare the dramatist risk hearing us laugh when he would wish us to weep? Can he risk diminishing the stature of his hero in order to ensure his individuality, as happens with Dr Stockmann of *An Enemy of the People*, whom Ibsen variously declared to be 'muddle-headed' and 'an extravagant immature fellow and a hothead'? Might not the narrowing of the frame and setting of the play limit the width of its appeal as seems to have happened with *A Doll's House*, but not with *The Master Builder*, concerned with those who will not accept the limitations of middle age, and so touching us all? As Desmond MacCarthy justly said of Hjalmar Ekdal of *The Wild Duck*, Hjalmar the small man and our representative of illusory happiness, 'Hjalmar is a wide shot that hits half the world.'[1] We may sense tragedy here, but we may not find it: we may be looking for the wrong evidence.

Thus tragedy 'in the full sense of the word' is missing today. Our present-day mongrel conventions, interbred with the spirit of naturalism, can better do other things, and do not encourage the exclusive consistency of purpose we ask of tragedy. Twentieth-century currents of contradictory thought and the mood of audiences do not permit it; the laws of tragedy belong to a world which is religious in its affirmation of human greatness. Today we hear only the uncertainty and the whimper of the ending of Jean Cocteau's Oedipus story, *The Infernal Machine*, as Creon and Tiresias watch the blinded king led away by his daughter Antigone and the ghost of his wife Jocasta:

CREON: And even supposing they leave the town, who will look after them, who will admit them?
TIRESIAS: Glory.
CREON: You mean rather dishonour, shame . . .
TIRESIAS: Who knows?

Curtain[2]

The play slips imperceptibly into 'tragicomedy'. In an age when tragedy is submerged in moral indifference, we may expect a kind of tragicomedy to come into its own.

The line between tragedy and its hybrid partner tragicomedy is often difficult to draw, and is a central concern in this essay. A technical point, however, invites attention here. The ironies which enforce the dialectical conflict of tragedy are simple in formula: each step the hero takes towards a supposed triumph is a step nearer his death, each step one which strengthens the audience's sense of a necessary end. The spectator, knowing or feeling this outcome, is wholly in the confidence of the author and the secret of the play; the characters are not. The spectator stands where the Gods themselves stand, in a happy position of omniscience. Therefore his excitement during the performance does not arise from a simple chemical mixture, as it were $x+y$, where x is each decision arising from the hero's wish to assert his personal responsibility, the positive element, and y is the tightening of the net of inevitable destruction, the negative element; but its source is in an active chemical compound, where the resulting passion is xy, imaginatively irreducible, a new substance with fierce properties of its own. It has even been given a name of its own: 'tragic irony'.

Yet its counterpart, 'comic irony', is not very different in kind. It may indeed merge at times into the more easily recognisable irony of tragedy. The spectator is equally omniscient, able by his presence in the comic theatre to perform a chemical experiment like his fellow in the tragic theatre. Within his mind he mixes the positive image of a character wishing to be and to assert himself, x, with another aspect of necessity's power to destroy – its power to belittle and undermine by suggesting commonplaceness and triviality, y. Comic irony, however, can prick with a thousand pins in the course of a play, and in its way be as all-pervading and relentless and irresistible in its effect as tragic irony itself. Nor need we assume that such tragicomedy as emerges carries less weight than tragedy, is any the less moral, or bears any the less relationship to the society which promotes it. Its philosophy may come equally from profound laws of feeling and understanding, just as important in themselves for our apprehension of the quality of life.

Both experience of life and familiarity with the best of twentieth-century drama constantly compel us to be aware of the blood relationship of the tragic and comic senses, of the interbreeding of tears and laughter. In an earlier essay, Ronald Peacock had declared with more justice that both tragedy and comedy 'spring from the tension between our imperfect life and our ideal aspirations. They exist together in their dependence on the contradictions of life. They are parallel expressions, in different keys, of our idea of what is good.'[3]

We may gladly defer to the sound judgement of Dr Johnson in his familiar defence of Shakespeare's tragicomedy:

Shakespeare's plays are not in the rigorous and critical sense either tragedies or comedies, but compositions of a distinct kind; exhibiting the real state of sublunary nature, which partakes of good and evil, joy and sorrow, mingled with endless variety of proportion and innumerable modes of combination; and expressing the course of the world, in which the loss of one is the gain of another; in which, at the same time, the reveller is hasting to his wine, and the mourner burying his friend; in which the malignity of one is sometimes defeated by the frolick of another; and many mischiefs and many benefits are done and hindered without design.

Dr Johnson is of course the last man to invite anarchy in literary or dramatic standards: the play must disclose its design if life will not. But even he allows that 'there is always an appeal open from criticism to nature': we must be well prepared to admit an endless variety of proportion and innumerable modes of combination.

SOURCE: extract from *The Dark Comedy* (Cambridge, 1962; revised edn 1968), pp. 31–8.

NOTES

1. D. MacCarthy, 'The Wild Duck' (1905), reprinted in P. C. Ward (ed.),
Specimens of English Dramatic Criticism, XVII–XX Centuries (London, 1945), p.
237. In his essay on 'Tolstoy: Tragedian or Comedian?' (1921), Shaw later
suggested that 'Ibsen was the dramatic poet who firmly established tragicomedy as a much deeper and grimmer entertainment than tragedy'.

2. J. Cocteau, *The Infernal Machine*, trans. C. Wildman (London, 1950). [The
original French version was first performed in 1934–Ed.]

3. R. Peacock, *The Poet in the Theatre* (London, 1946): chapter on 'Tragedy,
Comedy and Civilisation', p. 126.

Raymond Williams   Tragedy and Contemporary Ideas (1966)

. . . Tragic experience, because of its central importance, commonly
attracts the fundamental beliefs and tensions of a period, and tragic
theory is mainly interesting in this sense, that through it the shape and
set of a particular culture is often deeply realised. If, however, we think
of it as a theory about a single and permanent kind of fact, we can end
only with the metaphysical conclusions that are built into any such
assumption. Chief among these is the assumption of a permanent,
universal and essentially unchanging human nature (an assumption
taken over from one kind of Christianity to 'ritual' anthropology and
the general theory of psycho-analysis). Given such an assumption, we
have to explain tragedy in terms of this unchanging human nature or
certain of its faculties. But if we reject this assumption (following a
different kind of Christianity, a different psychological theory, or the
evidence of comparative anthropology) the problem is necessarily
transformed. Tragedy is then not a single and permanent kind of fact,
but a series of experiences and conventions and institutions. It is not a
case of interpreting this series by reference to a permanent and
unchanging human nature. Rather, the varieties of tragic experience
are to be interpreted by reference to the changing conventions and
institutions. The universalist character of most tragic theory is then at
the opposite pole from our necessary interest.

The most striking fact about modern tragic theory is that it is rooted
in very much the same structure of ideas as modern tragedy itself, yet
one of its paradoxical effects is its denial that modern tragedy is possible,

after almost a century of important and continuous and insistent tragic art. It is very difficult to explain why this should be so. Part of the explanation seems to be the incapacity to make connections which is characteristic of this whole structure. But it is also significant that the major original contributions to the theory were made in the nineteenth century, before the creative period of modern tragedy, and have since been systematised by men deeply conditioned, by their academic training, to a valuation of the past against the present, and to a separation between critical theory and creative practice. . . .

The argument that there is no significant tragic meaning in 'everyday tragedies' seems to rest on two related beliefs: that the event itself is not tragedy, but only becomes so through shaped response (with the implication that tragedy is a matter of art, where such responses are embodied, rather than of life where they are not); and that significant response depends on the capacity to connect the event with some more general body of facts, so that it is not mere accident but is capable of bearing a general meaning.

My doubts here are radical. I do not see how it is finally possible to distinguish between an event and response to an event, in any absolute way. It is of course possible to say that *we* have not responded to an event, but this does not mean that response is absent. We can properly see the difference between a response which has been put into a communicable form and one which has not, and this will be relevant. But, in the case of ordinary death and suffering, when we see mourning and lament, when we see men and women breaking under their actual loss, it is at least not self-evident to say that we are not in the presence of tragedy. Other responses are of course possible: indifference, justification (as so often in war), even relief or rejoicing. But where the suffering is felt, where it is taken into the person of another, we are clearly within the possible dimensions of tragedy. We can of course ourselves react to the mourning and lament of others with our own forms of indifference and justification, even relief and rejoicing. But if we do, we should be clear what we are doing. That the suffering has communicated to those most closely involved but not to us may be a statement about the suffering, about those involved, or (which we often forget) about ourselves.

Obviously the possibility of communication to ourselves, we who are not immediately involved, depends on the capacity to connect the event with some more general body of facts. This criterion, which is now quite conventional, is indeed very welcome, for it poses the issue in its most urgent form. It is evidently possible for some people to hear of a mining disaster, a burned-out family, a broken career or a smash on the road without feeling these events as tragic in the full sense. But the starkness of such a position (which I believe to be sincerely held) is of course at once qualified by the description of such events as *accidents* which, however painful or regrettable, do not connect with any general meanings. This view is made even stronger when the unavailable meanings, for a particular event, are described as universal or permanent.

The central question that needs to be asked is what kind of general (or universal or permanent) meaning it is which interprets events of the kind referred to as accidents. Here at least (if not at a much earlier stage) we can see that the ordinary academic tradition of tragedy is in fact an ideology. What is in question is not the process of connecting an event to a general meaning, but the character and quality of the general meaning itself.

I once heard it said that if 'you or I' went out and got run over by a bus, that would not be tragedy. I was not sure how to take this: as engagingly modest; as indifferent and offensive; or as a quite alien ideology. I remembered Yeats: 'some blunderer has driven his car on to the wrong side of the road – that is all'; or again: 'if war is necessary, or necessary in our time and place, it is best to forget its suffering as we do the discomfort of fever'.

This has come a long way from Hegel's description of 'mere sympathy', which he distinguished from 'true sympathy' because it lacked 'genuine content': 'an accordant feeling with the ethical claim at the same time associated with the sufferer'. It is also some way from Bradley's restatement of this: 'no mere suffering or misfortune, no suffering that does not spring in great part from human agency, and in some degree from the agency of the sufferer, is tragic, however pitiful or dreadful it may be'. Here the 'ethical claim', a positive and representative content, has been changed to the more general concept of 'agency'. But what is really significant is the subsequent separation of both ethical content and human agency from a whole class of ordinary suffering. . . .

We can only distinguish between tragedy and accident if we have some conception of a law or an order to which certain events are accidental and in which certain other events are significant. Yet wherever the law or order is partial (in the sense that only certain events are relevant to it) there is an actual alienation of some part of human experience. Even in the most traditional general orders, there has been this factual alienation. The definition of tragedy as dependent on the history of a man of rank was just such an alienation: some deaths mattered more than others, and rank was the actual dividing line – the death of a slave or a retainer was no more than incidental and was certainly not tragic. Ironically, our own middle-class culture began by appearing to reject this view: the tragedy of a citizen could be as real as the tragedy of a prince. Often, in fact, this was not so much rejection of the real structure of feeling as an extension of the tragic category to a newly rising class. Yet its eventual effect was profound. As in other bourgeois revolutions, extending the categories of law or suffrage, the arguments for the limited extension became inevitable arguments for a general extension. The extension from the prince to the citizen became in practice an extension to all human beings. Yet the character of the extension largely determined its content, until the point was reached where tragic experience was theoretically conceded to all men, but the nature of this experience was drastically limited.

The important element in the earlier emphasis on rank in tragedy was always the *general* status of the man of rank. His fate was the fate of the house or kingdom which he at once ruled and embodied. In the person of Agamemnon or of Lear the fate of a house or a kingdom was literally acted out. It was of course inevitable that this definition should fail to outlast its real social circumstances, in its original form. It was in particular inevitable that bourgeois society should reject it: the individual was neither the state nor an element of the state, but an entity in himself. There was then both gain and loss: the suffering of a man of no rank could be more seriously and more directly regarded, but equally, in the stress on the fate of an individual, the general and public character of tragedy was lost. Eventually, as we shall see, new definitions of general and public interest were embodied in new kinds of tragedy. But, meanwhile, the idea of a tragic order had to co-exist with the loss of any such actual order. What happened, at the level of theory, was then the abstraction of order, and its mystification.

One practical consequence intervened. Rank in tragedy became the name-dropping, the play with titles and sonorities, of costume drama. . . .

But the main effects were more serious. What had been a whole lived order, connecting man and state and world, became, finally, a purely abstract order. Tragic significance was made to depend on an event's relation to a supposed nature of things, yet without the specific connections which had once provided a particular relation and action of this kind. Hegel's insistence on ethical substance, and his connection of this with a process of historical embodiment of the Idea, was a major attempt to meet the new situation. Marx pushed the connection further, into a more specific history. But, increasingly, the idea of the permanent 'nature of things' became separated from any action that could be felt as contemporary, to the point where even Nietzsche's brutal rationalisation of suffering could be welcomed as specific. The whole meaning of 'accident' changed. Fate or Providence had been beyond man's understanding, so that what he saw as accident was in fact design, or was a specifically limited kind of event outside this design. The design in any case was embodied in institutions, through which man could hope to come to terms with it. But when there is an idea of design, without specific institutions at once metaphysical and social, the alienation is such that the category of accident is stressed and enlarged until it comes to include almost all actual suffering, and especially the effects of the existing and non-metaphysical social order. This is then either newly generalised as a *blind* fate, accident taking over from design as a plan of the universe, and becoming objective rather than subjective; or significant suffering, and therefore tragedy, is pushed back in time to periods when fully connecting meanings were available, and contemporary tragedy is seen as impossible because there are now no such meanings. The living tragedies of our own world can then not be negotiated at all. They cannot be seen in the light of those former meanings, or they are, however regrettable, accidents. New kinds of relation and new kinds of law, to connect with and interpret our actual suffering, are the terms of contemporary tragedy. But to see new relations and new laws is also to change the nature of experience, and the whole complex of attitudes and relationships dependent on it. To *find* significance is to be capable of tragedy, but of course it was easier to find insignificance. Then behind the facade of the emphasis on order, the substance of tragedy withered. . . .

When we look, then, for the historical conditions of tragedy, we shall not look for particular kinds of belief: in fate, in divine government, or in a sense of the irreparable. The action of isolating extreme suffering and then of reintegrating it within a continuing sense of life can occur in very different cultures, with very different fundamental beliefs. It is often argued that these beliefs need to be both common and stable, if tragedy is to occur. Some such argument lies behind the assertion that tragedy was dependent, in the past, on ages of faith, and is impossible now, because we have no faith. That the beliefs which are brought into action or question need to be reasonably common I would not deny. We have, as we shall see, our own beliefs of this kind, and we are surely capable of avoiding the simple trap of calling some beliefs 'faiths' and others not.

The question of stability is much more important. I would not deny the possibility of tragedy when there are stable beliefs, but it is in this direction that an historical examination seems to take us. What is commonly asserted, about the relation between tragedy and stability of belief, seems to be almost the opposite of the truth. Of course if beliefs are simply abstracted, and taken out of their context as lived behaviour and working institutions, it is possible to create the impression of stability, the reiteration of received interpretations, even when the real situation is quite evidently one of instability or indeed disintegration. The most remarkable case of this kind is the description of an Elizabethan and Jacobean sense of order – the persistence of late mediaeval beliefs – in almost total disregard of the extraordinary tensions of a culture moving towards violent internal conflict and substantial transformation. The ages of comparatively stable belief, and of comparatively close correspondence between beliefs and actual experience, do not seem to produce tragedy of any intensity, though of course they enact the ordinary separations and tensions and the socially sanctioned ways of resolving these. The intensification of this common procedure, and the possibility of its permanent interest, seem to depend more on an extreme tension between belief and experience than on an extreme correspondence. Important tragedy seems to occur, neither in periods of real stability, nor in periods of open and decisive conflict. Its most common historical setting is the period preceding the substantial breakdown and transformation of an important culture. Its condition is the real tension between old and new: between received beliefs, embodied in institutions and responses, and newly and vividly experienced contradictions and possibilities. If the received beliefs have widely or wholly collapsed, this tension is obviously absent; to that extent their real presence is necessary. But beliefs can be both active and deeply questioned, not so much by other beliefs as by insistent immediate experience. In such situations, the common process of dramatising and resolving disorder and suffering is intensified to the level which can be most readily recognised as tragedy. . . .

Human death is often the form of the deepest meanings of a culture. When we see death, it is natural that we should draw together – in grief, in memory, in the social duties of burial – our sense of the values of living, as individuals and as a society. But then, in some cultures or in their breakdown, life is regularly read back from the fact of death, which can seem not only the focus but also the source of our values. Death, then, is absolute, and all our living simply relative. Death is necessary, and all other human ends are contingent. Within this emphasis, suffering and disorder of any kind are interpreted by reference to what is seen as the controlling reality. Such an interpretation is now commonly described as a tragic sense of life.

What is not usually noticed, in this familiar and now formal procession, is precisely the element of convention. To read back life from the fact of death is a cultural and sometimes a personal choice. But that it is a choice, and a variable choice, is very easily forgotten. The powerful association of a particular rhetoric and a persistent human fact can give the appearance of permanence to a local and temporary and even sectional response. To tie any meaning to death is to give it a powerful emotional charge which can at times obliterate all other experience in its range. Death is universal, and the meaning tied to it quickly claims universality, as it were in its shadow. Other readings of life, other interpretations of suffering and disorder, can be assimilated to

it with great apparent conviction. The burden of proof shifts continually from the controversial meaning to the inescapable experience,
and we are easily exposed, by fear and loss, to the most conventional
and arbitrary conclusions.

   The connection between tragedy and death is of course quite evident,
but in reality the connection is variable, as the response to death is
variable. What has happened in our own century is that a particular
post-liberal and post-Christian interpretation of death has been
imposed as an absolute meaning, and as identical with all tragedy.
What is generalised is the loneliness of man, facing a blind fate, and this
is the fundamental isolation of the tragic hero. The currency of this
experience is of course sufficiently wide to make it relevant to much
modern tragedy. But the structure of the meaning still needs analysis.
To say that man dies alone is not to state a fact but to offer an
interpretation. For indeed men die in so many ways: in the arms and
presence of family and neighbours; in the blindness of pain, or the
blankness of sedation; in the violent disintegration of machines and in
the calm of sleep. To insist on a single meaning is already rhetorical, but
to insist on the meaning of loneliness is to interpret life as much as death.
However men die, the experience is not only the physical dissolution
and ending; it is also a change in the lives and relationships of others, for
we know death as much in the experience of others as in our own
expectations and endings. And just as death enters, continually, our
common life, so any statement about death is in a common language
and depends on common experience. The paradox of 'we die alone' or
'man dies alone' is then important and remarkable: the maximum
substance that can be given to the plural 'we', or to the group-name
'man', is the singular loneliness. The common fact, in a common
language, is offered as a proof of the loss of connection.

   But then, as we become aware of this structure of feeling, we can look
through it at the experience which it has offered to interpret. It is using
the names of death and tragedy, but it has very little really to do with
the tragedies of the past, or with death as a universal experience.
Rather, it has correctly identified, and then blurred, the crisis around
which one main kind of contemporary tragic experience moves. It blurs
it because it offers as absolutes the very experiences which are now most
unresolved and most moving. Our most common received interpretations of life put the highest value and significance on the individual
and his development, but it is indeed inescapable that the individual
dies. What is most valuable and what is most irreparable are then set in
an inevitable relation and tension. But to generalise this particular
contradiction as an absolute fact of human existence is to fix and finally
suppress the relation and tension, so that tragedy becomes not an action
but a deadlock. And then to claim this deadlock as the whole meaning

of tragedy is to project into history a local structure that is both culturally and historically determined. . . .

Source: extracts from *Modern Tragedy* (London, 1966), pp. 45–8, 48–51, 53–4, 55–8.

Dorothea Krook   'Heroic Tragedy' (1969)

. . . The ideal representativeness of the tragic hero finds a local habitation and a name in his high distinction – of character, mind, spirit, or whatever. The particular qualities making up the sum of an actual hero's distinction may be as multifold and various as it may please the dramatist to make them, and they may include some which would not normally be thought of as belonging to a tragic hero. Among the most striking of these is something which may be called charm: not in its diluted modern tea-party and drawing-room meaning, but as that charisma of personality which in literature as in life is part of the magnetism of the heroic character, and which properly belongs to the tragic hero as hero if not as tragic. This charismatic charm is, as it were, the outward radiance of a spirit brimming over with an energy of life, a superabundance of vitality, which is the sacred fount of all its gifts and graces. It expresses itself in a spontaneous delight in people; a rich, bright curiosity about the world; a keen responsiveness and receptiveness to all impressions; and often a gaiety, a good humor, which does not diminish but on the contrary reinforces and intensifies its profounder distinctions of mind and spirit. Shakespeare's Hamlet possesses it in an exemplary degree: in the scene with the players, in all his encounters with Horatio, in his supposedly mad colloquies with Polonius and his soliloquy over the skull of Old Yorick; and it is this charismatic quality which, I believe, has led people like Dover Wilson to speak of Hamlet as an 'adorable prince'. That may be an extravagant way of expressing one's sense of it, but has the merit at least of registering a response to something that is distinctly there to be responded to. ╱

In Shakespeare's tragedy as a whole the charisma of personality appears to have a specially prominent place. Shakespeare understands better than most its power to induce the Aristotelian pity:

> O! What a noble mind is here o'erthrown:
> The courtier's, soldier's, scholar's, eye, tongue, sword;

> The expectancy and rose of the fair state,
> The glass of fashion and the mould of form,
> The observ'd of all observers, quite, quite down.
>
> (*Hamlet*, III i 153–7)

He does not hesitate to exploit it to capacity, from the earliest tragic dramas, like *Richard II*, to the latest, like *Antony and Cleopatra*; it is part of the secret. of his deathless appeal, to the sophisticated and unsophisticated alike; and it is something the severer of his modern critics should take less trouble to resist. It is also a distinctly modern phenomenon – that is, of the Renaissance and after. In Shakespeare, besides Hamlet, Antony and Cleopatra, Romeo and Juliet, Cressida, Richard II, and Richard III possess it; in Webster, the Duchess of Malfi, and Vittoria and Brachiano; in Middleton, Beatrice-Joanna. It is no doubt one of the multifold products of the fusion of Renaissance humanism with the Romance tradition of medieval Europe; it sinks out of sight in the nondramatic, nontragic literature of the eighteenth century, re-emerges with Romanticism, in a somewhat etiolated form, and is powerfully revived again in the tragic literature of the later nineteenth century. It is there in the dramas of Chekhov, whose lovely ladies have all the charm that Ibsen's lack; still more in some of the great tragic novels of the period – in *Anna Karenina*, for instance, and in *Daniel Deronda*; and in all the works of Henry James, who is the true spiritual seed of Shakespeare in recognising the value for tragedy of heroes and heroines who are wonderfully, beautifully, prodigiously charming, and in succeeding with a Shakespearean genius in making them so.

However, though the charm I have been speaking of is a persistent feature of the tragic hero in Shakespeare and after, it is totally absent from Greek classical tragedy. There is plenty of the power of personality – the King Lear and Lady Macbeth power – but none of the Hamlet charm in an Oedipus, a Clytemnestra, a Medea, an Antigone, an Electra. Consequently, it cannot rank as a universal distinction of the tragic hero, nor therefore as a definitive distinction, and must regretfully be set aside as one of the delightful things a tragic hero may but need not be.

Of the universal, definitive distinctions of the ideal hero in tragedy, there are two which appear to encompass all others. These are courage and nobility (greatness of soul), where the courage is a function of the nobility and the nobility principally defined by the courage. The courage is best understood, I believe, if it is taken in Plato's sense: as the emblematic virtue of that part of the soul which Plato calls the 'spirited' element, or simply 'spirit'. In the Platonic psychology, the spirited element stands midway between the appetitive (the lowest) element and the reasonable (the highest), partaking of the nature of both but identical with neither. What this means is that, on the one hand, the spirited element, and *a fortiori* the courage which is its distinctive virtue, is grounded in the passions – in the non-intellectual, non-analytical, emotional, or impulsive side of man's nature. It has a physical, animal basis, and draws its strength and vitality from this primitive source. On the other hand, it is guided and controlled (in Plato's phrase) by the element of reason, whose distinctive virtue is wisdom (knowledge in the sense of insight); and more particularly, by that part of the element of reason which Plato calls the 'practical' reason (as distinct from the 'pure' or 'contemplative' reason) – wisdom in action, so to speak. Thus courage, though it is not itself wisdom, both serves the ends of and is informed by wisdom. In the Platonic scheme, however, wisdom as the supreme virtue incorporates goodness, that is, moral virtue. Thus courage, partaking of the nature of wisdom by its submission to and service of wisdom, ceases to be a purely physical, appetitive quality and becomes a moral virtue: a virtue of character, the domain of the practical reason, though never a virtue of mind, the domain of the pure or contemplative reason.

The Platonic analysis, sketchy and schematic though it is, does much to illuminate the courage of the tragic hero: what it is and how it operates in tragedy. By finding a logical place for all the components of the tragic hero's courage, it establishes firm connections between elements that would otherwise seem unrelated and even arbitrary.

To begin with, it finds a place for what one feels to be the physical basis of the tragic hero's courage. The superabundance of vitality, which I suggested was the source of his charisma, is also the source of his courage; and it is, in some sense, of the body: rooted in the physical, animal springs of life. This is true not only of the obvious men of action – an Othello, an Antony. We feel it equally in a Hamlet, a Lear, an Oedipus, in Antigone and Electra. Their courage is of course moral, not physical; but its exercise (to adapt a splendid phrase of Lionel Trilling's) appears to involve their sensations, their emotions, and their sex; and this aspect of it becomes more intelligible (and more interesting) if it is remembered that in Plato's analysis the spirited element by definition partakes of the nature of the appetitive.

There is an element in the courage of Plato's young warriors which is usually translated by the word 'anger', meaning the kind of impetu-ousness, irritability (in the somatic sense of 'quickness to react'), irascibility, peremptoriness which make up the high spirit of an aristocratic warrior class. This is the anger which leads Oedipus to commit his fateful crime, informs the passionate speeches of Antigone and Electra, sustains Medea in her savage heroism and Ajax in his resistance. It is rightly made much of in classical Greek tragedy because it is the chief outward sign of the hubris which brings the tragic heroes and heroines to disaster; yet it is always seen also as a function of their courage, and thus as a properly tragic flaw. Beyond the Greeks, one has only to think of the anger in which Hamlet kills Polonius behind the arras, or that in which Lear rejects Cordelia and Kent, or that in which Othello takes by the throat the circumcised dog, to recognise that this quality, which Plato identified in the courage of his 'spirited' young warriors, is a permanent feature of the courage of the tragic hero.

A more fundamental property of the courage suggested by the Platonic analysis is that it is pre-eminently *moral:* not a quality of mind but of character; not the courage or heroism of the contemplative spirit (the philosopher's, the scholar's, the scientist's) but that of the man or woman immersed in life and living; therefore, a courage practical, applied, active, characteristically expressing itself in immediate responses to concrete moral situations. Nevertheless, because the spirited element in the Platonic scheme partakes of reason, its end is knowledge. The knowledge is not indeed the wisdom, or perfect and complete knowledge, of the contemplative reason. It is the moral understanding (often misleadingly translated by the word prudence) of the practical or applied reason; and as such it exactly covers the case of the tragic hero's pursuit of knowledge as a function of his courage. It expresses itself primarily as the power to confront, without evasion or subterfuge, the pain and terror of the human condition as figured in his own representative situation, to explore this situation to its furthest limit, in order to see it steady and whole, and having seen it, in some sense to be reconciled to it, to come to terms with it. It is an enterprise which requires the exercise of courage in an extreme or absolute degree: as Oedipus exercises it in his relentless quest for the true knowledge of his situation, Antigone in her unyielding defiance of Creon, Electra in her ruthless pressure on her brother Orestes, Lear in his bitter uncompromising revulsion from his pelican daughters, Hamlet in his remorseless self-examination and heart-searching about whether to be or not to be, what to do or not to do about his mother Gertrude and the incestuous, adulterate beast Claudius.

To exercise courage in this way demands a capacity for suffering in the same extreme, unqualified, absolute degree. The tragic hero exposes himself, totally and without reserve, to the weary weight of all this unintelligible world, receives the full impact of its painful, terrible, humiliating unintelligibility, by the extremity of his conscious suffering, renders it intelligible, and by rendering it intelligible, effects the final reconciliation of tragedy. This is the supreme, overtopping distinction of the tragic hero; and whatever other specific distinctions he may possess – the passion for truth of an Oedipus, the passion for justice of a Lear, the moral sensibility of a Hamlet, the moral imagination (which is not the same thing as moral sensibility) of a Macbeth, the ferocious single-mindedness of an Antigone or Electra – are fully tragic qualities only as they are linked with a capacity for suffering which is as extreme and absolute as it is conscious.

The Platonic analysis, finally, also illuminates the nature of the knowledge that issues from, or is involved in, the suffering of the tragic hero. I have said that the suffering must be conscious, but need not be more. In spite of what our post-Shakespearean preconceptions lead us to believe, it need not involve or issue in self-knowledge. It need not even be articulate – that is, expressed in words or language. Clytemnestra's silent prayer near the opening of the *Agamemnon* as fully expresses her sense of her anguish of spirit as do the soliloquies of the Shakespeare heroes; and when Hedda Gabler moves silently about her drawing room, arranging and rearranging the flowers, drawing the curtains and pulling them back again, moving an ornament, glancing toward the portrait of her father the General, we are not only conscious of the desperate suicidal boredom that is moving her but conscious also of her awareness of her own desperation. The necessary condition to be satisfied is that the spectacle of suffering shall yield knowledge of the human condition, or some fundamental aspect of it, not necessarily to the tragic hero but to us, the readers or audience. The tragic hero's business is only to suffer, to the utmost capacity of a human being: consciously to register in his body and blood the horror, cruelty, and shame of the wheel of fire upon which he is bound; and the point of insisting that his suffering shall be conscious is that conscious suffering – the suffering of those made for both being and seeing – is, in fact, of all suffering the most intense.

This is not to say that a tragic hero with self-knowledge or insight may not be more interesting (that is, exemplary and instructive), especially to the modern mind, than one without. That is why Shakespeare's tragic vessels are to the modern mind more interesting than Aeschylus's, and Henry James's than Ibsen's. Nor (an important point) is it inconsistent with the view proposed to demand a high degree of self-knowledge in a tragic hero or heroine so conceived and presented as to lead us to *expect* it, and to judge the success or failure of the drama as tragedy, at least partly, by the kind and quality of the self-knowledge attained by such a hero through his suffering. This is likely to be true of modern tragedy in particular. Ibsen's *Hedda Gabler* is a case in point; . . . the failure of this play as tragedy is to be located partly at least in the final lack of insight – or worse, false insight – into her situation of Hedda Gabler, the highly self-conscious vessel of the potentially tragic experience. . . .

SOURCE: extract from *Elements of Tragedy* (New Haven, Conn. and London, 1969), pp. 39–46.

Jeannette King   From Tragic Drama to
the Tragic Novel (1978)

The decline of serious drama in Britain in the nineteenth century is a
well-known phenomenon. The relationship it bears to the corresponding rise of the novel is a problematic subject. Until the appearance of
Shaw's plays at the end of the century, no contemporary drama of any
stature or seriousness was produced in the theatre. It was not that
tragedy or tragic themes were neglected, as they largely were in the
eighteenth century, but works on tragic themes and subjects were
written for private reading only. All the great nineteenth-century
writers were poets or novelists, not dramatists. The separation from the
live theatrical tradition and the simultaneous development of the novel
as a tragic form are surely not simply coincidental.

It is important to remember, of course, that while serious drama
declined, the commercial theatre flourished, marking the increasingly
significant division of literature into 'highbrow' and 'lowbrow'. It
seemed that dramatists could no longer entertain as they taught, or *vice
versa*. As the stage was more and more given over to melodrama,
pantomime and even hippodrama – literally, horse-drama! – so more
serious writers turned to the creation of what has become known as
'closet-drama'. The fact that such 'drama' was intended to be read
rather than performed caused many contemporary critics to react as
John Gibson Lockhart did, in reviewing Lord Byron's *Sardanapalus*
(1821): 'in God's name, why call a thing a tragedy, unless it is meant to
be a play?' Closet-drama was, in addition, clearly intended for a literary
élite, while the playwrights designed their work for a popular mass
audience. The two strands which unite in great British drama – the
literary, aesthetic principle, and the feeling for the contemporary and
popular – were totally divorced. There could, therefore, be no great
drama.

When we remember that almost all the great Romantic and
Victorian poets attempted to write a poetic tragedy, for the 'closet', it
may seem surprising that none of them produced anything that even
approached real drama. But . . . their work was too often a mere
pastiche, reviving the style and themes of the drama of the past rather
than its spirit. Shakespeare was the commonest source of inspiration.
His own plays were almost the only serious dramas to achieve
popularity on the stage during this period. The fact that . . . his work
was rarely cited by critics as a model for tragedy is again indicative of

the increasing gulf between popular and critical taste. This popularity undoubtedly relates to that interest in character which made Shakespeare such a positive source of inspiration for many of the great nineteenth-century novelists. But this stage success had disastrous consequences for the contemporary drama, which so carefully attempted to render the Shakespearean style. Augustin Filon complained, in his contemporary survey of nineteenth-century drama, that Shakespeare's spirit could not be assimilated: 'this is impossible to a man of our time; one can but dress oneself up in the cast-off garment which served as a cover to his genius. This garment does not suit us.' And, by copying from the past, the dramatist lost sight of his own time, which it was his true function to reflect. As Filon put it, for contemporary drama to succeed, 'the choice has to be made between Shakespeare and life'.[1]

But Shakespeare was not the only model. Reviewing Matthew Arnold's *Merope* (1858), W.E. Henley objected that it was 'an imitation Greek play: an essay, that is, in a form which ceased long since to have any active life, so that the attempt to revive it – to create a soul under the ribs of very musty death – is a blunder alike in sentiment and in art'. The would-be tragedians were imitating older literary forms, when the demand everywhere was for a living drama that modelled itself on nature. A living drama should express the ideas and passions of the age, and reflect the national character. Each age must therefore develop its own methods and language as a vehicle for these ideas.[2]

In defence, Shelley [in 1821] claimed that it was precisely the inadequacy of the age that made it necessary for the dramatist to turn to the drama of the past:

In periods of the decay of social life, the drama sympathises with that decay. Tragedy becomes a cold imitation of the form of the great masterpieces of antiquity, divested of all harmonious accompaniment of the kindred arts; and often the very form misunderstood, or a weak attempt to teach certain doctrines, which the writer considers as moral truths.[3]

It was not the age that provided inadequate material for tragedy, but the old forms that were inadequate to convey the tragedy of the age. For the ideas, passions and character of the age were finding expression in the novels of the period. This was perhaps the only place where they could find expression. As Henry James put it:

The old dramatists . . . had a simpler civilisation to represent – societies in which the life of man was in action, in passion, in immediate and violent expression. Those things could be put upon the playhouse boards with comparatively little sacrifice of their completeness and their truth. Today we're so infinitely more reflective and complicated and diffuse that it makes all the difference. What can you do with a character, with an idea, with a feeling, between dinner and the suburban trains? You can give a gross, rough sketch of them, but how little you touch them, how bald you leave them! What crudity compared with what the novelist does![4]

James suggests that the novel penetrates the surface of modern life far better than drama can. And James's concern, like George Eliot's, was very much with the kind of tragedy which was not apparent on the surface. Until English translations of Ibsen's plays appeared in Britain towards the end of the century, many more critics claimed that realistic tragic drama was impossible. The heroism portrayed in many novels of modern life was essentially undramatic. In addition, the dramatist must constantly be making all processes of decision, all feelings, all communications, more articulate than they are in real life. If we want to see inarticulate people's decisions and experiences realistically portrayed, we must look to the novel, where direct speech can be amplified in narrative.

The novel obviously presented itself as a more satisfactory vehicle for modern tragedy than the drama had become. When serious drama was itself reduced to a form for private reading, the novel was a formidable rival. It combined its serious reflections on life with the popular appeal it shared with the theatre, healing – for a time – the breach between 'literature' and 'entertainment'. In the novel was also realised that ideal of interaction, of combining the dramatic and the narrative, the poetic and the contemporary reality, that critics of drama and the novel alike were demanding. . . .

The clash between the individual and the deterministic structure results in a dual movement of decline and regeneration. The tragic novels of George Eliot, Thomas Hardy and Henry James all retain this traditional pattern; the progression from egoism to altruism brought about by tragic suffering ensures that sacrifice is simultaneously salvation. Hardy's tragic novels also remain remarkably close to the tradition of tragedy in other respects, existing largely as stark outlines of events. In many aspects, therefore, they stand in contrast to the novels of George Eliot and James, who, in leading their reader's attention beyond the level of events, make the most radical attempts to redefine the nature of tragedy and of the heroism that accompanies it. Their more personal vision consists of an admiration for qualities which might seem essentially anti-heroic, and of an understanding of human suffering which gives real meaning to the phrase 'a fate worse than death'.

But Hardy introduces at least one new element into the traditional idea of tragedy. He uses working-class characters as material for tragedy – and far more successfully than George Eliot, because their tragedy arises, in part, out of their class, and he is not afraid to let their class experience, or the character, speak for itself. Hardy defends his concentration on the lower classes on aesthetic grounds. He claims that in tragedy social distinctions are unimportant, because 'education has as yet but little broken or modified the waves of human impulse on which deeds and words depend. So that in the portraiture of scenes in any way emotional or dramatic – the highest province of fiction – the peer and the peasant stand on much the same level.' If anything, social refinement stands in the way of the depiction of contemporary tragedy. It makes 'the exteriors of men their screen rather than their index'.[5] But, in extending the novel's range and shifting the focus of tragedy, Hardy is clearly involved with morality and society. His attempt to arouse the same pity and fear for the fates of his humbler characters that is traditionally experienced over the fates of noble leaders is no mere academic exercise.

George Eliot's theory of tragedy is based on an ideal of realism which links it with her theory of the novel. She believes that the novelist's aim should be the 'extension of our sympathies'. This can only be achieved by a realistic representation of that life of which her largely middle-class readers hold false or unsympathetic views. An idyllic portrait of the working-class merely reinforces the reader's predilection for the picturesque or admirable, encouraging his ignorance and social apathy. George Eliot attacks Dickens for failing to match his truthful de-lineation of idioms and manners with psychological truth, so that when passing on to an emotional or tragic plane he becomes 'transcendent in his unreality', encouraging the 'miserable fallacy that high morality and refined sentiment can grow out of harsh social conditions, ignorance and want'.[6] The situation most likely to arouse sympathy for this alien reality is a tragic one, based as it is on the most elemental forms of suffering. George Eliot's avowed method is 'to urge the human sanctities through tragedy – through pity and terror as well as admi-ration and delights'.[7]

But if George Eliot's artistic and moral purposes can only be achieved through tragedy, they also require the re-education of her public, to whom her idea of tragedy is new. In her first work of fiction, *Scenes of Clerical Life* (1858), she constantly makes explicit comparisons between her own vision of tragedy and the ideal modes of contemporary fiction. This is not simply a defence of her own fictional mode. Her ridicule of the literary tastes of readers like Mrs Farthingale [in 'Amos Barton'] 'to whom tragedy means ermine tippets, adultery and murder' *Scenes of Clerical Life*, 1, p. 66)* is also an attack on their moral sense. It is an attack on what she calls 'otherworldliness', on the inability to associate heroism or tragedy with the contemporary or familiar. George Eliot deplores this limited understanding of human suffering and this blindness to real human dignity. She is not merely a literary innovator, fusing tragic with realistic themes and methods, but a moral teacher, awakening her readers to a greater awareness of the sorrows and aspirations all around them.

Heroism is, for George Eliot, to be found in . . . 'wise passiveness' . . . . Her work does not celebrate any heroic transgressions of the law, because she accepts the morality of that inexorable law of consequence. The nobly heroic is, in her eyes, inevitably tinged with egoism; it disregards the reverberating complex of society. Like Henry James, she is suspicious of the dramatic gesture, the act of sacrifice so ostentatious that it defeats its own purpose. The heroine of *Romola* (1863) is, at the beginning of the novel, a beautiful, noble young Florentine, with a vision of a proud and heroic future. But when the gradual knowledge of her husband Tito's baseness forces her to abandon the ideal of her love, she finds – under the influence of Savonarola – 'a new presentiment of the strength there might be in submission' (*Romola*, II, p. 102). While Hardy shares George Eliot's view of 'wise passiveness' as the safest course of action in a deterministic universe, he does not see it as the heroic course. If his heroes also display stoicism, it is the stoicism of endurance, of passive resistance, rather than of resignation and acceptance. Endurance is perhaps the greatest of the traditional tragic virtues, as exemplified in Oedipus and King Lear. The endurance of Hardy's characters often stems from that indignation which W. B. Yeats calls 'a kind of joy', the joy that must accompany tragic suffering.[8] George Eliot's heroes, in contrast, are educated by their suffering into abandoning indignation, which she believes is frequently mistaken for virtue. The modern world denies all opportunity for such heroic action or outlets as were available to a Saint Theresa in her time. It therefore creates both its own forms of suffering and the need for new forms of heroism.

Because they adopt this attitude of resignation, George Eliot's heroes rarely face the crises of traditional tragedy. But they do not escape from tragic experience. Tragedy can arise from the trivial as much as from the important events: 'it is in these acts called trivialities that the seeds of joy are forever wasted, until men and women look around with haggard

* Here and subsequently, quotations from George Eliot's novels are from the Cabinet edition of the *Works of George Eliot* (Edinburgh and London, 1878–80) – Ed.

faces at the devastation their own waste has made'. George Eliot wishes to convey 'that element of tragedy which lies in the very fact of frequency' (*Middlemarch*, II, p. 231; I, p. 297). She suggests that such monotonous daily suffering is as great a tragedy as (if not greater than) death itself. Having sacrificed all egotistical hopes and desires, having ceased to live as an individual, it seems relatively easy to die in fact. George Eliot's novels suggest how superficial are our notions of tragedy, and question our habit of giving so central a place in it to death. 'It is a sad weakness in us, after all, that the thought of a man's death hallows him anew to us; as if life were not sacred too' ('Janet's Repentance', *Scenes of Clerical Life*, II, p. 176). Her work anticipates Yeats's recognition that 'Only the dead can be forgiven' (*A Dialogue of Self and Soul*). It is again worth noting the contrast with Hardy, for whom it is death that gives life significance: 'the most prosaic man becomes a poem when you stand by his grave at his funeral and think of him'.[9] His attitude typifies the much more traditional concept of tragedy to which he adheres.

Henry James exploits the same preconceptions of heroism and tragedy as George Eliot, although far less explicitly. He presents both familiar and new versions of the tragic experience, so that the reader is forced to ask which relates most convincingly to his own experience. On the one hand there is the traditional tragic ending (the hero's death) and on the other the modern 'unfinished' ending (life goes on). In George Eliot's words, 'life must be taken up on a lower stage of expectation' (*Middlemarch*, III, p. 181). Catherine Sloper of *Washington Square*, another victim of a fortune-hunter, Maurice Townsend, experiences this kind of finality to all her hopes and daydreams. After his return as a man who no longer has the power to move her in any way, she, picking up her embroidery, 'seated herself with it again – for life, as it were'. In this case, there is no contrasted ending, and this is relevant to the form of the work as a whole. But in *The Portrait of a Lady*, Isabel Archer's continuing life is set against her cousin Ralph Touchett's death; *Roderick Hudson* sets Rowland Mallett's future life against Roderick's death; and *The Wings of the Dove* sets Merton Densher's against Milly's. These juxtapositions suggest that death and life under such terms are very much the same thing. Discussing the idea of '*too late*' which is central to his concept of the unlived life, James states that 'the wasting of life is the implication of death'.[10] Death even seems a release compared with the daunting prospect of continuing without change, without hope, a life that has lost its motivation. On his deathbed Ralph, at last able to show his love to Isabel, pities her because she has to go on living and suffering in a loveless marriage.

But while James's concept of tragic suffering might seem close to George Eliot's, his concept of heroism is less like hers than might at first appear. Just as George Eliot's conception of heroism centres on resignation and duty, so James's novels offer apparently similar values in the form of renunciation and disinterestedness. But his 'renunciation' is a far less moral and more individualistic concept than George Eliot's 'resignation'. It is primarily a means to fulfilment and freedom, in favour of which James rejects duty. His heroes often refuse to commit themselves either to another individual or to any specific course of action, showing a desire for a more impersonal kind of fulfilment which renounces personal happiness. Such characters wish to avoid any involvement which will require them to take sides or compromise their freedom, which will corrupt their idealism into that morality known as 'being realistic'. In *The Spoils of Poynton* (1897) Fleda Vetch refuses to declare her affection for Mrs Gereth's son, Owen, or to give him any kind of encouragement, while he is in any way attached to Mona Brigstock, in spite of her awareness of Owen's growing fondness for her, and Mrs Gereth's encouragement. Fleda will not commit herself to the man if this involves breaking her greater commitment to the ideal of acting unimpeachably. Fulfilment can only be measured in terms of such freedom. 'The free spirit, always much tormented and by no means always triumphant', James observed, 'is heroic, pathetic or whatever, and, as exemplified in the record of Fleda Vetch, for instance, "successful", only through having remained free.'[11] Moral value does not transcend the individual, as it does in George Eliot's novels. But James clearly shares that novelist's belief that it is far easier – as well as more irresponsible – to embark upon some heroic act of self-expression than to acquire the strength to remain passive. When Christina Light attempts to renounce Roderick Hudson for his own good, she is incapable of this kind of heroic self-effacement. She must make her act a dramatic gesture, and she thereby renders it ineffective.

The apparent negativity of the concepts of heroism of both George Eliot and James presents the novelists with difficulties. And these concepts are, of course, so essentially untheatrical as to be totally unsuited to drama. The successful outcome of the Jamesian quest for freedom is almost inevitably – in any practical sense – failure. The more the free spirit refuses to meddle with the lives of others, the more pathetic he is liable to appear in his inactivity. If renunciation and disinterestedness are heroic qualities, they are nevertheless in themselves not enough to turn James's energetic little spinster feminist, Miss Birdseye, into a heroine in the fictional sense. The individual must feel his sacrifice for it to be truly heroic. The heroic activity, as opposed to inactivity, lies in the mind which James shows assessing the picture. It is here, too, that the tragedy is wrought and intensified. In the living death with which he is concerned, unlike physical death, the consciousness survives, 'so that the man is the spectator of his own tragedy'.[12]

The sharper the individual's perceptions, the greater the irony of his inability to act upon them. Because he observes and understands the passing of his own unhappy life, his passivity is not pathetic, but tragic, offering as it does a comment on and explanation of the blind suffering of the helpless. James's heroes are able to transcend their involvement in their own situation, to see its wider relevance, because their consciousness turns naturally – through education and intellect – to analysis and abstraction. It is the relative rareness of such a consciousness that makes George Eliot's images of passive heroism – particularly among her working-class characters – pathetic rather than tragic.

S O U R C E : extracts from *Tragedy in the Victorian Novel* (Cambridge, 1978), pp. 36–9, 43–9.

NOTES

[These have been revised and renumbered, with some deletions, from the original–Ed.]

1. Augustin Filon, *The English Stage: An Account of the Victorian Drama* (1897), pp. 175, 176.

2. W. E. Henley, *Views and Reviews*, I, p. 85 (*Collected Works*, 1908).

3. John Shawcross (ed.), *Shelley's Literary and Philosophical Criticism* (1909), p. 136.

4. *The Tragic Muse* (1921), I, p. 59.

5. Thomas Hardy, 'The Profitable Reading of Fiction', *Forum*, v (1888), 89.

6. George Eliot, 'The Natural History of German Life', *Westminster Review*, LXVI (1856), 58, 61.

7. G. S. Haight (ed.), *The George Eliot Letters*, IV (1954–55), p. 301.

8. Allan Wade (ed.), *The Letters of W. B. Yeats* (1954), p. 128.

9. Evelyn Hardy (ed.), *Thomas Hardy's Notebooks* (1955), p. 37.

10. F. O. Matthiessen and Kenneth B. Murdock (eds), *The Notebooks of Henry James* (1947), pp. 182–3.

11. Henry James, Preface to the one-volume edition of *The Spoils of Poynton, A London Life, The Chaperon*, p. xvii.

12. *Notebooks of Henry James*, op. cit., p. 144.

R. P. Draper   'Ane Doolie Sessoun': Lyric Tragedy (1980)

In Aristotle's view tragedy is essentially something which manifests itself in action. He prefers the plot which mounts to a climax of 'recognition' and 'reversal', and brings about a clearly identifiable catastrophe. For him tragedy is exclusively dramatic; it must manifest itself in the theatre to an audience, and involve a collective response. It is questionable whether he would admit the possibility of such a thing as 'lyric tragedy'.

But if the emphasis is shifted from structure to meaning, from tragedy in its formal aspect to tragic vision, the essence of tragedy – or 'the tragic' – appears as a certain feeling for the human condition, and its embodiment in dramatic action as only one of a number of possible ways of giving it expression. Not that the feeling is to be regarded as absolute and the expression as accidental; the feeling is itself changeable and the expression something which changes relatively to it; or, rather, such is the subtle relationship between substance and form, feeling and expression are mutually interacting. From this point of view 'lyric tragedy' becomes quite conceivable as a mode of tragic expression quite different from the Aristotelian in that it is more dependent on mood and atmosphere than on action and characterisation, and conducive to an individual and introspective rather than a public, collective response. In many tragic novels more than a step in this direction has already taken place; plot and character necessarily remain paramount, but a heightening of mood and atmosphere, and a tendency to transfer action to the theatre of the mind, indicate a change in the manner of expression which points towards a more lyrical mode. But in lyric tragedy proper these become dominant. Narrative and dramatic elements may remain, but in subordination to a pervasive tone and quality of feeling created through the poetic resources of language. It is a case of action indicating state of mind rather than of state of mind manifesting itself in action.

The argument, here presented hypothetically, becomes a more convincing reality if one looks at a number of examples of English poetry. The purpose of this essay, indeed, is not to make a theoretical statement about the variable nature of tragic form, but to illustrate certain aspects of the tragic sense which, it seems to me, are more suitably expressed in the poetic texture of lyric than in any other mode.

A good point of departure is Robert Henryson's *The Testament of Cresseid* since it represents a half-way house between the Aristotelian and lyric forms of tragedy.[1]It is a narrative poem which has its obvious action, but which approaches tragedy through its poetic organisation. And it is especially useful from the present point of view that Henryson opens with a statement about the relationship between tragic subject and tragic atmosphere:

> Ane doolie sessoun to ane cairfull dyte
> Suld correspond, and be equivalent.
> Richt sa it wes quhen I began to wryte
> This tragedie, the wedder richt fervent,
> Quhen Aries, in middis of the Lent,
> Schouris of haill can fra the north discend,
> That scantlie fra the cauld I micht defend.   (p. 19)

The *Testament* has sufficient of an Aristotelian structure for the tragic sense to be seen as manifesting itself in action. Indeed, its climactic moment is a highly original semi-'recognition' scene: the encounter of Troylus with the leprosy-afflicted Cresseid. Though 'not witting quhat scho was', he is nevertheless reminded of

> The sweit visage and amorous blenking
> Of fair Cresseid sumtyme his awin darling.   (p. 38)

Prompted by this sight he makes an unusually generous donation of alms, and when Cresseid afterwards realises who is the donor (hers, too, is a slightly unorthodox 'recognition'), she is pierced with remorse. She at last understands how little she has hitherto appreciated the real worth of Troylus, and, at the same time, to what extent she is herself to blame for her own downfall:

> 'Thy lufe, thy lawtie, and thy gentilnes,
> I countit small in my prosperitie,
> Sa elevait I was in wantones,
> And clam upon the fickill quheill sa hie:
> All Faith and Lufe I promissit to the,
> Was in the self [*] fickill and frivolous: [* = myself]
> O fals Cresseid, and trew Knicht Troylus.' (p. 39)

As a result, she ceases to complain against the gods and rail on Fortune. Like Richard II, who in Pomfret castle comes to the realisation that 'I wasted time and now doth time waste me', Cresseid turns her attention inward upon her own self: 'Nane but myself, as now, I will accuse.'

It is at this point that Cresseid becomes a truly tragic character; but this moment is a precipitation of the tragic feeling which is present throughout the poem. The opening does more than provide a suitable setting for the story which is to follow. The 'doolie sessoun', made physically real by the onomatopoeic language evoking the hail, frost and arctic winds of the Scottish winter, is associated with the poet's age and the fading of love and youth; and when he retreats to the warmth of his chamber to take up a book, it is one that deals with the aftermath of romantic love: 'the fatall destenie / Of fair Cresseid, that endit wretchit-lie' (p. 21). Love is thus placed in the perspective of experience and a tragic awareness of life which sees it in terms of chilling seasonal change. Though the poet, previously dedicated to Venus, trusted that his 'faidit hart of lufe scho wald mak grene' (p. 20), he finds that he is frustrated by the 'greit cald'; and the fire in his chamber – where he will study the tragic story of Cresseid – becomes an ironic substitute for the fire of passion.

Again, Cresseid's protest against Cupid and Venus is voiced in words which echo the poem's wintry theme:

> 'Ye causit me alwayis understand and trow
> The seid of lufe was sawin in my face,
> And ay grew grene throw your supplie and grace.
> Bot now allace that seid with froist is slane,
> And I fra luifferis left and all forlane.'   (p. 24)

The juxtaposition of 'grene' and 'froist' deepens the meaning of this protest for the reader, who connects it with what has gone before; but for Cresseid herself this deeper meaning is something of which she is as yet unaware. Or, to continue the metaphor of the poem itself, it is a seed planted in her consciousness, but not yet growing. That growth can, however, be sensed in the dream of the seven planetary deities which comes to her after her faint. These gods are the embodiment of forces, some evil, some beneficent, which control the life of man; collectively they present an allegorical pageant of the human condition. But individually they are also touched with the colours of Cresseid's still dormant tragic awareness and feeling of guilt. This is most apparent in the description of Saturne, a wintry figure who can be directly related to the opening of the poem:

> His face [fronsit], his lyre was lyke the Leid,
> His teith chatterit, and cheverit with the Chin,
> His Ene drowpit, how sonkin in his heid,
> Out of his Nois and Meldrop fast can rin,

> With lippis bla and cheikis leine and thin;
> The Iceschoklis that fra his hair doun hang
> Was wonder greit, and as ane speir als lang.　(p. 25)

Mars, 'Wrything his face with mony angrie word' (p. 26), reflects something of the anger which led Cresseid to her protest; and, more pertinently, Venus, characterised in terms of dissimulation and inconstancy, reflects Cresseid's own faithlessness – the quality for which she is destined to become a byword. The climax of this description also takes up the theme of seasonal change once more:

> Now hait, now cault, now blyith, now full of wo,
> Now grene as leif, now widderit and ago.　(p. 28)

Finally, the portrait of Cynthia, most junior of the planetary deities, but joined with Saturne in pronouncing doom on Cresseid, is a melancholy study in leaden colouring, or absence of colour, and 'full of spottis blak' – a touch which seems to hint at the disease which will be visited on Cresseid as punishment for her offence. And it is indeed Cynthia, following and reinforcing the judgement of Saturne depriving Cresseid of her youthful 'wantones', who reads the bill blighting her with leprosy:

> 'Thy Cristall Ene minglit with blude I mak,
> Thy voice sa cleir, unplesand hoir and hace,
> Thy lustie lyre ouirspred with spottis blak.'　(p. 32)

In the conventional language of compliment Cresseid is earlier called 'the flour and A per se / Of Troy and Grece' (p. 22). Now the 'frostie wand' (p. 31) of Saturne is laid on that flower, and its beauty is turned by Cynthia into ugliness. In the 'Complaint' which expresses her woe as a leper, Cresseid employs the *ubi sunt* formula of medieval poetry to stress this theme once more ('Quhair is thy garding with thir greissis gay? / And fresche flowris . . .' (p. 35); and she warns the ladies of Troy and Greece 'Nocht is your fairnes bot ane faiding flour' (p. 36). This is part of a great commonplace about the instability of earthly life, but it also reveals a gathering sense of the destructive force inherent in nature – especially in the insistent alliteration of 'Your roising reid to rotting sall retour' (p. 36). The commonplace, aided by its context in the poem's recurrent seasonal imagery, is in process of becoming a feelingly experienced tragic reality.

　　As already indicated, it is in the climactic meeting with Troylus that this gathering sense bursts into Cresseid's consciousness as an immediate personal truth. It is there that the pervasive lyric feeling and the specifically narrative and dramatic structure fuse into one. The

subsequent action is brief and sparely expressed, but, because of this
fusion, made powerfully symbolic. There are two simple episodes:
Cresseid makes her Testament; and Troylus erects a tomb to her
memory. The Testament sums up the theme of decay:

> 'Heir I beteiche my Corps and Carioun
> With Wormis and with Taidis to be rent'   (p. 40)

and the ring which is to be returned to Troylus is the means by which his
'discovery' is to be completed. Yet, as if to emphasise that what has been
done cannot be undone, the broach and belt which he gave her remain
irretrievably with Diomeid; Cresseid touchingly dies in admitting this,
her Testament broken off in mid-line with words that refer to Troylus's
love:

> 'O Diomeid, thou hes baith Broche and Belt,
> Quhilk Troylus gave me in takning
> Of his trew lufe', and with that word scho swelt.   (p. 41)

The tomb erected by Troylus, appropriately of 'Merbell gray', carries
an inscription, in contrasting 'goldin Letteris', which sums up the
fading flower theme:

> 'Lo, fair Ladyis, Cresseid, of Troyis toun,
> Sumtyme countit the flour of Womanheid,
> Under this stane lait Lipper lyis deid.'   (p. 41)

In itself this is cliché, but – as the gold of the letters betokens – it is cliché
redeemed by the context which the complete poem provides.

   The medieval *de casibus* view of tragedy, with its central image of the
wheel of Fortune, is reflected in *The Testament of Cresseid*, but also
transcended, through the self-discovery of Cresseid. The link between
the two is the seasonal imagery, at once commonplace and penetrating,
which makes external nature mirror a personal crisis. Though a
narrative poem, ostensibly carrying on from where Chaucer left off in
his *Troilus and Criseyde*, the real concern of *The Testament* is with a
moment of lyrical intensity when the prevalent condition of humanity is
made feelingly real to a woman who has hitherto been essentially
unaware. The movement from 'doolie sessoun' through protest and
subconscious dream-expressed guilt to the final awareness that 'Nane
but myself, as now, I will accuse', has both narrative and dramatic
power, but is fundamentally lyric in that it constitutes a welling-up of
feeling to a moment of revelatory insight. In this, despite the remoteness
in time, and considerable difference in length and structure, it is akin to
Gerard Manley Hopkins's 'Spring and Fall':

> Margaret, are you grieving
> Over Goldengrove unleaving?
> Leaves, like the things of man, you
> With your fresh thoughts care for, can you?
> Ah! as the heart grows older
> It will come to such sights colder
> By and by, nor spare a sigh
> Though worlds of wanwood leafmeal lie;
> And yet you will weep and know why.
> Now no matter, child, the name:
> Sorrow's springs are the same.
> Nor mouth had, no nor mind, expressed
> What heart heard of, ghost guessed:
> It is the blight man was born for,
> It is Margaret you mourn for.

Hopkins, of course, makes his approach through the comparatively innocent child: one whose intuitive insight into the intimate connection between human and natural decay is greater than it will be when the film of custom has overlaid it in adult life. (Though Catholic and conservative, Hopkins in this is clearly post-Romantic: the heart 'will come to such sights colder' – the vision will fade into the light of common day.) Henryson, more convincingly, sees the insight as something pressed in on Cresseid by a bitterly resisted, but inevitable, deepening of consciousness as experience moves her towards the recognition of that wintry season which is the present time of the poem (and of the poet himself) and the underlying reality of human life. But though the route, and the perspective from which it is viewed, are dissimilar, the sense of pressure building up to a tragic epiphany is the same. The climax of Hopkins's poem –

> It is the blight man was born for,
> It is Margaret you mourn for.

– could be the climax of Henryson's. Both move from a general sense of the inevitability of the winter condition to a particular realisation of it which precipitates a connection between tragedy and personal feeling.

Henryson and Hopkins are both Christian poets, but neither *The Testament of Cresseid* nor 'Spring and Fall' is in itself a specifically Christian poem. The doctrine of original sin is most probably what 'the blight man was born for' means to Hopkins, but in this particular poem Christ's countervailing grace is not mentioned. Likewise, Henryson, though he balances his moral condemnation of Cresseid – 'how was thou fortunait! / To change in filth all thy Feminitie' (p. 22) – with humane sympathy (the same stanza ends with the line: 'I have pietie thou suld fall sic mischance'), offers her no Christian salvation. The simple explanation may be that it would have been anachronistic to do so. The fact, however, remains that the poem is non-redemptive, except in some possibly metaphorical sense that Cresseid's final acceptance of her guilt reinstates her in the eyes of Henryson and his readers. But in both poems the absence of this Christian redemptive principle is a necessary part of the tragic effect. It is the sense that life decays and destroys and that the human being must come to a cruel awareness of this fact – pain giving birth to consciousness, consciousness giving birth to pain – which makes the poems tragic.

Such consciousness is the stuff of lyric tragedy and nowhere more evident than in the poetry of Keats. His consciousness of tragedy, however, is usually set in contrast with an alternative world of fancy or romance. Thus the sonnet, 'On Sitting Down to Read King Lear Once Again', begins with a farewell to 'golden tongued Romance' as unsuited to the encounter with reality which here, as in *The Testament of Cresseid*, is signified by 'this wintry day'. The need is for that 'bitter-sweet' combination of pain and delight which the reading of *King Lear* involves, and Keats submits himself to it in the spirit of one undergoing a purgatorial cleansing which, he hopes, will prepare him for the writing of a tragedy of his own:

> Let me not wander in a barren dream,
> But, when I am consumed in the fire,
> Give me new Phoenix wings to fly at my desire.

However, in spite of attempts to create tragedy in the Shakespearean mould with plays like *Otho the Great* and the unfinished *King Stephen*, Keats comes nearest to successfully 'flying at his desire' in the lyrical form of 'La Belle Dame Sans Merci' and the Odes. The seasonal metaphor of Henryson and Hopkins is the basis of 'La Belle Dame'. Autumn is on the verge of winter:

> The squirrel's granary is full,
> And the harvest's done.

But the dominant feeling is of chilled, withering loss – memorably caught in the sense of desolation engendered by the truncated last line of each stanza and the enclosing of the whole poem within the repeated

> The sedge has wither'd from the lake,
> And no birds sing.

Characteristically for Keats, the sense of loss is heightened by contrast with a dream-world of 'faery' – the world of the 'belle dame' and her 'honey wild, and manna dew' – which tempts escape from the chill reality only to end by intensifying awareness of it:

> And I awoke and found me here,
>   On the cold hill's side.

The tragedy of the knight-at-arms is made what it is by this contrast. To have experienced his dream only to lose it again is the very source of his pain; as such it is a paradoxically compelling poison.

A similar poison is the subject of the 'Ode on Melancholy'. The opening is an exhortation to avoid the 'poisonous wine' which would only 'drown the wakeful anguish of the soul'. Consciousness, for Keats, is a necessary condition of that 'bitter-sweet' experience which converts the 'melancholy fit' into tragedy. The imagination must dwell intensely on its simultaneous awareness of beauty and decay to distil another kind of poison which seems to exude from the rich, luxuriating language which constitutes the poem itself:

> Then glut thy sorrow on a morning rose,
>   Or on the rainbow of the salt sand-wave,
>   Or on the wealth of globed peonies.

The word 'poison' is re-introduced in the third stanza, but in a way that makes it apparent that its meaning is no longer the negative one of the first:

> She dwells with Beauty – Beauty that must die;
>   And Joy, whose hand is ever at his lips
> Bidding adieu; and aching Pleasure nigh,
>   Turning to Poison while the bee-mouth sips.

The antithesis between 'Pleasure' and 'Poison' is not a simple one, since the 'Pleasure' is qualified by 'aching' and the 'Poison' is a process that goes on 'while the bee-mouth' (with strongly creative connotations) 'sips'. Such poison is destructive-creative. Melancholy has her shrine 'in the very temple of delight', and what is needed to perceive it is the savour of 'Joy's grape' on the palate of an intensely sensitive and positive awareness of mutability. This – to take up again the phrase of the first stanza – is a 'poisonous wine', but one which is directly opposed to the sluggish, Lethean associations of the phrase in its original context. The accent is on effort and energy; the shrine will be seen by 'none save him whom whose *strenuous* tongue/Can *burst* Joy's grape'.

Such melancholy is not evasive, but, as the image of the last two lines seems to hint –

> His soul shall taste the sadness of her might,
> And be among her cloudy trophies hung

– almost heroic. It involves the accepting of a challenge not unlike that with which Moneta, using another version of the 'none save him' formula, confronts the dreamer in *The Fall of Hyperion: A Dream*:

> 'None can usurp this height,' return'd that shade,
> 'But those to whom the miseries of the world
> 'Are misery, and will not let them rest.'   (147–9)

There are some striking similarities between the two poems. The poet's dream in *The Fall of Hyperion* comes to him after drinking from 'a cool vessel of transparent juice / Sipp'd by the wander'd bee' (42–3), and the danger of 'thoughtless sleep' (*Fall*, 151) is common to them both. Above all, the emphasis in both poems is on tragic awareness. The ambivalence of a drug-like poison and a pleasure-pain poison acknowledges the temptation for imaginative creation to be used as a means of blunting the awareness of suffering, but the emphasis comes down firmly on the importance of recognising, and being fully and sensuously involved in, the phenomenon of simultaneously created beauty and pain.

This theme, once more in association with a cluster of words suggestive of drug and wine ('opiate . . . Lethe-wards . . . vintage'), also recurs in 'Ode to a Nightingale'. Here, however, the 'bitter-sweet' movement is one of alternation between the nightingale image of imaginative creation aloof from human suffering and the compelling image of tragic reality. Numbing of consciousness is invoked in the first two stanzas to blunt the force of the tragic image, but in the third the very naming of what the unconscious nightingale has never known, aided by the insistently repeated parallel constructions, gives that negative an unavoidably positive emphasis:

> Fade far away, dissolve, and quite forget
>   What thou among the leaves hast never known,
> The weariness, the fever, and the fret
>   Here, where men sit and hear each other groan;
> Where palsy shakes a few, sad, last gray hairs,
>   Where youth grows pale, and spectre-thin, and dies;
>   Where but to think is to be full of sorrow
>   And leaden-eyed despairs,
>   Where Beauty cannot keep her lustrous eyes,
>   Or new Love pine at them beyond to-morrow.

Stanza IV renews the movement away from this world, though now 'on the viewless wings of Poesy', in terms redolent of the 'golden tongued Romance' of the Lear sonnet, and continues it into the imaginatively re-created sensuousness of stanza V. But what is moon-lit in stanza IV becomes 'embalmed darkness' in V, with a funereal overtone that leads, in stanza VI, to the wish for 'easeful Death' and, in stanza VII, to the transformation of the nightingale into an 'immortal' singer: an apotheosis of the earth-freed poet, who is, if not unconscious of, then immune from, human suffering. The line with which stanza VI concludes – 'To thy high requiem become a sod' – is nevertheless an ominous development of the preceding darkness and death. It exalts the song of the nightingale to the splendour of a great musical ritual only to contrast it with the mere 'sod' which the poet's death would have made of him. In fact, we have returned to the world of tragic reality. The 'No hungry generations' of stanza VII make us acutely aware of deprivation and decay, and the nightingale's song as it is imagined finding a path 'Through the sad heart of Ruth' seems to derive what value it has, not from itself, but from its poignant relationship to her, standing 'in tears amid the alien corn'. It lifts again, in the remaining richly evocative lines of the stanza, towards 'the foam / Of perilous seas, in faery lands', but it is the tragic human perspective which is once more asserted in that ultimate, post-positioned adjective, 'forlorn'. 'Forlorn' also bridges the gap to the last stanza and leads to a monosyllabic line – 'To toll me back from thee to my sole self' – which, like the word 'sod' at the end of stanza VI, brings the poet, and the reader, firmly back to reality. Even so, the song is not simply silenced: the 'plaintive anthem' (a diminutive form of the 'high requiem' of stanza VI) grows less and less as, in recessional, it

> fades
> Past the near meadows, over the still stream,
> Up the hill-side; and now 'tis buried deep
> In the next valley-glades;

and its status as 'vision' or 'dream' is left in equal, undecided poise.

To speak of all this in terms of reality versus escape is to oversimplify. Escape is partly what the Ode is concerned with, especially in stanzas I, II and VI, but that to which the poet would fly in stanzas IV and V, and the 'perilous seas' on which those 'magic casements' open in stanza VII, represent a creation of the imagination which is valid in its own terms. Those terms are, however, too absolute for Keats. The poem is written precisely as it is – i.e. with a constantly shifting perspective – in order to emphasise its nature as a *dialogue* between mortality and immortality.

The alternation and contrast between the two reveal what the imagination may conceive, but also emphasise the bounds within which the human being is none the less confined. A connection is thus established between the opposite poles of 'Thou wast not born for death, immortal Bird!' and 'Adieu! the fancy cannot cheat so well / As she is fam'd to do, deceiving elf', which allows the immortality of the bird its ecstatic truth, while, in consequence of that very allowance, bringing home more sharply the pain of disenchanted reality.

The most tragic of the Odes, however, is one in which this characteristic alternation seems to have given way to acceptance of transience as a kind of fulfilment. 'To Autumn' is saturated with images of fruitful completion; the language, particularly of the first stanza, is that of natural ripening: 'mellow fruitfulness', 'maturing sun', 'load and bless / With fruit', 'fill all fruit with ripeness to the core', 'swell', 'plump'. The other seasons are included. Summer and spring are mentioned at the end of the first and the beginning of the third stanza respectively, and the remarkable lines which represent autumn as conspiring with the sun

> to set budding more,
> And still more, later flowers for the bees,
> Until they think warm days will never cease,

seem to extend the budding process of spring so far into the year as almost to promise its perpetuity. But, of course, 'think' is ominous; and the 'never cease' is an illusion. The reference to summer in the following line intensifies the saturating fruitfulness to the point where it all but topples over into a sticky rottenness: 'For Summer has o'er-brimm'd their clammy cells'. Arrest and drowsiness is the key-note of the second stanza, and its culmination is again in a line which is full to the verge of being repellent: 'Thou watchest the last oozings hours by hours'. The question, 'Where are the songs of Spring?' which opens the last stanza is also tinged with melancholy. Behind it lingers the traditional ubi sunt theme. This is immediately deflected by the thought that autumn has its 'music' too, but that music is sadly intoned by a 'wailful choir' of mourning gnats, lifted or allowed to fall by a wind associated with death as well as life. Natural music dominates the last four lines with the bleating of sheep, the singing of crickets, the whistling of the robin, and the twittering of swallows; but again each has a melancholy tinge which is reinforced by other associations. The sheep are, in fact, 'full-grown lambs' ('Where are the lambs of Spring?'); the 'red-breast' is a bird of winter (the only season not actually named); and the final line, a companion to the lines of implied excess which end stanzas II and III, hints at winter again as the swallows gather for migration.

Death is ultimately as much the theme of 'To Autumn' as fulfilment. Retrospectively this can be seen to be present in the very first line as well as the last: Autumn is apostrophised as the season of 'mists' as well as 'mellow fruitfulness'. The melancholy music of death, sounding through the almost overpowering assonance and consonance and packed metrical stresses, is heard as an undertone even when the poem is in its major key, and comes quite naturally into its own, therefore, with the modulation into the minor which occurs in stanza three. The point about this death, however, is that it is inseparable from life. Winter, though implied only, wells up as an overflow from excess of fruitfulness; ripeness spills into rottenness. What makes the poem tragic is the embodiment of this recognition in its own poetic substance. The 'I' of 'Ode to a Nightingale' has apparently disappeared, replaced by personification of the season, addressed as 'thou', and this may seem to deprive the poem of a consciousness in which to focus the tragic awareness. But what has happened is that the 'I' has transcended itself (though its more personal tone can just be heard in the first line and a half of stanza three), losing its pity for its own, and human, mortality in a more objective contemplation of the natural condition. Yet the result is not objectivity as such. The poem it still an intensely personal lyric in which Keats's own feeling for transience attaches to the sensuous details. His very submission to their reality involves his recognition of their transitory nature, and the process of creating them with such loving care brings out the essence of their bitter-sweetness. Delight in the fertility of autumn thus merges with the pain which comes from acknowledgement of its simultaneous existence as the season of death; the two are fused, and the poetry in which this fusion is realised becomes the expression of the poet's own acceptance of it.

The special achievement of the 'Ode to Autumn' is that it creates tragedy out of the pathos of transience by avoiding the self-pity which consciousness of transience so easily produces. Pathos is an important element in tragedy; but only when there is also resistance to it does it issue in authentically tragic feeling. The danger of inadequate resistance can be felt in the 'Ode on Melancholy' and even the 'Ode to a Nightingale'. In Arnold's 'Dover Beach', where the pathos derives from the Victorian loss of faith rather than awareness of transience, this inadequacy becomes a serious defect as far as the poem's tragic status is concerned. The scene is set for tragedy in the opening lines which build convincingly to the 'eternal note of sadness', and the allusion to Sophocles strengthens the impression that Arnold is reaching for a distinctively tragic expression; but the mutual comfort suggested by

Ah, love, let us be true
To one another!

has too much the tone of a babes-in-the-wood pathos to balance the 'melancholy, long, withdrawing roar' of the retreating Sea of Faith. The epic image of the final lines –

> And we are here as on a darkling plain
> Swept with confused alarms of struggle and flight,
> Where ignorant armies clash by night.

– is also alien to the would-be tragic feeling. The 'we' is feebly unequal to the 'ignorant armies'; nothing could grow from resistance, which is felt to be inherently futile.

A quite different effect is created by such poems as Hopkins's so-called 'terrible sonnets' (for example, 'Not, I'll not, carrion comfort . . .', 'No worst, there is none . . .', 'To seem the stranger . . .', 'I wake and feel the fell of dark . . .' and 'Thou art indeed just, Lord . . .'). The wrestling with doubt is here creatively energetic. 'No worst' ends with what is once more a form of pathos:

> Here! creep,
> Wretch, under a comfort serves in a whirlwind: all
> Life death does end and each day dies with sleep.

But this pathos is the result of exhaustion after an immense struggle – one which is as unequal and unavailing as Arnold's, but which has nothing of the barren feebleness of 'Dover Beach'. (The implied allusion in 'Here! creep, / Wretch, under a comfort serves in a whirlwind' is to the hovel in which King Lear takes refuge during the storm on the heath. There is the same devastating, but fundamentally invigorating, turmoil in both Shakespeare's and Hopkins's verse, and it is this which offers a convincing source of resistance).

The questioning of God's justice in 'Thou art indeed just, Lord' involves a pathetic personal consciousness, caught, for example, in the poignant antithesis of 'birds build – but not I build', but this, too, is transcended by the implications which the poetry expressive of that pathos generates. The 'I' of this poem who 'contends' with his 'Lord' is man alienated from God and nature; he is both individual and generic. His sense that his life is unproductive makes him 'Time's eunuch', a phrase that is at once boldly metaphorical and universalising; and the final line, 'Mine, O thou lord of life, send my roots rain', though it contrasts the natural fertility of 'banks and brakes', 'fretty chervil', 'fresh wind' and 'birds' with the poet's own personal condition (an effect redoubled by the syntactic displacing of 'Mine' and its emphatic position at the beginning of the line), also connects him with natural processes. He is both tragically divorced from nature, set in personal isolation from it, and dignified by the universal need so strongly communicated through the conjunction of 'roots rain'.

Henryson, Keats, and especially Hopkins, are all, of course, helped by a traditional language connecting nature and the spirit which enables such a prayer as 'send my roots rain' to work on two levels at once. The loss of faith with which Arnold is concerned in 'Dover Beach' cuts him off from that tradition. Nature, for him, in 'The Scholar Gipsy' or 'Thyrsis', becomes a retreat rather than a means of creating a tragic tension through universalising the personal condition. Yet it is in Arnold that lyric tragedy begins to emerge in a distinctively modern form. 'Dover Beach' leads on, for example, to T. S. Eliot's *The Waste Land*. Whether that poem expresses 'the disillusionment of a generation', or merely expresses for certain 'approving critics' – as Eliot tartly commented in 'Thoughts After Lambeth' – 'their own illusion of being disillusioned' (Eliot himself, as quoted in the *Waste Land* facsimile, called it 'the relief of a personal and wholly insignificant grouse against life . . . a piece of rhythmical grumbling'), it is certainly a poem in which the traditional language of nature is used to emphasise the pathos of modern man's spiritual isolation from the past. The quester for the Grail cannot ask the question necessary to save the blighted land, which therefore remains dead and sterile:

> A heap of broken images, where the sun beats,
> And the dead tree gives no shelter, the cricket no relief,
> And the dry stone no sound of water. (22–4)

The seasons are reversed: 'April is the cruellest month', whereas winter, like the Keatsian drug-like wine, protects from the bitter truth which it traditionally embodies:

> Winter kept us warm, covering
> Earth in forgetful snow, feeding
> A little life with dried tubers. (5–7)

The most dreaded event is the disinterring of the seed-like corpse planted last year in the garden:

> 'Has it begun to sprout? Will it bloom this year?
> 'Or has the sudden frost disturbed its bed?
> 'Oh keep the Dog far hence, that's friend to men,
> 'Or with his nails he'll dig it up again!' (72–5)

The scarcely conscious wish of the modern protagonist is to keep the
corpse buried. He fears death by water; and his intensest moments are
moments of lyrically expressed spiritual failure:

> . . . when we came back, late, from the hyacinth garden,
> Your arms full, and your hair wet, I could not
> Speak, and my eyes failed, I was neither
> Living nor dead, and I knew nothing,
> Looking into the heart of light, the silence.
> *Oed' und leer das Meer.* *
>
>   (37–42)

If a sense of tragedy hangs over him it is expressed as an anti-tragic
evasion. A hope remains for the poet himself that he might set his own
lands in order, but for his more representative protagonist there is only
the pathos of his half-life in the waste land, reluctantly stirred from time
to time by echoes from a tragically more exalted past – 'aethereal
rumours' which 'Revive for a moment a broken Coriolanus' (415–16).

If one turns to the poetry of Thomas Hardy – more clearly still than
Eliot a post-Arnoldian writer – one finds the natural language used
most typically to reflect a bleakly godless universe which, however, is
not matter for pathos or evasion, but stoic acceptance. 'Winter in
Durnover Field' is one such example:

SCENE – *A wide stretch of fallow ground recently sown with wheat, and frozen to
iron hardness. Three large birds walking about thereon, and wistfully eyeing the
surface. Wind keen from north-east; sky a dull grey.*

<table>
<tr><td></td><td colspan="2" align="center">(Triolet)</td></tr>
<tr><td>Rook –</td><td>Throughout the field I find no grain;</td><td></td></tr>
<tr><td></td><td>The cruel frost encrusts the cornland!</td><td></td></tr>
<tr><td>Starling –</td><td>Aye: patient pecking now is vain</td><td></td></tr>
<tr><td></td><td>Throughout the field, I find . . .</td><td></td></tr>
<tr><td>Rook –</td><td></td><td>No grain!</td></tr>
<tr><td>Pigeon –</td><td>Nor will be, comrade, till it rain,</td><td></td></tr>
<tr><td></td><td>Or genial thawings loose the lorn land</td><td></td></tr>
<tr><td></td><td>Throughout the field.</td><td></td></tr>
<tr><td>Rook –</td><td></td><td>I find no grain:</td></tr>
<tr><td></td><td>The cruel frost encrusts the cornland!</td><td></td></tr>
</table>

A critic determined to do so might possibly find religious overtones in
this: the grain of grace denied to the fable-like birds by the 'cruel frost'
making the scene one of damnation, but with a hint of salvation to come
with the 'genial thawings' of spring. If such an interpretation has

---

* 'Waste and empty the sea.'

relevance, however, it is only the relevance of irony. The voice of the Rook is the most insistent (he speaks three times to the Starling's and Pigeon's once each), and he monotonously repeats, 'No grain'. Like the Flintcomb Ash episode of *Tess of the D'Urbervilles,* which it seems to echo, the scene is unrelievedly bleak, and its tone at best stoic. The grain, though recently sown, lies hidden and inaccessible to the birds; their chance of getting at it is no greater than Vladimir's or Estragon's chance, in *Waiting for Godot,* of actually encountering Godot. Some comradeship exists among themselves, and it is that which, Arnoldian fashion, they have to rely on. 'Rain' and 'genial thawings' likewise appear in this context, though existing (and even so only as possibilities) on the natural, not supernatural, level. The self-pity of 'Dover Beach' is, however, completely eradicated. Even these simple birds will take the strain of tragedy uncomplainingly. They will endure.

Less typical, but demanding attention since it is one of the most remarkable examples of tragedy compressed into the narrow space of the lyric, is Hardy's 'The Convergence of the Twain'. It opens with the great luxury liner – the supposedly unsinkable *Titanic* – lying on the ocean bed. The tragic drama has already been enacted, and what therefore is emphasised is the lyric mood of ironic discord – heightened by the grandiloquent poetic diction and symbols of modern opulence (the very name of the liner clearly struck Hardy as implying a twentieth-century *hubris*) – between the wrecked ship and the weird sea-creatures surrounding it:

I

In a solitude of the sea
Deep from human vanity,
And the Pride of Life that planned her, stilly couches she.

II

Steel chambers, late the pyres
Of her salamandrine fires,
Cold currents thrid, and turn to rhythmic tidal lyres.

III

Over the mirrors meant
To glass the opulent
The sea-worm crawls – grotesque, slimed, dumb, indifferent.

IV

Jewels in joy designed
To ravish the sensuous mind
Lie lightless, all their sparkles bleared and black and blind.

V

Dim moon-eyed fishes near
Gaze at the gilded gear
And query: 'What does this vaingloriousness down here?'

The remorseless catalogues of 'grotesque, slimed, dumb, indifferent',
and 'bleared and black and blind', which form the climaxes of stanzas
III and IV respectively, particularly catch the note of absurd meaninglessness which is the burden of the first half of the poem. From stanza VI
onwards some sort of meaning is offered in answer to the question,
'What does this vaingloriousness down here?'. Yet the explanation
which is offered explains comparatively little: it tells, in mockingly
grand, philosophical terms, *how*, but not *why*. The 'one august event',
which is the collision of the *Titanic* with an iceberg and its sinking, could
only seem 'august' to a sick mind; indeed, this marriage (the hints for
calling it such are there in 'sinister mate', 'smart ship' and 'con-
summation') is a sharp satiric comment on the respectable, Imperial
society which produced it, as well as a deliberate replacement of the
idea of Christian providence by a blind fate which Hardy here, as in *The
Dynasts*, calls the 'Immanent Will'. If the tragedy of 'Winter in
Durnover Field' is akin to that of *Tess of the D'Urbervilles*, the novel to be
associated with 'The Convergence of the Twain' is that saga of
mismating, *Jude the Obscure*. And like *Jude*, it is satiric tragedy.

As the coupling of the two genres into the one phrase 'satiric tragedy'
implies, there is a risk in 'The Convergence of the Twain' of attack
taking over from pity. The poem is perhaps more sardonic than
compassionate. (Nothing, oddly enough, is said about the appalling loss
of human life.) The preoccupation of tragedy with human anguish and
the human condition is a little too narrow for this poem; it has other
interests in mind.

Hardy's poem perhaps points the way to the feeling, characteristic of
many twentieth-century writers (though not of Hardy himself), that
tragedy is in some ways a limiting genre, that it gains its intensity – as
Aldous Huxley argues in his essay, 'Tragedy and the Whole Truth' –
from an exclusiveness which falsifies the truth, or, at any rate, 'the
whole truth'. The un-intense, colloquial casualness of much modern
poetry (for which Hardy is also a precedent), whether cause or effect,
might also be associated with this view. The notion of the high, pure
language of tragedy, exemplified at its best in Racine, has certainly
gone, and even the conception of a tragic focus, still essential to the quite
different tragic style of Shakespeare, is questioned. Tragedy looks
straight forward at the sufferer and his suffering. The modern poet finds

this too much like tunnel vision. He wants to see what is going on to the left and to the right, and he is content with a looser synthesis than is to be found in his predecessors.

Yeats is a comparatively lonely voice crying out against this view. The aristocratic *frisson* of 'An Irish Airman Foresees His Death', expressed in a taut, concentrated rhetoric, proclaims a self-consciously tragic exclusiveness:

> Nor law, nor duty bade me fight,
> Nor public men, nor cheering crowds,
> A lonely impulse of delight
> Drove to this tumult in the clouds.

And though the political considerations which are explicitly denied in 'An Irish Airman' form the subject, and generate the emotion, of the more profoundly tragic 'Easter 1916', its 'terrible beauty' is born out of a violent adjustment of vision which suggests that commonplace experience, and its 'Polite meaningless words', have had to be superseded.

Above all, in 'Lapis Lazuli', where Yeats enunciates his mature view of tragedy, he insists on an heroic stance which is single and uncompromising. The protagonists, he declares,

> If worthy their prominent part in the play,
> Do not break up their lines to weep.

The accent is on concentration and transfiguration: 'Gaiety transfiguring all that dread'. His Chinamen carved in lapis lazuli are figures of dignity and wisdom. Incidental flaws in the stone, the work of time and natural imperfection, do not diminish or deflect their tragic vision; imagination dominates the substance in which it is expressed, purifying it and transforming it:

> Every discoloration of the stone,
> Every accidental crack or dent,
> Seems a water-course or an avalanche.

The Chinamen, as depicted in the carving, appear to be climbing towards a 'little half-way house', but the climax of the poem comes, significantly, in a scene not there depicted, but imagined by the poet. He delights, he says, to imagine them having reached their goal and from that vantage point staring on 'all the tragic scene'. The Chinamen then become a symbol for the artistic consciousness which transmutes suffering into exultant wisdom. One of them asks for appropriately tragic music ('mournful melodies'), and, as 'Accomplished fingers begin to play', the gaiety which insistently recurs throughout the poem as an expression of the transfiguring power of tragic art glitters in the eyes of these mythic figures:

> Their eyes mid many wrinkles, their eyes,
> Their ancient, glittering eyes, are gay.

In W. H. Auden's 'Musée des Beaux Arts', however, it is the casual un-focused view suggested by Huxley which prevails. This poem begins with a seemingly traditional emphasis:

> About suffering they were never wrong,
> The Old Masters –

but, in the same way that Huxley sets Homer against the tragedians, Auden chooses his old masters with malice aforethought. His preference is for those who give suffering its wide, ordinary human context – who understand

>   how it takes place
> While someone else is eating or opening a window or
>   just walking dully along;

and who never forget

> That even the dreadful martyrdom must run its course
> Anyhow in a corner, some untidy spot
> Where the dogs go on with their doggy life and the
>   torturer's horse
> Scratches its innocent behind on a tree.

Thus in Brueghel's painting Icarus falls, and the ploughman 'may/ Have heard the splash, the forsaken cry', but, says Auden, unemphatically and prosaically, 'for him it was not an important failure'. Likewise, the sun continues to shine indifferently, and

>   the expensive delicate ship that must have seen
> Something amazing, a boy falling out of the sky,
> Had somewhere to get to and sailed calmly on.

Indifference, here, is not Hardy's indifference of a godless universe, but that dispersed attention which characterises a democratic world. 'Something amazing' is perhaps an arresting spectacle, but its very uniqueness guarantees that for most people it will hold attention only for a moment; the routine of life demands that they move on to other things. Moreover, in the post-Arnoldian world no one figure can gather up in himself the values which are meaningful to all: Icarus cannot be seen as everyone's self at its highest intensity. Arthur Miller may offer as an alternative the tragedy of the common man; but if this works, it works because each member of the audience sees in the predicament of a hero like Willy Loman something of the pathos of his own commonplace situation rather than an image of his highest self. Icarus is the tragic figure asking for recognition as the highest self, but failing to get it.

Nevertheless, 'Musée des Beaux Arts' retains at least semi-tragic status. Although Icarus is deliberately demoted from his heroic, central position in the composition, and the 'doggy life' of each individual goes on in its separate dogginess, the artist is able to give them some relation to each other. And what the artist sees becomes what the reader sees. The indifference which suffering encounters thus achieves a pitiable reality of its own, and though the protagonist may fail to achieve representativeness, his isolation does.

It may well be that the contemporary tragic artist cannot hope to achieve much more than this, at any rate with regard to the presentation of Icarus. His focus may have to be on the ploughman instead – though not in the sense urged by Miller, i.e. that every ploughman is a potential Icarus. If the ploughman cannot find his tragic reality in Icarus, he may have to find it in other ploughmen, and in the rediscovery, within his seemingly un-tragically commonplace surroundings, of the presence of that 'wintry' theme which is the traditional subject of lyric tragedy. Such a discovery would have to come about by a process of gradual defamiliarisation – a sense of growing strangeness, begetting pity and fear, in an experience that nevertheless seems an inevitable and universal feature of strictly contemporary existence.

A poem which works precisely in this way, and towards this end, is Philip Larkin's 'The Building' (published in *High Windows*, 1974). The high-rise structure given this anonymous title is at once a commonplace of the contemporary urban scene and a disturbing intrusion upon it. It is, of course, a recently built hospital, but, in keeping with the evasiveness that characterises the modern attitude to illness and dying, it is never named as such. It has its affinities with the tall hotel or the airport lounge, but, while stranger than either, it is also much nearer home, and

> those who tamely sit
> On rows of steel chairs turning the ripped mags
> Haven't come far.

It is a building which sits in the middle of their familiar surroundings; and, as a look from its windows shows, the unlovely, ordinary life of everyday goes on as doggily around it as the daily life in 'Musée des Beaux Arts'. But there is something indefinably menacing in its relationship to that world:

> what keep drawing up
> At the entrance are not taxis; and in the hall
> As well as creepers hangs a frightening smell.

Those who have come to it have been subtly set apart from others; they are

> Humans, caught
> On ground curiously neutral, homes and names
> Suddenly in abeyance . . .

Their restlessness combines with resignation, and, without evidently being deprived, they seem to have lost some essential control over their comings and goings: 'Every few minutes comes a kind of nurse' – and then a curiously disrupting jump to a new stanza – 'To fetch someone away'. They are a mixture of young and old, but the majority, significantly, are 'at that vague age that claims / The end of choice, the last of hope . . .'.

Larkin's poem is particularly concerned with the way this sense of dislocation from ordinariness, in perfectly ordinary surroundings, generates an almost guilty unease, an incipient tragic recognition. Those who are waiting have a mute sense of being part of a congregation (in the eighth stanza some of them actually join the 'unseen congregations'), and 'all' – with another disturbing stanzaic jump – are 'Here to confess that something has gone wrong'. The 'error', it is added, must be

> of a serious sort,
> For see how many floors it needs, how tall
> It's grown by now . . .

The size and remoteness of the building seem to grow as the poem develops, like an externalisation of whatever disorder it is from which the (unacknowledged) patients suffer:

> For past these doors are rooms, and rooms past those,
> And more rooms yet, each one further off
> And harder to return from . . .

This incipient tragic recognition is, of course, the realisation of mortality. All those here

> know they are going to die.
> Not yet, perhaps not here, but in the end,
> And somewhere like this.

Life itself is the disease, and 'the building' waits for everybody. But with this recognition also comes awareness of a need for something which may console in the face of mortality. The religious implication hidden in the earlier use of '*confess* that something has gone wrong' and 'unseen *congregations*' at last breaks into consciousness in the final lines:

> That is what it means,
> This clean-sliced cliff; a struggle to transcend
> The thought of dying, for unless its powers
> Outbuild cathedrals nothing contravenes
> The coming dark, though crowds each evening try
>
> With wasteful, weak, propitiatory flowers.

Whether this consolation is the consolation that religion traditionally has to offer is uncertain. Like so much in this poem, it is not explicitly named. All that can be said for sure is that 'the building' wakens its inmates from the 'self-protecting ignorance' which congeals round their lives as a protective cover to enable them to go on with the business of living. This awakening is akin to the religious sense of sin; but if in any way the 'clean-sliced cliff' may be regarded as a latter-day cathedral symbolising 'a struggle to transcend / The thought of dying', there is no assurance that such a struggle will succeed. With its white-rowed congregations it is an ironic cathedral only; to outbuild the cathedrals of the past it would need to shed its irony and be instilled with a faith which, in the circumstances of the poem, seems unlikely to be attained.

The crowds who come each evening to visit those whom the building has already claimed are equally vulnerable, for they are also potential patients. The single line on which the poem ends – 'With wasteful, weak, propitiatory flowers' (the only line left to stand thus exposed, in frail isolation from a complete stanza) – shows that their attempts to ward off the knowledge of mortality are doomed to the same ineffectiveness; and it is the inevitability of this defeat which makes it so moving. The visitors are united with those they come to visit in their affliction with the same basic human sickness, which the building is supposedly there to relieve, but which, in fact, it can only press into their reluctant consciousness. Like Henryson's Cresseid and Hopkins's

Margaret, the building's visitor-patients arrive at an awareness of the 'the blight man was .born for', and it is their participation in the common tragic condition of man which they are learning to mourn for. They learn that they are all creatures of 'Ane doolie sessoun'.

SOURCE: written for, and first published in, this Casebook.

NOTE

1. The text used here is that printed in Hugh MacDiarmid (ed.), *Robert Henryson: Selected Poetry* (Penguin, 1973), and the page numbers attached to excerpts from the poem relate to that edition.

SELECT BIBLIOGRAPHY

Students are advised to consult the complete books from which extracts have been reprinted in this collection. The following additional studies are recommended.

Geoffrey Brereton, *Principles of Tragedy: A Rational Examination of the Tragic Concept in Life and Literature* (University of Miami Press, Coral Gables, Florida, 1968).

Joseph N. Calarco, *Tragic Being: Apollo and Dionysus in Western Drama* (University of Minnesota Press, Minneapolis, 1968).

Robert W. Corrigan (ed.), *Tragedy, Vision and Form* (Chandler, San Francisco, 1965).

W. MacNeile Dixon, *Tragedy* (Arnold, London, 1924).

T. R. Henn, *The Harvest of Tragedy* (Methuen, London, 1956).

Jean Jacquot (ed.), *Le Théâtre Tragique* (Centre National de la Recherche Scientifique, Paris, 1962).

Murray Krieger, *The Tragic Vision: Variations on a Theme in Literary Interpretation* (Rinehart, New York, 1960).

Clifford Leech, *Tragedy* (Methuen, London, 1969).

David Lenson, *Achilles' Choice: Examples of Modern Tragedy* (Princeton University Press, Princeton, N.J., 1975).

Richard Levin (ed.), *Tragedy: Plays, Theory and Criticism* (Harcourt, Brace, New York, 1960).

F. L. Lucas, *Tragedy: Serious Drama in Relation to Aristotle's 'Poetics'* (Hogarth Press, London, 1927; revised edition, 1957).

Laurence Michel, *The Thing Contained: Theory of the Tragic* (Indiana University Press, Bloomington, Ind., 1970).

Laurence Michel and Richard B. Sewall (eds), *Tragedy: Modern Essays in Criticism* (Prentice-Hall, Englewood Cliffs, N.J., 1963; reprinted Greenwood Press, Westport, Conn., 1978).

Elder Olson (ed.), *Aristotle's 'Poetics' and English Literature: A Collection of Critical Essays* (University of Chicago Press, Chicago, 1965).

Richard B. Sewall, *The Vision of Tragedy* (Yale University Press, New Haven, Conn., 1959).

Brian Vickers, *Towards Greek Tragedy: Drama, Myth, Society* (Longman, London, 1973).

NOTES ON CONTRIBUTORS
TO PARTS ONE AND THREE

R. P. DRAPER: Professor of English, University of Aberdeen. His publications include *D. H. Lawrence* (Twayne's 'English Authors' series, 1964); *D. H. Lawrence* (Profile series, 1969), the edited volume on Lawrence in the 'Critical Heritage' series (1970), and the Casebooks on *Hardy: The Tragic Novels* (1975) and George Eliot's '*The Mill on the Floss*' and '*Silas Marner*' (1977).

NORTHROP FRYE: Professor of English, University of Toronto. His publications include *Fearful Symmetry* (1947), *Anatomy of Criticism* (1957), *The Well-Tempered Critic* (1963), *The Educated Imagination* (1963), *T. S. Eliot* (1963), *Fables of Identity* (1963), *A Natural Perspective* (1965), *The Return of Eden* (1965), *Fools of Time* (1967), *The Modern Century* (1967), *A Study of English Romanticism* (1968), *The Stubborn Structure* (1970), *The Critical Path* (1971), *The Secular Scripture* (1976) and *Spiritus Mundi* (1976).

HUMPHRY HOUSE (1909–55): Former Senior Lecturer in English Literature, University of Oxford. His publications include *The Notebooks and Papers of Gerard Manley Hopkins* (1937), *The Dickens World* (1941), *Coleridge* (1953), and *Aristotle's 'Poetics'* and *All in Due Time* (posthumously, 1956).

ALDOUS HUXLEY (1894–1963): Novelist and essayist.

JOHN JONES: Senior Lecturer in English Literature, University of Oxford; elected Professor of Poetry at Oxford, 1979. His publications include *The Egotistical Sublime* (1954), *On Aristotle and Greek Tragedy* (1962) and *John Keats's Dream of Truth* (1969).

JAMES JOYCE (1882–1941): Irish novelist and literary pioneer.

JEANNETTE KING: After graduating from Cambridge she gained her Ph.D. at Aberdeen University, and is currently a tutor in English at the Scott-Sutherland School of Architecture, Aberdeen.

DOROTHEA KROOK: American scholar. Her publications include *Three Traditions of Moral Thought* (1959), *The Ordeal of Consciousness in Henry James* (1962) and *Elements of Tragedy* (1969).

ARTHUR MILLER: American playwright and critic.

I. A. RICHARDS, C.H. (1893–1979): Critic and poet, and a powerful influence in twentieth-century literary studies, especially through his two classic works, *The Principles of Literary Criticism* (1924) and *Practical Criticism* (1929), which were the fruit of his early teaching in Cambridge. His collaboration there with C. K. Ogden produced *The Meaning of Meaning* and *The Foundation of Aesthetics*. After a long period in America, where he became Professor of English, Harvard University, he returned to Cambridge in 1973 and was made Honorary Fellow of Magdalene College.

GEORGE STEINER: Professor of English and Comparative Literature, University of Geneva, and Fellow of Churchill College, Cambridge. His publications include *Tolstoy or Dostoevsky* (1958), *The Death of Tragedy* (1961), *Anno Domini* (1964), *Language and Silence* (1967), *Extraterritorial* (1971), *In Bluebeard's Castle* (1971), and *After Babel* (1975).

J. L. STYAN: Andrew Mellon Professor of English, University of Pittsburgh; previously on the teaching staff of the University of Hull. His publications include *The Elements of Drama* (1960), *The Dark Comedy* (1962), *The Dramatic Experience* (1965), *Shakespeare's Stagecraft* (1967), *The Challenge of the Theatre* (1972), *Drama, Stage and Audience* (1975) and *The Shakespeare Revolution* (1977).

RAYMOND WILLIAMS: Professor of Drama, University of Cambridge; his publications – embracing works on literature and society, and novels – include *Drama from Ibsen to Eliot* (1952), *Culture and Society* (1958), *The Long Revolution* (1961), *Modern Tragedy* (1966), *The English Novel from Dickens to Lawrence* (1970), *The Country and the City* (1973) and *Keywords* (1976). The most widely read of his novels is probably the first, *Border Country* (1960).

VIRGINIA WOOLF (1882–1941): novelist and literary critic. Her main critical writings are in the two volumes of *The Common Reader*.

W. B. YEATS (1865–1939): Irish poet, playwright and essayist. Some of his most important critical essays are included in *Essays and Introductions* (1961).

INDEX